WARRIOR HERDSMEN

WARRIOR HERDSMEN

by *Elizabeth Marshall Thomas*

With photographs by Timothy Asch

W · W · NORTON & COMPANY

New York · London

Portions of this book have appeared in *The New Yorker*.

Library of Congress Cataloging in Publication Data
Thomas, Elizabeth Marshall, 1931–
    Warrior herdsmen.
1. Dodoth (African tribe)   I.   Title.
DT433.245.D63T46   1981   967.6′1   80–21126
ISBN 0–393–00040–0 (pbk.)

W. W. Norton & Company, Inc. 500 Fifth Avenue,
New York N.Y. 10110
W. W. Norton & Company Ltd. 25 New Street Square,
London EC4A 3NT

1 2 3 4 5 6 7 8 9 0

Introduction to the Norton Paperback Edition

Between 1961, when I lived among the Dodoth, and now, many changes that were expected to take place in Karamoja did not take place. After Uganda's Independence in 1962, Karamoja was expected to move from a pastoral economy to a money economy; literacy was supposed to rise; and medical care was supposed to be made available even in the remote, back country of the North.

However, so far the progressive kinds of assimilation and deculturalization have not taken place. Even though cattle overgraze the land, the Karamojong peoples hold their herds in the same high esteem that they have traditionally, are willing to give their lives to keep or increase their cattle, and have little inclination to change a cattle economy for a money economy.

Karamoja is a land beset with famine. Reports currently appearing in the press suggest that famine is new to the area. It is not. It was present when we visited in 1961, and its continued presence explains some of the dependence of the Karamojong peoples on their herds—livestock can often survive when planted crops cannot; people living from the produce of their herds can survive in arid, famine-ridden lands long after people who live from gardens or from subsistence agriculture have starved.

In the eighteen years since Uganda's independence, almost nothing has been done to induce change in the

pastoral economy of Karamoja. The government presented
no viable programs for Karamoja, and the people who run
the government, most of whom are from urban or agricul-
turalist peoples of southern Uganda where the land is far
better for farming than the land in the North, look upon
the Karamojong peoples—the Karamojong, the Dodoth, and
the Jie of Uganda and the Turkana of Kenya—as backward,
ignorant, undeserving, a blight on progress, and a black
eye to what little national pride is left after the regime of
Idi Amin.

In 1961, when I was camped in Karamoja among some
of the Dodoth people's stockaded dwellings about five
miles south of Kalapata on the only road, I occasionally
met representatives of the new government of independent
Uganda who could barely hold their tempers when speaking of the Karamojong peoples. That the Karamojong men
insisted upon going naked was as infuriating to progressive Ugandans as the Ku Klux Klan is to progressive
Americans. That the Karamojong peoples raided their
traditional enemies for cattle was also infuriating and
should, some Ugandans thought, be punished very severely. The attitude of fighting violence with violence
came to characterize the treatment the pastoral peoples of
the North received at the hands of the westernized peoples
of the South. The westernization of the Karamojong peoples received low national priority: the money and per-
sonnel that would have been required to convert the
reluctant pastoralists into literate participants of a money
economy were not available; and the resistance to change
on the part of the Karamojong peoples, who regarded the
agricultural and urban Ugandans with scorn, was very
strong. As a result, the change that came to northern

Uganda was not the change that had been hoped for, or that people like me tentatively foresaw—a progress in which the few educated Karamojong, Dodoth, and Jie could serve their people as leaders in the new government and new economy. The change that actually took place was more in keeping with trends already at work. The southern Ugandans in general and Idi Amin in particular treated the northern pastoralists with such ferocity that the northern pastoralists had to reexamine their warlike ways, not necessarily with an eye to abandoning these ways, as the southern Ugandans might have liked, but with an eye to upgrading their weapons.

Furthermore, many of the northern pastoralists served in the army, which was first the King's African Rifles, then the Uganda Rifles, and thus gained experience in western military tactics, which are somewhat different from the traditional pastoralist military tactics. Then, after Independence, many of the northern pastoralists in Uganda acquired rifles. While formerly the Ugandan Karamojong peoples had fought the rifle-equipped Turkana of Kenya with spears, their acquisition of rifles now brought them closer to military equilibrium.

There were many signs in 1961 of what the future was to bring for the Karamojong peoples. After a short truce encouraged by the Protectorate Government, cattle raiding between the Dodoth and Karamojong allied against the Jie and Turkana had resumed. That year, the King's African Rifles, called upon to put a stop to it, established a presence in the Karamojong hills. The detachment near my camp was under the command of a black colonel. Because the creation of black officers hadn't had high priority in this particular army organized by the British, only two

Ugandans had, by 1961, achieved the rank of colonel, and when the need arose for disciplinary military action that would be perceived as nonracist or non-British in origin, only two Ugandans had sufficient rank to command.

When some Turkanas came from Kenya to attack and raid the Dodoth, the King's African Rifles responded with such ferocity that the ensuing massacre is remembered to this day. The colonel personally pursued the raiders back across the border from Uganda to Kenya. He personally slaughtered Turkana men and women and he even executed children with his bare hands.

Dodoth whom I knew followed the King's African Rifles and witnessed the massacre. Their accounts are given in this book on pages 229 to 235. The soldier who on page 234 is described killing a little girl was the colonel himself. In this book he is called a soldier, which is what the Dodoth called him. His rank, of course, meant nothing to them, and I learned of it after the book was published. I also learned after the book was published that the colonel was none other than Idi Amin.

Although Amin had illegally led troops across an internatonal border and had massacred civilians, and although his deeds became known to the Protectorate Government, no effective steps were taken to remove him from command. After Independence, he deposed Milton Obote and became head of state. His bloodstained dictatorship rivalled Hitler's. During the years that he was in power, very few outsiders traveled to remote parts of Uganda, and therefore little is known, at the time of this writing, about his activities in Karamoja since he came to power. It has been suggested that his methods of suppression were so extreme that he kept intertribal warfare to a minimum. Perhaps so. He kept, it appears, a staggering supply of weapons, ammunition, and even artillery pieces in Moroto, the small town that is the capital of Karamoja.

In the spring of 1980, the famine that seemed endemic to Karamoja worsened to take on the proportions of the 1970s famine of the western Sahel. The need for cattle became very great. Raiding appeared to be increasing, and in early June, 1980, Karamojong men broke into Idi Amin's arsenal and took it all—twelve thousand rifles, two million rounds of ammunition, and the artillery pieces, according to a news report. This extraordinarily large amount of arms, with more bullets than there are people in the countryside, surely will, with the famine, open a new and terrible chapter in the history of Karamoja.

I tried to keep in touch with the people about whom I have written in this book and succeeded in doing so for a few years, but after Amin came to power communication .stopped. I learned, however, that several people whom I knew well are dead. Among them is Lopore, to my infinite sorrow.

Elizabeth Marshall Thomas

June, 1980

Acknowledgments

THE NEW YORKER made it financially possible for us to go to Uganda to acquire material for this book, and a fellowship from the John Simon Guggenheim Memorial Foundation provided us with the necessary time to write the book. I would like to thank both these organizations and in particular William Shawn and those who sponsored me for the fellowship.

Between the time the trip was made and the writing finished, so many people helped me that I may not be able properly to thank them all, and if I should overlook someone, I would ask that person to excuse me; my gratitude and obligation are no less.

For the idea to visit Karamoja, I would like to thank Edward and Marguerite Mason. I would like to thank my parents, Laurence and Lorna Marshall, for the survey trip they made on our behalf in Karamoja and Dodoth. For the inestimable help of source material once the area was selected, I would like to thank Doctors Neville and Rada Dyson-Hudson. The Dyson-Hudsons spent many years in Karamoja and gave so generously of advice and information, showing us photographs and the then unpublished manuscript of *The Karimojong*, that my gratitude cannot be sufficiently expressed, nor can my debt be measured for the understanding gained by this help. I also read *The Family Herds* by Dr. Phillip Gulliver, and "The Central

Nilo Hamites" in *The Ethnographic Survey of Africa,* by Dr. Gulliver and Dr. Pamela Gulliver, works which enabled me better to understand life in Dodoth. I am much indebted to Dr. Walter Deshler for sending us his publication, "Livestock Tripanosomiasis and Human Settlement in Northeastern Uganda," a valuable article concerning the very neighborhoods we knew, which appeared in the October 1960 issue of the *Geographical Review* (Vol. 50, No. 4). Father Farina of the Verona Fathers wrote a dictionary of Akarimojong which we read and found helpful. James P. Barber gave us copies of his very interesting articles, "The Murder of Chief Achia" and "The Karamoja District of Uganda," which were also very helpful. I would like to thank all these people and acknowledge my debt to them all and would also like to stress the fact that errors and misinterpretations which may occur in this book in no way accrue to any of them.

While in Entebbe and Kampala, we received warm hospitality, help, and advice from nearly everyone we met. I would like in particular to thank Mr. and Mrs. Christopher Melmouth, Mr. and Mrs. Sam Ntiro, Mr. Macoun, Mr. Powell-Cotton, Mr. Burgess, and Mrs. Fley.

In Moroto, too, we were accorded gracious help, friendship, and hospitality without which we would have been unable to continue our trip. For this I would like to thank our friends June and Jim Barber, also Mr. Allen for almost unlimited assistance and favors, also Dr. Gowan, Mr. James Locut, Mr. and Mrs. David Morris, Mr. and Mrs. Pat Howard, Mr. Robeson, Father Franco Petrocelli, Mr. Ray Cauderay, and Mr. Ishverbahi.

As we traveled north, we received kind assistance from the A.D.C. of Jie, Major Charles Lamb. When we arrived in Kaabong, we were received, fed, and housed for more than two weeks by the Kaabong Catholic Mission, whose generosity toward us was very great indeed. For this I would like to thank Father Danielli, Father Berginini, and Brother Fortunato.

For assistance and cooperation I would like to thank Chief Kamarri, Jackait Lokol, and Rose Ironga, and for hospitality I would like to thank Mr. J. B. Patel.

When we left Kaabong, we went to our own camp in Lokoki. It was there the material for this book was gathered. Not a word of the book could have been written without the information, hospitality, cooperation, and gracious friendship given us by the neighbors—men and women whose courtesy and generosity can neither be measured nor repaid. For these favors I thank in particular Lokwal Lopore and his family, especially his wife Rengen, his wife Nabilo, and his daughter Chuchu; also Lotiang Uri and his family, Mora, Nakade, Lokwang and his brothers, Lotido and his family, Nadolupe and Lokorimoe. For further information and assistance I would like to thank Lomotin, Major Groom, Mather Ojwang, Kalisto Agen, and last but by no means least, Amos J. Bala, whose interpretation of material we gathered and brought home was of inestimable value. Here again, it should be stressed that none of these people is responsible for any mistake which may be in the book.

I should also like to thank the offices of the Protectorate government, Moroto, for information on tax collection, and the office of the Protectorate Police for data and information on raiding.

To the people in our camp, I owe an inestimable debt. Tom Johnson and his late wife, Kirsti Johnson, I thank for the success of the entire venture. David B. Lotukei, interpreter and field assistant, I thank for the care and brilliance he gave to his work, for the understanding, then far beyond his years, of the project at hand, and for the pleasant graciousness of his character, through which filtered most of the work we did in Dodoth. Our debt to Timothy Asch is obvious; the beautiful photographs in this book were taken by him. Yet beyond that, I would like to offer particular thanks to him for his cooperation, for the ease in the language which he achieved very quickly, and which proved of great help, and for his assistance in gathering material. It should again be stressed that any mistakes which may well be in this book are mine and should not accrue to him. I would also like to thank Daniel Lopote, and William Aginga, with special thanks to Filomon.

I received many kinds of help with the manuscript. For their help with its typing and preparation, I would like to thank Montie Johnson and also Marilyn Wood, whose precision and encouragement speeded the work to its conclusion. For encouragement, advice, and for her expert opinion, I would like to thank Marie Rodell. For editorial assistance and for the good faith they have shown in me I would like to thank Harold Strauss, and in this context, thank William Shawn again.

I would also like to thank my children, Stephanie and John, for their serenity and patience, for the discomforts and the disruptions of their young lives which they endured, and for having made the trip with me. But my deepest thanks must go to Steve Thomas, my husband. I won't estimate everything he did to help this book forward, or list the material he collected for it, but will only venture to hope he likes it, especially the parts of it he wrote himself.

Contents

Illustrations

A Note

MOST of the personal names in this book have been changed. For some people I made up names. For some people I substituted other people's names. And to some people I gave the names of places in Dodoth and in the southern Sudan. In Dodoth, because of the system for naming children, men and women use the same names interchangeably. A newborn baby is offered its mother's breast as a name is suggested. If the baby likes the name, it sucks. Both men's and women's names are suggested; the baby is free to choose whichever it likes.

Most Dodoth words are accented on the last syllable. In words of five syllables or more, there are sometimes two accents, one on the middle syllable and one on the last. The sound *ng* is common in Dodoth, and is often the first sound in a word. Most words take *ng* to form the plural, always at the start of the word. This syllable is pronounced as a single sound, like the *ng* in si*ng*er; it is never two sounds as in fi*ng*er.

Personal Names

Abibu	girl taken by ivory hunter
Adupa	son of Nabilo and Mustafa
Adwong	third wife of Lopore
Akikar	son of Lopore and Rengen
Akou	a rich camp owner near Morukore
Akral	youngest son of Lopore and Rengen
Alaina	daughter of Lopore and Ngira
Angerengmoe	a senior elder of Lokoki
Apan	neighbor of Lopore
Asch, Tim	photographer of our group
Assuman	son of Nabilo and Mustafa
Bakimoe	a senior elder of Lokoki
Barber, Jim	Assistant District Commissioner in Moroto, and a friend of ours
Bilo	elderly brother-in-law of Rengen; the man to whom Lopore had given refuge
Botia	Lopore's late father
Botia	son of Adwong and Lopore
Botia	Lokorimoe's retainer
Carlo	grown son of Uri, who kept a dhuka in Kalapata
Chuchu	daughter of Rengen and Lopore
David	David Lotukei, our interpreter

Dyson-Hudson, Neville and Rada	ethnologists who spent years in Karamoja
Elijah	Suk prophet
Emuthugut	Uri's dog
Gulliver, P. and P. H.	ethnologists who spent years in Turkana-land and Jie
Ibongo	a mysterious figure, a prophet who may or may not be living
Ikwaibong	another name for Ibongo
Ikwal Thonal	Rengen
Iloshabiet	granddaughter of Lopore
Iruata	late wife of Mora; sister of Uri
Johnson, Tom and Kirsti	friends who came to Dodoth with us
Juma	Swahili foreman of roadwork in Dodoth, around 1925
Kalingemala	young brother in a compound household, whose cattle were confiscated
Kapoi	eighth living wife of Lokorimoe
Kiten	friend of Lopore
Lokiding	Lokorimoe's first name
Lokorimoe	the millionaire—He of the Spotted Enemy
Lokwal	Lopore's first name
Lomotin	famous prophet who lived in Lokoki
Lopole	householder killed at Kamion
Lopore	central figure in the book
Lothimidik	rich young householder of Morukore
Lotiang	Uri's first name
Lotukei, Davia	interpreter for our group
Macdonald	first Britisher to enter Dodoth
Manumiss	adopted name of Nabilo

Marco Pole	Acholi friend of Lokorimoe
Miriam	daughter of Nabilo and Mustafa
Mora	poorest householder of Morukore; brother-in-law of Uri
Mustafa Bin Jaddin	first husband of Nabilo
Nabilo	fourth wife of Lopore
Nadolupe	the woman doctor, the only relative of Lopore
Nakade	a neighbor of Lopore
Nathigiria	the old man to whom Lopore married Alaina
Ngira	second wife of Lopore
Ngoriamoe	Jie householder who knew Lopore's mother
Okware	Dodoth householder who lived near Kaabong, who gave refuge to Lopore's mother
Remi	householder who had a camp in Morukore
Remi	deceased elder sister of Uri
Remi	a youngster, son of Nathigiria
Rengen	senior wife of Lopore
Rogo	brother of Kalingemala
Sokot	married into Ngira's family; his dwelling annexed Lopore's
Thonal	Rengen's father
Tim	Tim Asch, a photographer
Toperi-peri	young Teutho spy
Torori	son of Lopore and Ngira
Tupona	first governor of Dodoth; the term may come from the word "governor" or from his name, Tufnell

Tupona   second governor of Dodoth; the word
             may come from the word "governor" or
             from his name, Turpin

Uri   central figure in Morukore

Words and Place Names

abuthia	the mass at the end of the raiding formation; the word comes from "wide-mouthed gourd"
Acholi	the people west of Dodoth, and their land
akachierit	small bright star
Akarimojong	the language of Karamoja
akibak	stand in line
Akuj	God
angerenger	eviscerate
amuron	(f. of emuron) a woman doctor
apolon	important, big
aremong etop	shooting star
Arri	the Watershed, the Milky Way
arri	a fence
askari	policeman
atom	elephant
Baganda	a people in central Uganda
dhuka	a shop or store
Didinga	a people of the southern Sudan
Dodoth	a nation of 20,000 people, offshoots of the Karamojong and third tribe of the Karamojong Cluster
Donyiro	another name for the Nginyangatom, a nation of 5,500 people, seventh tribe of the Karamojong Cluster
ejie	fight
ekamuran	in-law

ekapolon	a word coined from *ekile apolon,* now used for first-degree chief, a government-appointed office
eketoi	tree, wood, bark, branch, medicine, poison, venom, spell
ekichot	the arm of a raiding formation
ekile	man
ekipi	water spirit
ekori	giraffe-like spots
emanik	bull
emoit	enemy, foreigner
emong	ox
emuron	prophet, doctor, diviner
emuthugut	European
Entebbe	political capital of Uganda
etem	the sitting place for men, outside the dwelling
etop	large, soft, bright star
Iteso	language of the Teso
Jackait	second-degree chief—a coined word
Jie	the second tribe of the Karamojong Cluster, numbering 18,000 people, hostile to Dodoth and their immediate neighbors to the south
Jiye	the fifth or sixth tribe of the Cluster, inhabiting the southern Sudan
Kaabong	capital of Dodoth
Kailele	a hill and neighborhood west of Morukore
Kalapata	a small town north of Morukore
Kamion	place in northern Dodoth, smaller than Kalapata
Kampala	industrial capital of Uganda
K.A.R.	King's African Rifles
Karamoja	the northeastern district of Uganda
Karamojong	the first tribe of the Karamojong Cluster, numbering perhaps 55,000, allies of the Dodoth

Karamojong Cluster	seven tribes, all with more or less the same language, all offshoots of each other or of the Karamojong
Kitgum	a town in Acholi
Lara	the month corresponding to November
lokapa	"he of the father's place" (*lo* = he *ka* = place *pa* = father); the father's place is the dwelling; hence, half brother
lokato	"he of the mother's place" (*lo* = he *ka* = place *to* = mother); the mother's place is the court; hence, full brother
Lokijuka	the time the Protectorate government pushed north into Karamoja and Dodoth
Lokoki	the district of which Morukore is a neighborhood
lothiru	a soft-leafed plant
Lotim	a mountain, west across the plain from Morukore
Loyoro	a town in southern Dodoth
Luganda	language of Buganda
mkungu	third-degree chief; the name for this appointed office comes from Baganda
moru	mountain
Morukore	neighborhood of four households and one camp in eastern Lokoki—the neighborhood in which we lived
Morunyang	a hill in western Lokoki
Ngadodotho	language of Dodoth
ngakuliak	the Pleiades
ngapulei	indentations in the Rift Valley
Ngidiko	They of the Warthogs, a clan name
ngimoe	enemies, foreigners
Nginyangatom	They of the Yellow Trumpet, a clan name
Nginyangatom	a people in the Sudan; see Donyiro
ngipian	plural of *ekipi;* water spirits
nyang	yellow, tan

Suk	a people east of Karamoja
Teso	a people south of Karamoja
Teutho	a hunting and gathering people living in the Escarpment hills
Timu	a vast forest in Dodoth
Toposa	a nation of 34,000 people, the sixth tribe of the Karamojong Cluster, who live in the southern Sudan
Turkana	a nation of 85,000 people, the third tribe of the Karamojong Cluster, who live in the Rift Valley; allies of the Jie, hostile to the Dodoth and the Karamojong

NOTE: Population figures in text and glossary are based on "The Central Nilo Hamites" by Pamela Gulliver and P. H. Gulliver, in *Ethnographic Survey of Africa*, ed. Daryll Forde (London: International African Institute; 1953).

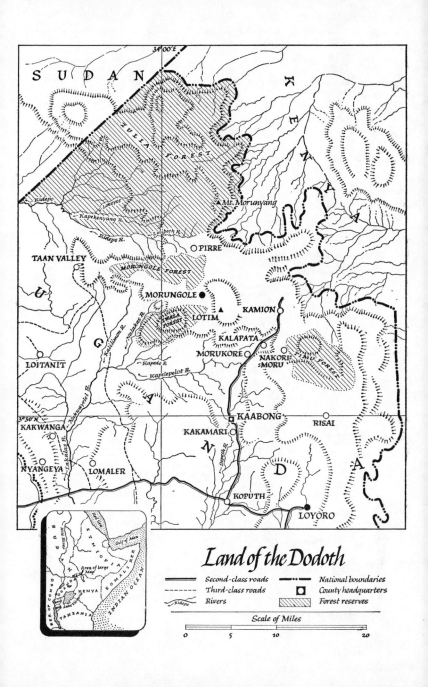

Land of the Dodoth

Second-class roads	National boundaries
Third-class roads	County headquarters
Rivers	Forest reserves

Scale of Miles

0   5   10   20

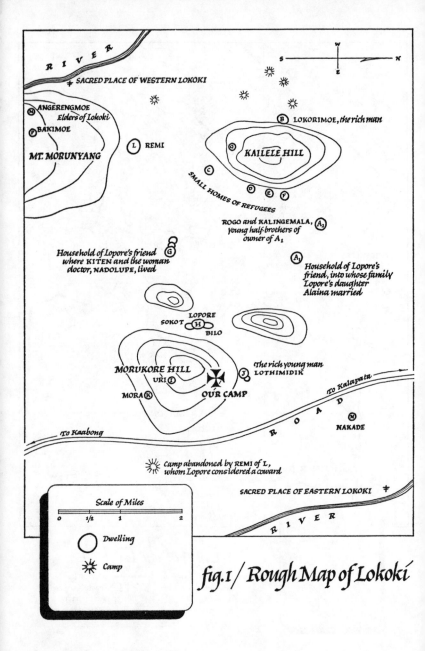

fig. I / Rough Map of Lokoki

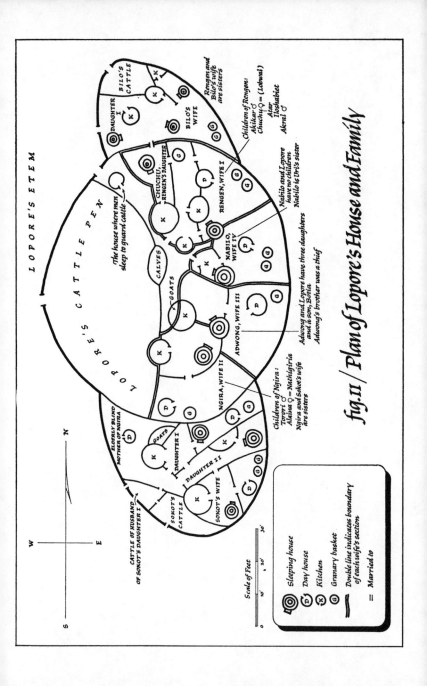

LOPORE'S ETEM

LOPORE'S CATTLE PEN

BILO'S CATTLE

Rengen and Bilo's wife are sisters

DAUGHTER I

BILO'S WIFE

Children of Rengen:
Akikar ♂
Chuchu ♀ = (Lotwel)
Atar
Akrwl ♂
Iloshabiet ♂

CHUCHU, RENGEN'S DAUGHTER

The house where men sleep to guard cattle

RENGEN, WIFE I

Nabilo and Lopore have no children
Nabilo is Uri's sister

CALVES

NABILO, WIFE IV

GOATS

ADWONG, WIFE III

Adwong and Lopore have three daughters and a son, Bitia
Adwong's brother was a thief

ELDERLY BLIND MOTHER OF NGIRA

DAUGHTER I

GOATS

Children of Ngira:
Torori ♂
Alaisa ♀ = Nathigitia
Ngira and Sokot's wife are sisters

NGIRA, WIFE II

CATTLE OF HUSBAND OF SOKOT'S DAUGHTER I

SOKOT'S CATTLE

DAUGHTER II

SOKOT'S WIFE

N
W — E
S

Scale of Feet
0   10'   20'   30'

◉ Sleeping house
Ⓓ Day house
Ⓚ Kitchen
Ⓖ Granary basket
╪ Double line indicates boundary of each wife's section
= Married to

fig. II / Plan of Lopore's House and Family

WARRIOR HERDSMEN

CHAPTER ONE

Morukore

MORUKORE, though not on any map, is a neighborhood in southeast Dodoth, a high, green land that is today the northernmost county of Uganda. The neighborhood takes its name from a hill called Morukore, and the name comes from a word describing cattle who have markings like giraffes. Giraffe Spotted Mountain, it could be called, because of the yellow stones that lie on its pale sides and make it, from a distance, as spotted as any ox or bull or cow. Its name is no wonder, for the Dodoth who named it are of the Nilo-Hamitic pastoralists, proud warrior herdsmen whose numbers include the Masai.

The Dodoth have existed as a people for perhaps two centuries, from the time a band of colonists broke from the parent tribe that lives to the south, a tribe that today numbers 55,000 and is called Karamojong. The word *Dodoth* is said to come from the Karamojong word for "yolk," perhaps in memory of the colonizing nucleus. The colonizing band

increased to more than 20,000 people, who, in the last two
centuries, have not chosen to change their customary ways
for new ways. Most of the changes in Dodoth have been
evolutionary and internal, for the people have resisted outside government; efforts of police and missionaries to
pacify or convert the Dodoth have for the most part met
with failure, and today these conservative pastoralists live
with their herds as they have always lived. They are
Ugandans now.

As a people they are rather formidable. Most men are
enormous: they stand six feet tall or taller and have long
arms and legs, yet are not lanky, as are some East Africans,
but husky, heavy-boned, broad-shouldered, and strong.
Most women are somewhat shorter, but are also heavy-
boned and graceful, handsome rather than soft and pretty,
for the strong jaw of the nation, the lean face, and the deep,
wide eyes create a beauty that lasts into old age.

A group of Dodoth seems larger than life, for everyone
speaks very loudly and ornaments glitter in the crowd. The
men stud their ears with earrings, wear bracelets, belts,
necklaces, and anklets, and increase their height with
headdresses. Young men's headdresses are long red baskets
in the shape of sugarloafs; older men wear buns of their
own felted hair plastered with stippled, painted sacred
clay, with ostrich plumes or cock feathers standing above
and bright chains asway below. Apart from ornaments,
Dodoth men usually wear nothing, except occasionally
sandals, and cloth capes over their backs. Women wear
their hair in tightly coiled ringlets like Dutch bobs; they
wear leather capes, ankle-slapping, fluted leather skirts,
towers of loose neckrings, very many earrings, anklets,
bracelets, chain belts, and bibs of necklaces. Both sexes
wear the lip plug. This, a small bone or metal disc, or a

knob of precious ivory, fits in a hole below the membrane of the lower lip. To accommodate the plug, the lower incisor teeth are pried out of youngsters. To be rude, a woman may remove the plug and thrust her tongue out through the hole at you.

The Dodoth ornament their persons beautifully, but almost nothing else. They are austere, and not artistic, and even the ornaments, in the case of men, are sometimes put aside. Hence it is not unusual to meet a Dodoth man far from home and wearing nothing, no headdress, not a feather, no sandals, nothing in his hands.

Of weapons the Dodoth have almost too many. The primary weapon is the nine-foot spear, made with a metal foreshaft and a sharp, leaf-shaped blade, a short wooden center piece, and a tapered metal tail, the spear straight and light and perfectly balanced. There are different kinds of bows, arrows, slingshots, axes; also sticks, clubs, and shields for different kinds of fighting; and at least four different kinds of knives: hooked knives worn as rings on the fingers, round knives worn like bracelets, ordinary daggers worn around the neck, and thin stilettos thrust in the hair. But the owners paint no pictures, carve no figures, weave no fabrics, and make no dishes, baskets, or jars. Halves of dry calabashes serve as containers until they become trash, and no one bothers to draw designs on these. The great music of Africa, the contrapuntal singing and the intricate, weaving, thirty- and forty-beat rhythm periods, are not found in Dodoth, where there are no musical instruments, not even drums. Even the religion seems austere compared to religions that embody saints or heroes, ancestors, or angels or a hierarchy of gods, for the Dodoth have but one God whose name is God, Akuj. He is so remote and vague a figure that very little is known about him, except that he inhabits the air and sometimes settles in the tops of certain trees. But he has no kingdom populous with spirits, and for the dead maintains no paradise.

Yet the culture of the Dodoth is complex, and the people are highly imaginative. The care and passion, the artistic expression, and the materialism that other people devolve on other things are fixed, by the Dodoth, on their cattle.

The owner of a herd does not have to paint or sing. It is enough to watch his cattle come home in the evening, and stand chest deep among them as in a slow, deep stream. It is enough to watch the gentle, ambling cows and oxen and see the herd bulls jostling each other, enough to rub a spotted back or to touch a ticklish ear, a lyre-shaped, warm horn, to know the cattle all by sight, to hear their bawling voices, to smell the rising dust mixed with the grassy, milky scent, to see them pass and pass as if the herd would never end, to be their owner.

It is said that among African people some of those who own and value cattle are the most resistant to change. This is true of the Dodoth, who are proud of themselves because of their cattle, who hold people without cattle in contempt, and who see no reason to change as the government wishes them to by reducing the size of their herds to improve the stock and to increase the grazing. Every few months a government cattle buyer comes to Kaabong, administrative center of Dodoth, to buy any cull, any rack of bones that can walk to the auction. There is a tax in Dodoth that must be paid in cash, and people must sell cattle to pay it. There is a serious need to reduce overgrazing. But for the Dodoth, cattle are not items to be bought and sold, or beasts to be slaughtered. Dr. Neville Dyson-Hudson, an anthropologist who studied the related Karamojong, says of these pastoralists that to ask a man to cull his herd is like asking a man to destroy the dirty dollar bills in his pockets. Cattle do not represent wealth; they are wealth.

For the Dodoth, cattle are the warp of life. They are the only wealth, the foundation of economic and social stability, the origin of all human ties. If drought comes, if the gardens and the grain crops fail, cattle provide food. Cows give milk. This is drunk daily, and churned into butter, or curdled with cow's urine into a salty cheese. Oxen give their blood. A man wishing to bleed an ox tightens a cord around its neck until its eyes and veins are bulging. While his sons hold the ox by the tongue, tail, and horns, he shoots its bulging neck vein with a blocked arrow. Blood pours in a steaming arch and is caught in a basin. When a quart or two is in the basin, the cord around the ox's neck is jerked away, the vein collapses, the bleeding stops as the ox runs off shaking its head and the blood is eaten. People drink the blood raw, after squeezing it with their fingers to break the clots, or cook it with green millet flour into a delicate, delicious pudding, as airy as soufflé.

Cowhides make sleeping mats and clothing. Cow dung makes flooring. Fresh cow urine in its sterile stream washes dirty hands or cleans utensils, or softens leather or curdles milk for clabber or speeds the making of ghee.

The first morsel a baby ever eats in his life is a drop of butter. From then on, he is involved with cattle. Every day and night of his life, his nostrils will be filled with their sweet odor, his ears with their vibrant voices; to tend his herd is his life's occupation, and when he dies, if he dies at home, his body may be wrapped in the hide of one of his oxen and buried in the soft earth of their pen.

If a cow dies, it is eaten. But no one would kill so valued a creature just for meat when it gives milk or blood already. No matter how small or poor a little cow is, she can

bear a calf yearly and increase the herd. Thus, numbers of
cattle are important. The condition of each cow is not.
There is a government farm in Moroto, administrative center of Karamoja District, of which Dodoth is a county, and
on the farm are beautiful prize livestock—just a few, in
pasture that is not overgrazed. But those who uphold the
farm as a good example are regarded by pastoralists with
the same superiority with which we regard a person who
prefers a nickel to a dime because the nickel is larger.

With cattle, men marry. The Dodoth are polygamous,
and a man gives twenty or fifty or a hundred and fifty
cattle for each wife, wanting to pay as much as he can
rather than search for a bargain, for he not only gains a
woman to live with him and bear his children but also
forms a strong and deep connection with her family, especially her father. When a man dies, his widows can become
the wives of his brother, if they like, and usually they do,
since cattle have been given to join the women to their
husband's family. By exchanging cattle with friends, a man
can gain supporters. When they marry, he contributes to
their bridewealth; when he marries, they contribute to his;
and an indestructible network involving friendship, marriage, and property is formed, to last for the rest of his
life.

Cattle are admired. Derogatory words such as *moo* do
not exist in Ngadodotho; the sounds people make in imita-
tion of cattle are majestic, deep, loud cries, exactly like
cows' voices. And the songs that young men sing while
dancing, songs about cattle, begin and end with muffled
cries like bulls or oxen bellowing.

Cattle are part of religious life. During all important
ceremonies, an ox or many oxen are speared as sacrifices.
Cattle are part of emotional, personal life. Every man owns

a special ox from which he takes one of his names, being
called the ox's father. He burns stripes upon his ox's hide
and beats its horns into extraordinary shapes with a stone.
He ties a necklace around its neck and composes songs in its
honor, songs that confide to it his fears or griefs or victor-
ies. In later life, at moments of danger or triumph, a man
holds up his arms to represent his ox's horns, and during a
battle he cries its name. After a battle he slits its ears, one
slit for each of his victims, so the ox will know its owner has
killed in its name, and will rejoice with him. "A bull is
father of the herd," say the Dodoth, "but an ox encourages
a man."

People hostile to the Dodoth live at their borders. These
people, the Jie to the south, numbering 18,000, and the
Turkana to the east, numbering 85,000 and occupying most
of the northern parts of Kenya, are related to the Dodoth
through the fact that the Jie also sprang from Karamoja as
the result of a tribal fracture. The name Jie comes from
ejie, to fight. The Turkana later rose peacefully from the Jie
to form the fourth tribe of what is called the Karamojong
Cluster, which has seven tribes in all. All the tribes of the
Cluster own and value cattle; when drought and disease
deplete the herds of one of these people, the people must
have more. Even today there is raiding, the Karamojong
and Dodoth against the Jie and Turkana, or any one of
these people against some of the other, less closely related
pastoral tribes unfortunate enough to live within reason-
able distance. Thus battles are fought, and crops and dwellings burned, and human lives risked and lost for the little
lyre-horned cattle. Now and then *The New York Times*
carries an article about the raiding; one, in 1962, concerned
a raid mounted by a thousand Karamojong against a
neighboring people, the Suk. That there are only 55,000

Karamojong shows the size of the army. More than a hundred people were killed during that raid, which lasted all day. The government sends police and soldiers to stop the raiding, confiscates cattle as punishment for raiding, calls a curfew, and forbids the carrying of spears, but still raiding goes on.

When we first arrived in Uganda, we were told by an African resident of Kampala that it was "risky in Dodoth for people with your color skin." Not so. Raiding is often misunderstood by the more sophisticated people of Uganda, for the political complexities and the feelings against Europeans and the Protectorate which sometimes affect the emergent state were not at work in Dodoth. We had an eerie immunity from the pastoral wars and came and went like birds in the air. Though we possessed vehicles and many other useful, desirable things, all this was as nothing to the proud Dodoth pastoralists, nothing in comparison to cattle, and of these we had none.

We stayed in Dodoth from early summer 1961 until the first weeks of December, and during that time we lived on Morukore. We made a camp in a grove of trees, with tents and a brush fence to keep the livestock out. It was a nice camp—some of its ruins may be there still—and its site was lovely because, of all the hills for miles around, Morukore was the highest.

Morukore forms a peak on a ridge and is one of the chain of volcanic Escarpment hills, all tumbled and rock-strewn, which stand 5,000 feet above sea level near the eastern border of Dodoth. A few miles beyond the hills in the east, the high land falls so sharply as to be almost a precipice, and drops 2,000 feet to Kenya on the Rift Valley floor. In western Dodoth, the country becomes level, and reaches fifty miles to Acholi over great grass plains.

The hills begin rising in the south of Dodoth almost at the Jie border and, growing higher and wilder, extend eighty miles north into the corner of Dodoth formed by Kenya and the Sudan. Morukore is about fifty miles south of that.

Standing on Morukore, one could look north and south along the chain of hills. To the west, one could see out over a narrow plain, a flat valley with acacia trees on it, to a range of mountains with forests on their sides. From June to September in the mountains, during the heaviest rains small waterfalls showed here and there, white like plumes amid the dark green, but in January and February, during the drought, the leaves and waterfalls were gone and the slopes were red and bare.

East of Morukore was a forest. It stretched for miles over rolling land to the edge of the Escarpment. No one lived in the forest—at least, no Dodoth—but they would graze their cattle in its green shade and water them in a river that wound there. In the dry season, when the riverbed was sand, it served as a roadway for cattle, leading to a well that the Dodoth had dug twenty or thirty feet below the surface, where there was always water. During a heavy rain the river would swell and boil in a brown torrent that broke the banks and drowned the roots of trees. Branches would trail in its current, wetting the birds' nests that were dangling. After the rain, the floods receding left the riverbed damp and bare, as the brown water went by way of larger rivers, swamps, and lakes to join the River Nile. The forest was a lovely place, still and wild. All day in the hot season doves called in its thickets and in the dark earth hyenas slept in their holes.

Most of the Dodoth population gathered itself in the
Escarpment hills. The western plains, reaching to Acholi,
were not inhabited, being partly reserved for grazing and
partly overgrown with elephant grass so coarse and harsh
that cattle cannot eat it. There is not enough wood on the
plains for building, but besides that, the Dodoth like to live
with a view. The residential section in the hills was therefore long and thin, extending from a few miles north of the
Jie border to perhaps twenty miles south of the Kenya-
Sudan corner. The section was divided into districts, which
were in turn divided into neighborhoods. The Dodoth do
not live in villages. Each household, each large family, oc-
cupies its own enormous dwelling, so self-sustained, so
independent as to seem almost autonomous.

From the top of Morukore one could see more than
thirty of these dwellings, some near, some very far away,
standing like crowns on the ridges, like bristling rings, for
the dwelling walls are made of uneven, heavy poles thrust
upright in the ground to form vast circles, the walls of the
usual dwelling standing perhaps seven feet high and en-
closing perhaps ten thousand square feet. The upright
poles of the dwelling walls are densely wound with
branches, forming an impenetrable barricade several feet
thick, the mass broken here and there with a forked pole
thrust prongs down into the earth to form a tiny door, so
low and narrow that the broad-shouldered occupants must
crawl and squeeze to enter. These low doorways keep the
livestock out by day as the heavy fences keep them in at
night. But also each dwelling is a fort. Spears cannot penetrate the bristling walls and a person wishing to enter a
dwelling must enter alone on hands and knees, presenting
the back of his neck.

One dwelling stood at the foot of Morukore. From the

top of the hill one could see inside, for the enormous encircling ring was open to the sky. Though not exceptionally
large, the dwelling was the home of forty people. Inner
walls, delineating courtyards, divided its uphill half in pie-
shaped sections, and in the courts the thatched roofs of
houses clustered so that, like a fortified village which had
swelled inside its walls, the dwelling seemed crowded. The
houses were round and were made of the hard, red, almost
rainproof plaster that people dig from white-ant hills. The
thatches, bundles of grass sewed tightly to a wooden frame,
were tiered.

There were no courts or houses in the downhill half. This
was the cattle pen, empty during the day while the cattle
were grazing, but just before dawn, all night, and in the
evening, the cattle pen was crowded too, with white and
red and spotted backs. The cattle pen was divided from the
part for people by a low rail fence that in the very center
forked into a circle to form a small round pen for calves,
the heart of the house. The rail fence is called *arii*. The
Watershed of East Africa, which divides the rivers that
feed the Nile from those that feed the Indian Ocean, is also
called Arii, and so is the Milky Way.

Early in the morning, when the sky was cold and pale
and the morning wind rising, the heavy poles that closed
the cattle gate, the one large opening in the outer wall,
were moved away and the cattle would emerge in procession, one or two at a time, until fifty of them stood outside.
They were very small and of all combinations of colors, red-
brown, black, white, dappled, brindle, and roan. The cows
had humps on their shoulders, the little bulls were humped
like walruses, and bulls and cows alike bore the graceful,
lyre horns like the horns of the little cattle depicted in
Egyptian tombs, perhaps of the same ancient species, having

a zebu strain. With the cattle would come a group of tiny isabella donkeys, a mother, a father, and a long-eared fuzzy colt, and always the herd was followed by its herdboys, three dark-skinned, naked little sons of the household, each carrying the smoldering end of a log, a remnant of his mother's nightime fire. Warm smoke would blow back over the little boys to mix with the cold, gray mist rising from the earth around them. They were like little boys in clouds. The boys would flourish sticks at the cattle and the cattle, eating as they went, would start their slow procession toward pasture. Their warm breath would be rising, warm dung they dropped made steam, and the little boys, their protectors, would follow the track the cattle left behind them in the wet, dew-covered grass. To defend the cattle against wild creatures, the oldest boy carried a short, sharp spear.

The cattle, following two little gray-brindle cows—a mother and her daughter, who often led the herd—would take a cattle road that went east to the forest or west through the fields and valley below, out toward the open plain where there were no fields or dwellings, only the blowing grass. It was a wide path, hard and dusty, tramped by many sharp feet. It wound between thornbush fences with stiles as gates to protect the fields, past huge old trees with deep round shadows, and through ravines, and it was crossed with footpaths, some leading from Morukore through the fields to other nearby dwellings, some leading farther, across the plain to the far mountains, the paths joined as they went by other footpaths that you could follow to any settled part of Dodoth.

Later in the day and as their schedules required, the women of the house, their many metal earrings chiming on their neckrings and their leather skirts asway, would go to the fields to spend the day gardening. As there were nine industrious women in the house, they had many acres under cultivation and many different crops. They grew a type of corn that stands ten or fifteen feet high and bears huge ears with tough yellow kernels. They grew finger millet, which bears small tender heads of grain, and bulrush millet, for all the world like huge cattails. They grew sorghum, the stalks of which are sweet and wet and can be eaten like sugarcane, while the heads, large clusters of round kernels in beautiful combinations of red, orange, purple, and white, can be ground into flour. Among the grain crops, pumpkins grew, and gourds, and many types of beans and squashes.

There is a great deal of work to be done to maintain a Dodoth household and to feed all its members. Little boys, too young to tend cattle, herd sheep and calves and goats around the dwelling's ragged walls. Little girls help their mothers with the digging, planting, hoeing, and weeding in the fields: even three-year-old children are not too young to chase birds out of the grain. For most of the day, then, the house stood empty, quiet, and warm in the sun. Brown hawks balanced in the air above it, stooping now and then for rats or lizards, each household's unseen population; sometimes ravens flew from nearby hilltops to sit on the roofs, and if no one was at home, to drop to the hard, earth floors of the courtyards and eat spilled grain.

But in the evening, when the sun was low and casting shadows from the peaks of the hills, when the valleys were cold and blue and the hawks and ravens had flown away, the women would come home, each with a load of firewood on her head, or a pumpkin, or a bowl of string beans or tomatoes for the evening meal. Each woman would crawl through the low doors of the dwelling, follow the maze of

passageways to her court, fling down her load in her courtyard, sweep its floor with a twig broom, and build her fire,
and when the hungry little boys would drive home the
cattle, each woman would send her children with clean
gourds to milk those cattle which were assigned to her.

Then the gates were closed, stuffed tight with poles and
branches, the cattle in the pen would bawl and crowd together, the goat pen would be full and closed, and the
many people would then eat and talk, each woman with
her children in her own court, and through the straw roofs
gray smoke lifted to the sky as the nighttime fires were
kindled in the houses to keep the sleepers warm.

All this of the dwelling below Morukore—the house with
its crowded courts and rooftops, the women, the children,
the cattle, calves, goats, sheep, and donkeys, the crops in
the round fields, even the hills and trees around the dwelling—was the domain of a tall man named Lokwal Lopore.
He built the house, married four women who bore him
many children, found husbands for his daughters, named
his grandchildren, and took in two families of his wives'
relatives whom he now protects and feeds from his herd.

Lopore was a fierce old man. Though he was in his six-
ties, and had short, iron-gray hair, his body was tall and
muscular. Veins and sinews stood out on his arms; ribbed
muscles showed on his belly. His arms and legs were long
and strong and his strength was obvious. He could walk
sixty miles in a day if he wanted to, or throw an ox down if
he wanted to doctor it, or throw a long spear so that it flew
with an eerie hum into the distance, to stand up just where
he said it would, trembling in the ground.

For a man of property, even in Dodoth, Lopore was
austere. He often wore no more than an amulet on a string
around his neck—and the amulet's invisible, enveloping

charm, a spell against witches. He also wore a lip plug, a flat, bone disc. Resistance to its weight for fifty years had make his face muscular and his mouth severe, a deceiving expression, for he was a volatile person whose moods changed easily. When one of his grandchildren would come up behind him to take his finger, a great softness would come over his face as he smiled down. But his own sons feared him. If one of them lost a calf or a goat during the day Lopore might fly into a rage and beat the child; but on the other hand, if his mood was milder, he might wait to hear the explanation, then excuse the child entirely and help him find the lost animal. Remembering their youth, his grown sons respected him, his married daughters obeyed him. And of his wives, two loved him, one adored him, and one no longer cared for him and today merely resides in his house.

Lopore spent a good deal of time at home. He would sit amid a pile of boulders near his dwelling. This was his *etem*, his sitting place. All households have one because each court or group of courts, each house within the uphill portion of a dwelling's walls is the place of a woman; and the lower portion is for cattle. The man who owns it has no place inside, so sits outside and oversees it all.

Lopore's etem was at the edge of the hill, where, at a small cliff, the hill dropped to the fields below. Like an eagle in his aerie, he watched his domains, seeing that no harm came and that everyone who ought to be was working. If he saw that his youngest wife had not gone to the river for water, he might come down from his rocks to catch her by the arm and scold her, and if he noticed, in the valley below, that one of his little daughters was playing when she should have been on the sod platform of her mother's field house throwing stones at birds, he would

shout out such a loud scolding that the girl in the distance
would leap to her feet, climb quickly on the platform, and
fling so many pebbles into her mother's grain that birds
would fly out in all directions.

Lopore liked the work of his dwelling to be done well,
but if he was harsh he was also passionately protective. He
would, for instance, challenge any strange passerby in a
rather insulting way, assuming, often wrongly, that the
stranger was up to mischief. When the surprised stranger
demeaned himself by explaining his presence—he would
have to explain or fight, for no one could ignore Lopore—
Lopore would dismiss him with an impolite grunt and watch
him out of sight. By no means do all Dodoth act this way.

In his protectiveness, Lopore could be frightening. One
night, without hesitation, he rushed into the darkness of his
cattle pen, where he thought he heard a hyena, and finding
a leopard, clubbed it so heavily that he not only killed it
but destroyed the skin, which angered him because if it
were not so ragged he could have worn it himself.

One night again, he heard a noise outside his wall and,
looking through a little space between the poles, he saw a
strange man standing in the moonlight. The man fell to one
knee, stood up, and fell again. Lopore, quietly unwind-
ing the branches of his door, crawled out, and leaping
on the stranger, killed him too, beating and beating him
with his club, although the stranger cried out and begged
him not to. But Lopore knew that the stranger was a witch
who, with a heart filled with spite, was trying to kill one of
Lopore's children perhaps, or some of his cattle, surely
some creature or person of his house.

A witch comes riding on the back of hyena. When near
the dwelling, the witch dismounts and begins to encircle
the walls. People who have seen a witch encircling de-

scribe the motion as stumbling and rolling, like a dog playing, for the witch moves up and down in a halting, tumbling
manner until he has cast his spell. Then he goes away.

The Dodoth do not bury all their dead. Most bodies are
placed in the bushes. Lopore, in the morning, carried off
the witch's corpse and threw it in the bushes, and before
many nights had passed, the body had disappeared. It was
removed by other witches; Lopore found the long, splayed
footprints of their mounts.

When we first met Lopore, he was trying a thief whom
he had caught robbing his field of a pumpkin. We were
looking for a place to camp. We, who that day were my
husband, myself, and our interpreter, David Lotukei, had
driven from Moroto, where we had left the rest of our party
—our friends, Tom and Kirsti Johnson, and our two children—and were walking in the mist that hung on Morukore, looking for a flat place where we could pitch our
tents. We found one in a grove of trees and, noticing a
group of people gathered on the slope below, went down to
ask permission. It was July, the rainy season. The men, a
large group, were seated on Lopore's boulders all close together in a dark company, for their skins were wet and
their black cloth capes were clinging to their shoulders
with the rain. Some men had removed their capes and
folded them over their headdresses, for rain dissolves the
clay and mats the feathers, and one man wore a bowl upside down over his head. The bowl I took at first to be a
helmet, for all the men were armed. They sat in a thicket of
clubs and spears, and spear blades and knife blades shone
in the gathering, dull gleams against the men's dark skin
and clothing.

In the midst of this, a young Dodoth in European clothes
crouched on the ground. His face was composed and he

seemed unconcerned, though his arms were bound behind
his back so that his shoulders thrust forward uncomfortably, and a tall man who was speaking in a loud voice, slow
and full of anger, stood over him with a club. These two
were the thief and Lopore, and of the two, the thief noticed
us first.

He seemed hopeful. Perhaps he thought we would inter-
vene on his behalf. Europeans in Uganda are known for
showing kindness in situations such as this. But we could
not possibly have tried to help him, to have had our first
gesture in Dodoth be in favor of a thief against his judges,
the householders and society, so when he looked at us we
looked away. We stood uncertainly nearby, listening to
what was said. The people were trying to decide whether
to beat the thief right where he was or take him to
Kaabong, administrative center of Dodoth, where the police, they thought, would beat him. It seemed unlikely that
anyone would want to walk the man to Kaabong, almost
twenty miles by road, when he could be punished where he
was, and I think our presence caused the indecision. Presently Lopore left the trial to have a look at us. "You want to
live here?" he asked when we had made our request. We
said we did. He thought it over, then answered: "Very
well," and excusing himself, saying he had a matter to attend to, he went back to his etem in the rocks.

We did not want to meddle, or to see the thief beaten, so
we went up the hill and began to clear ground to pitch the
tents. Near the end of the day, we were visited by Lopore.
He was so nice, so kind when he came to see us, bringing us
a calabash of fresh, delicious milk and seizing me by the
wrist to force my hand open so that he could give me a
pinch of soft, green powder, his burning snuff, that I was
emboldened to ask what had happened to the thief. He

seemed surprised. "The thief!" he said. "I helped him."
Lopore had said to the gathering: "If he wants a pumpkin,
let us give him a pumpkin," and sending to the garden for
another pumpkin, he had cut the young thief's bonds and
at spearpoint had made him eat every bite of the other
pumpkin raw before letting him run away.

Lopore had a hard, short, rather mirthless laugh and
was, we later found, an influential person not only in his
neighborhood but in surrounding neighborhoods as well.
He had a seemingly unlimited number of friends, who
came in a steady stream to visit him. They came for hospitality, which he gave generously, but also because they
liked his wit and valued his opinions. The Dodoth admire
those among them who are forthright, positive, and sound.

Morukore was in the eastern section of the district of
Lokoki. Lokoki was divided in two: the eastern section and
the western section, neither of which had names. People
called themselves the people of the east and the people of
the west. There were, as far as I could find, five neighborhoods in the eastern section. Morukore neighborhood was
small and round, with the diameter of half a mile. Besides
Lopore's dwelling, there were three dwellings in it, and one
cattle camp which stood in the trees beyond the eastern
slope of the hill. This camp, a large, thornbush enclosure,
contained just one small structure, a flat sod roof supported
by four poles like a woman's garden shelter. The camp
belonged to a man named Remi who had more cattle than
he could keep at home. But the camp on Morukore was
only one of several that Remi owned. He drove his herds
there only when he felt they would enjoy the grazing; for
most of the time the camp stood empty, with only the flies
on the dung inside it and a thornbush in its gate. Remi was
a man of forty who never wore a shred of clothing, but

whose blue clay headdress was always beautifully kept. He
occasionally visited us to ask for a stick of laundry bluing,
which gave the clay its color. He was one of the few people
in Dodoth who cared for European things, and once asked
us for gasoline. Since its advent in the country, it is used as
medicine, for the fumes relieve chest congestion by induc-
ing coughing, and the hot, slick feeling as the gas goes
down is thought of as a poultice. But we were afraid to give
it. Once he asked us the price of our specially made tents.
We told him. "Not much," he said. "A few oxen would buy
them." He asked us to sell them, but for cash, not oxen, as
he would sell the few oxen to the government cattle buyer
when he came to Kaabong. We had to refuse, though he
made a good offer, and he was disappointed but not surprised. The tents, he said, would have been good for his
calves; the canvas floors would have prevented foot rot and
the nylon screening would have kept out the flies. I was
surprised. I thought he had wanted a tent for himself. But
then, why would he, when the Dodoth houses are snug and
dry and spacious, cool in summer and much warmer
than tents when a fire is kindled inside. Later Remi asked
to buy the tent cable and its toggle bolt to help him train
the horns of his ox in the shape of a valentine.

Not counting the people who used Remi's camp, the
population of Morukore was ninety-two when we arrived,
ninety-three when we left, due to the births of a baby girl,
a baby boy, and the death of a very old lady. The livestock
population was over five hundred, more than half of which
were cattle, not counting the cattle at the camp. The rest
were sheep and goats, whose milk is drunk by children.
Donkeys are not included in the census, for they are not
considered useful animals. They are not milked, because
they kick the milker. Once in a while a donkey will be

made to carry a burden but never a person—although people sometimes eat their little donkeys, only witches ride.

The richest man in Morukore, who owned more than half the cattle, was Lothimidik, whose dwelling stood on the northern slope of the hill. He was hardly over thirty, very young to be so rich. No young man breaks away from his father's home before his father dies. But Lothimidik had no father. His father and his brother had been fiery warriors who, it was said, had raided the Turkana often and had amassed a fortune in cattle. But they were killed while raiding, and gentle, young Lothimidik had inherited the cattle and his brother's three wives as well. He had had a wife of his own, and a small herd, then suddenly he found himself with four wives and an enormous herd, and no children old enough to tend it, so he lent some of his cattle to relatives, and some to friends, and had to spend his days walking here and there, visiting the fragments of his great herd, to hear the news of his cattle and to see how they were. He was so often away we never really came to know him. When once he visited to bring us a gourd of milk, I mistook him for a householder's son and kept him waiting. Often when we saw him it was night, and he was coming over the brow of the hill. He never left the same cattle with any friend or relative for long, but was always shifting them, and when we saw him at night he was usually driving a few of the cattle before him. Lothimidik would seem like a shadow in the moonlight, the cattle would seem gray, and the tortoiseshell bells around their necks would knock and clack as they trotted home.

Lothimidik was born far away and had his origins and connections elsewhere. Also, he was a young man in a land where age, above all, is respected. He wore an elaborate,

old-man's headdress, and when he had time, attended
men's gatherings at etems, but when opinions were expressed, his own was not among them; he listened to his
elders in silence. He had very little influence in the neighborhood.

The poorest house of Morukore belonged to a man
named Mora who lived south of the hill. There was no
woman in his house, for his wife, Iruata, was dead. He
lived with his two grown sons and four young children,
with only eight cattle, only three of which were milking
cows.

Mora was tall and thin, perhaps ten years younger than
Lopore. His hair was dressed with sacred clay in which
stood two tufts of rooster feathers, iridescent black and
brown. He was a handsome man who carried himself
proudly, but his brown cloth cape was ragged, his ornaments were chipped and broken, and he was too poor to
buy more. His dwelling had but one court and a small
muddy cattle pen enclosed by a broken wall. It was a man's
house, a bachelor's quarters, with used gourds and pumpkin rinds drawing flies in the corners, and piles of cinders
here and there; Mora and his sons cooked wherever they
wanted and did not sweep afterwards, so white ashes blew
about. As gathering wood is woman's work, the men seldom
did it but broke their firewood from their wall, which explained its raggedness. Mora had only one field, and without a wife he was the gardener, but he had no talent for
gardening and no green thumb—he strewed his seeds before the rains came, but he seldom hoed and never weeded
—mostly he tended his field by watching it from atop his
broad, flat etem stone. If a dove or a little blackbird from
the forest would fly into his crop, he would scrape up a
handful of dirt to fling at the bird morosely.

The household was not a happy one. For most of the day it was empty except for his youngest children, his delicate, three-year-old daughter, quiet and large-eyed, who wore a necklace of green seeds, and her husky, five-year-old brother, who wore nothing at all. The girl was the little boy's victim; they fought, and she was always bested, but their father couldn't do everything—he couldn't tend his cattle, watch his garden, go to gatherings at etems, and stay with his children too. Every evening he would cook their food for the next day, but they were too young to divide the food into several meals or equally between them, so after breakfast they sometimes ate nothing else all day.

Except for the little girl, the only womanly thing in the dwelling was the house of Mora's married daughter, a tightly thatched, neat little house under a pepper tree. But the married daughter, a very beautiful girl, rarely had a chance to visit her father; though traditionally after marriage a girl lives with her family until she has two children able to walk, she was the exception. She seldom stayed, and her house stood very quiet and empty. Flies buzzed inside it, little red peppers dropped to the thatch and rolled to the ground. No one swept them away.

A woman was badly wanted. But marriage and property are so closely linked that Mora's proverty worked in several ways against his chances to remarry. He had no herd to give for a wife. He had few if any of the formal friends obtained by the exchange of stock, friends who might contribute to his bridewealth, for few men wanted to exchange stock with such a poor man. Because he had always been poor, and had only one wife, he had only one family of in-laws. If he had had many families of in-laws, they might have contributed enough stock. Because of all this, he was not considered well connected, his daughter was not considered a good match, and he had not received many cattle at her wedding.

His poverty worked against everyone in the family. His two grown sons were also ready to marry, and had less prospects than Mora. In their frustration they turned to petty crime, stealing useless objects from us, pumpkins from fields, and milk from cattle camps. The oldest was caught stealing milk from a camp and was beaten by the camp owners almost to death.

Being poor, Mora was not an influential person. The envy that the poor must feel toward the rich is feared, and other men seldom came to visit him. When he attended gatherings at other men's etems, he would sit quietly, seldom speaking, listening to what was said. However, he was a thoughtful person who bore his poverty well. Some poor men beg, but Mora never did. Some poor men become the retainers of rich men, but Mora preferred his independence. He was an experienced, wise person, and had two very helpful friends. One of them was Lopore. The other was the fourth householder of Morukore, a man named Uri, who lived on top of the hill.

Uri was the central figure in the neighborhood. Mora's late wife, Iruata, had been his youngest sister. Because Uri had lost his father at an early age, he had taken the place of his father and had accepted the marriage cattle for his sisters, thus forming the deep connection with Mora and Lopore that belongs to a father-in-law. Uri even looked like the central figure of the neighborhood when one saw him sitting, as he often did, on a rock atop the hill.

He was perhaps fifteen years older than Mora and five years older than Lopore, and was a short man with a slight frame and wrinkled skin. He was much respected, and his name was known afar. Travelers would come to his house to spend the night; once a group of policemen, who are afraid of the Dodoth, asked to bivouac in the corridor between his courtyards and his cattle pen. They would have felt safe there. Uri was able to refuse them politely, saying he regretted having neither food nor space. Twice he was asked to intercede between the Dodoth and the government, but he refused this too, saying he hadn't time.

Uri's dwelling was gray with weather but, like an old mansion, it was carefully tended and had many spacious courts and shady passageways within its walls. He had lived there a long time. His herd numbered about fifty head. He also had about twenty sheep and goats, and a small flock of chickens that scratched in the weeds around his dwelling and at night slept in a basket-shaped chicken house atop a pole, twelve feet high, beside the cattle pen. Uri also kept bees. Most men in Dodoth do not bother with bees, but Uri and his two grown sons had fifteen hives. The hives, sections of hollow logs, were chopped from the bee trees in the forest and carried home, to be set up in the trees on top of Morukore hill. When the time came, Uri would take the honey. He also had a little white dog who had two names, Ekori because of his pale yellow spots and Emuthugut, from the Swahili *muzugu,* which means *European.*

The fields of Uri's wives were large and productive. Their fences were well tended and the stiles where the public paths crossed were solid and high. The enormous storage baskets that stood in the fields were roofed with thick thatches. These baskets are used to hold harvested grain before it is threshed and winnowed. Most people do not roof their storage baskets because it seldom rains during the time the unthreshed crops are stored. However, it sometimes rains in the harvest season, and when it does, the grain in the unthatched baskets of Uri's neighbors rots, while Uri's harvest is dry. He was also protective of the crops as they were growing. It was his custom to get up long before sunrise and climb to the very top of the hill, where he would sit with his pair of spears propped against his shoulder. As the stars would disappear and the gray light in the east would show, Uri would see his gardens revealed to him slowly and would take by surprise any marauder, a thief, a wild pig, a monkey, that the gathering light would show to be there.

There may have been a mystery about Uri. He had as one of his names a name unlike that of other Dodoth as far as I know. It implied that its owner had killed a dangerous animal, such as a buffalo or an elephant. The Dodoth, however, are not a hunting people. Though they speak of hunting, they seldom try it, not only because they are uninterested in any beasts but cattle but because the only wild animals that can live in the populous residential areas are small creatures such as dik-diks, or predators such as leopards and hyenas, which like city sparrows can coexist with man. There is, however, a hunting people who live in the wild forest and in the mountains of the Escarpment, where there is lots of game. These are the Teutho, who look like the Dodoth and dress somewhat like the Dodoth, and about whom very little is known. Only a few words of their language have been recorded; no one has studied their lives or customs or visited them for long in their mountain homes. The Teutho may have occupied the land before the Dodoth came. If they did, they yielded space to the pastoral warriors and today live in wild places where no one else will go. They are famous as hunters, famous as magicians, and famous for keeping bees. It is they who have honorary names gained during hunting and I sometimes wondered if Uri was one of them. Sometimes it seemed unlikely; Dodoth families do not marry into Teutho families because the Teutho have no cattle. But they have goats and gather wild food, and Uri once mentioned vaguely that his father had goats but no cattle and that, at least once, he had lived by gathering berries and roots.

When we knew Uri, however, he was a Dodoth. His two wives, now elderly ladies, were well connected; he had given a hundred cattle for each one. As he guarded his lands and cattle, so he guarded his family. He helped his nephews, Mora's sons, out of many difficulties. Each year when the dry season came and Mora found the yield of his garden inadequate, Uri gave him grain. Uri brought up his own children carefully—they were respectful and polite; his daughters' suitors were expected to converse with the elder people in the household before visiting the girls, and his younger children were not allowed to loiter in Kaabong, picking up bad habits from the partially Westernized, detribalized youngsters who lived there. Uri had kept his second son at home to learn pastoralism. The young man, who was married, lived with his father, as most Dodoth men do, went to men's meetings, and wore a black cape and a black, feathered headdress. He was a serious, intelligent young man who was accumulating his own herd and his own formal friendships, which, until change comes to the country, will serve the family well.

Foreseeing the day when the Western world would change Dodoth, Uri had sent his eldest son to school. It was a school run by Catholic missionaries in Kaabong, where the eldest son was given the name of Carlo. He learned to read and write and to speak some English, and he was Western in his outlook. He too was married and had become the keeper of a tiny store, one of six mud dhukas that stood beside the road at a place called Kalapata, a flat place, as the name implies, perhaps five miles north of Morukore. He lived in the back of his store with his wife and child—a modern, nuclear family. He was interested in Uganda's politics, in Uganda's political parties, and in Uganda's impending choice of allegiance to Russia or the United States. He wore European clothes and though his brother, if asked, would refer to himself as a Dodoth, Carlo would speak of himself as an African. When change comes to Dodoth, Carlo will be able to help his family with the outside world.

Uri himself could read and write, though he seldom cared to. Sometimes, when I visited him on top of Morukore, where he sat, gaunt and naked under his etem tree, I would misunderstand or mispronounce something he told me. Then he would break a twig and scratch the word on the bare, brown skin of his thigh so I could read it, then lick his thumb and rub the letters out.

CHAPTER TWO

Neighbors

LOPORE was born in his uncle's house on the slope of
Mount Lotim. Its peak, rising across the valley in the west,
can be seen from Morukore, and in the evening, because
the peak is high, its shadow falls over the other mountains
near it and on the valley floor. The slopes of Lotim are
forested, and near the top are rocky cliffs where, in the
rainy season, the waterfalls shine. The dwelling was near
the foot of the mountain, on its eastern slope and long ago,
morning suns warmed the courtyards where Lopore played.

The members of the house where Lopore was born were
originally members of one court in another great house that
existed so long ago that no trace or memory of it remains,
but it belonged to Lopore's grandfather. He was a rich old
man and a well-known diviner, with a large herd and several wives. Today very few people remember his name. His
house was a traditional Dodoth house, with a section for

each of his wives, and his family was a traditional Dodoth family, a patriarchy. The permanent members of such a house are a man and his wives, his brothers and his brothers' wives but not his sisters, his sons and their wives but not his daughters. Men are the basis of families. Women marry in.

While Lopore's grandfather lived, all his sons lived with him. They married and brought their wives to his house. But when he died, his household fractured after the pattern of the Dodoth. Each set of full brothers, the sons of each wife, took their shares of inherited cattle and founded new dwellings, for a group of brothers is the nucleus of a new family, and their mother's court the nucleus of a new home.

Lopore's father, whose name was Botia, was his mother's youngest son, and so did not become head of the new household but only of the section where his family lived. His elder brother became the householder. This man, as Lopore remembers him, had a small body but a very fierce nature and never hesitated to fight with people larger than himself. As a middle-aged man, says Lopore, his uncle would beat men who would easily have beaten him if he had lacked his surprising temper and ferocity. Lopore remembers him with amusement and a certain pride, and calls him a very bad man. But when his uncle died, Lopore remembers, many people did not conceal their pleasure.

Botia had one wife, one son, and two daughters, and rather few cattle, perhaps twenty when his fortunes waned, forty when he was richer. But his elder brother had a large herd, several wives, and many children, and Lopore grew up with the advantages of a wealthy, prosperous house. He called both men "Father" and all their wives "Mother," a Dodoth custom which reflects the unity of brothers, and when as a little boy he tended the two men's calves, he tended the stock whose offspring were to be his inheritance. Lopore was given a little ox which he named Longurakori, adding to his own names the name Apalongurakori, Father of Longurakori. He composed several proud songs about Longurakori as it ran with the calves, and when, on moonlit nights or in the afternoons, people were dancing, Lopore, thin and naked, would leap behind the grownup dancers and sing his ox's songs, as children do today, though no one listens.

When the hot dry weather of December came, if the grass died near Lotim, he would accompany his father and uncle and the herds in search of better pasture. He went with his father to the far corners of Dodoth, up to the northern mountains by the Sudan border, and west, toward Acholiland, across the great grass plains. He watched the cattle as they grazed by day, and at night slept with the cattle under the sky of his father's camps. Thus he learned pastoralism. He learned the many details of veterinary knowledge, the names and values of the many kinds of grass, and how and where to find water in dry rivers, but most important, he developed the sensitivity to pastoralism which Dodoth men must have. When faced with the decision of which would most benefit his cattle, to stay in good pasture but to spend most of the day making a long, debilitating march to water, or to stay in a poor pasture near the water, Lopore could, as a grown man, consider the many factors involved, such as the distance, the types of grass, the competition from other herds in either the good or the poor pasture; he could estimate the physical condition of his herd, and far more likely than not, make the best decision. Some men seem to have a talent, a genius, for such decisions, while other men blunder. Lopore did well, for often enough, when the land was dry and the grass dying, the life of his herd and the well-being of his family depended on his judgment.

For the rest of his education, he watched the people of his house and neighborhood and listened to the advice of his father, who told him: "If you don't have cattle, you won't be a person."

Lopore's mother advised him to respect old men and to "live with other people slowly."

His father said to him: "Don't mistreat old men, and fear old people," which Lopore feels today was good advice. He has seen that those who mistreat old people die.

His mother said: "You must respect your fathers-in-law, and if you speak angry or bad words to them, God will hear you and kill you." She said: "If old men want something from you, kill them an ox. Or if children come to you, kill something for them. If people your own age come to you, give them something, and even if women come to you, give them something to eat."

His father said: "Take honey and milk to the old men so they will pray for you."

This advice stayed with Lopore all his life. Once, when he was a boy, living at his father's camp, he noticed that his father was hungry. He asked: "What is it, Father? Are you hungry?"

"No," said his father.

"But may I kill a sheep for you?"

"Yes," said his father. So Lopore killed a ram and gave it to his father, and when his father saw this, he asked: "Lopore, have you killed for me?"

Lopore answered: "Yes."

"Live," said his father. "Live, and even if trouble comes, you will escape it, to live with your cattle and be happy."

When Lopore was fourteen, he was at his father's camp,

which they were sharing with nine other men and boys. At dawn one morning, when the men were driving the cattle out of the thorn enclosure, a band of Turkana warriors ran from a nearby grove of trees and surrounded the camp. Lopore's father was speared to death before his eyes and all the cattle from the camp were stolen, driven far toward Turkanaland before the boy could give the alarm, before the men of neighboring camps could rally for pursuit.

Lopore remembers hiding alone in the bush after the cattle were gone, then walking alone the long miles to Lotim, to find the news had traveled before him. Everyone was weeping, except his mother, who sat in her court with her cape over her head and her daughters around her. When she was told that Lopore had come, she stood up and, taking off her cape, she poured water over him to bless him, saying: "My husband has not yet come."

Someone asked Lopore: "Where is your father?"

His mother said: "If we hear he is dead, I will not be with you any longer."

But surely it was obvious that he was dead. Lopore remembers everyone weeping except his mother, who began to cook a meal for him. Lopore said: "The enemies have killed him." To his uncle he said: "They have killed your son also. Everyone is dead. No one is living." When the food came, Lopore remembers that it made his empty stomach ache, and he remembers his mother repeating over and over that her husband had not yet come.

Lopore and his mother and sisters remained in his uncle's house. His mother could have become his uncle's wife if she had chosen, but she did not. If she had, the union would have been brief. The uncle's herd was severely diminished during a series of raids on the district, and he, the old warrior, wanting to replace his stock, organized a raid on

the Turkana during which he was fatally wounded and left
to die on the Turkana plains.

After that, the household fractured. The sons and wives
and little children went where they could and good luck
did not follow them—Lopore remembers searching the
bush for wild food, which the Dodoth scorn but eat when
they are starving. Of all the people of that house, only
Lopore and one of his uncle's daughters are alive today.
Her name is Nadolupe, and she is a doctor, a diviner. She
sucks poison spells from her patients and divines the
sources of their spells in dreams—it is God's gift to do
so—but she married unhappily and today, except for her
sons, she is alone in the world. She lives very near Lopore.

Lopore's lonely mother, when his uncle died, found herself without husband or household or protector, and turned
then to the man who had brought her up as if he were her
father. He was a Jie, and was called Ngoriamoe, an honorary name which indicates that he had killed an enemy—
the word for which is *emoeit*—quite possibly a Dodoth.
When Lopore's mother was a girl, a raiding party of Jie had
attacked her dwelling and killed everyone except her.
Ngoriamoe, one of the raiding warriors, had saved her and
brought her to Jie with the captured cattle.

The capture of children is a custom practiced occasionally by the nations of the Cluster. If a man has children of
one sex and wants children of the other, he may capture
some. If his children have died, he may try to replace them,
or if one of his wives is barren and longs for children, he
may bring her one as a gift. But oftener than not, the children found by a raiding party are put to death. Little boys
grow up to be warriors, little girls grow up to be the
mothers of warriors; children are considered in potential
and Lopore's mother was lucky.

Perhaps Ngoriamoe hoped eventually to be given a bride price for her—men treat captured girls as their daughters, not as their wives—but before she was old enough to marry, there came a period of truce between Dodoth and Jie, during which her father's brother came to Jie to take her home. Ngoriamoe gracefully released her, and when many years later she returned to Jie, she a middle-aged widow with children and Ngoriamoe an old man, when he could not possibly gain anything from her, he took her in.

Lopore hated it in Jie. The language, although easily intelligible to a Dodoth, has differences that disturbed his ear, differences that he ridicules to this day. Jie dwellings have thinner inside walls and less secure privacy than Dodoth households; and whereas the land of Dodoth is high and cool and often misty, the Jie plains are flat and bare; a hot east wind blows dust like a harmattan, and except for the dwellings, the gardens, and some small trees, there is nothing on those vast, baked plains to please the eye or relieve a young person who desires to go home.

Lopore herded goats with the sons of Ngoriamoe, but though his work and life were outwardly the same as before, his position was not. No more was he the son of a large household, but a supplicant in an enemy country, with an enemy benefactor, though whose household Turkana friends of the family often came and went. Ngoriamoe treated Lopore well, but Lopore did not like him. As if Ngoriamoe were to blame for the shame of dependent, impotent youth, the poverty, and the bites of prejudice that Lopore must have felt, to this day Lopore never calls him by his name but refers to him as "the Jie."

Lopore remembers a time when the goats he was herding with Ngoriamoe's sons broke into a woman's garden and began to eat the crop. The woman ran up, singled Lopore from among the Jie boys, and threw her hoe at him. He says of the incident: "I knew then that the woman was my enemy," and he waited for his mother, who was visiting Dodoth at the time, to tell her that he, too, wanted to go home. Feeling that she had settled him in the best place, she was reluctant to take him to Dodoth, where a famine persisted. But he refused to stay, he refused to let her go again without him, and because he insisted so strenuously, he prevailed. His mother took her children from Ngoriamoe's household and brought them home.

After that, Lopore says, "I lived in Dodoth and lived in Dodoth and lived in Dodoth, and never again did I go back to Jie."

His mother took her children to her sister, the last of many wives of a huge, rich, burly elder named Okware, who lived beside the river in Kaabong. Kaabong was then, as it is now, administrative center of Dodoth county, then as now it consisted of a few mud-walled shops or dhukas, a police post, and the stockaded Dodoth dwelling of the government-appointed county chief who represented British government in the country. Okware was related to him. The relationship may have given Okware's family a slight leaning toward foreign ways. Sometimes, for example, they would consult the chief for judgment, as the Protectorate government wanted people to do, instead of the traditional Dodoth court, which is a gathering of men and elders.

Though glad to be in Dodoth, Lopore was not happy to live with Okware. He herded cattle for Okware while his sisters helped in the gardens of Okware's wives, and once again Lopore's family was dependent. He was in the house of relatives, but he was connected through two women, his mother and her sister. Not in this relationship did he call

the householder "Father," but addressed him as *Ekamuran,*
which means in-law, in this case a term of remoteness and
respect. The cows Lopore herded for Okware would never
belong to him. When he gathered the cattle to give for his
bride, he might hope that Okware would help him with a
few head, but probably no more—unless Okware were a
warmly generous person, which he was not.

Even so, the period he spent with Okware was one of the
most important in Lopore's life. He was sixteen or so, an
age when young men in Dodoth are still called "boy" and
"child." Too, Lopore was very slight and thin; but before
the year was out he was a man, with a young and violent
ferocity and a herd of his own.

He captured the cattle during a raid on the Turkana.
Having heard that a raid was being planned, he went off to
join the raiding party, though when he left, his mother
cried for him as if he were dead. He found himself by many
years the youngest member, but he had a shield and spear
and joined them anyway, "a man in my own right," he said.
On the raid, he speared to death a Turkana man, and after
the raid, as the Dodoth were whipping the captured cattle
up through the rocks and thornbush of the steep Escarpment, fighting their pursuers as they climbed, Lopore
showed such bravery that when the party reached home
and divided the spoils he was awarded eight of the cattle
and fifteen captured goats. The eight cattle, gained by his
own hand, became the parents of some of the hundred cattle he paid for his first bride.

Not withstanding what he had done, he was, according
to Dodoth custom, still called "boy" and "child." Though he
had killed an enemy and could have taken an honorary
name, he would first have had to kill an ox to feast the

elders. Lopore had no ox and Okware didn't help him, so another man killed an ox, feasted the elders, claimed the victim, and took the name that might have been Lopore's. Later, two men who were distant relatives of Lopore's father arrived at Okware's to claim Lopore's cows. Lopore has forgotten the reason for the claim, but he never forgot his father's request to honor old men—to obey one's father and to honor old men being two of the strongest and best-kept precepts of the Dodoth—and he did not offer much resistance.

Seeing how things were with Lopore, Okware then claimed the fifteen goats. Again, Lopore could do no more than protest. The goats went to Okware. But as such strict obedience makes Dodoth boys smolder, Lopore continued to milk the goats when Okware was not at home.

Surely, Okware must have wondered why the goats mysteriously went dry. One day he caught Lopore milking them outside the dwelling. For protection, Lopore ran to his mother's court, but Okware fetched a fighting stick and a wicker stick-fighting shield, and crawling through the door of the courtyard, gave Lopore a beating. His elderly aunt and mother tried to catch Okware's arm. Lopore remembers that they cried: "Why do you want to kill him for his property? Didn't he go on his own feet to get these goats?" The two elderly sisters succeeded in loosening Okware's grip on Lopore, whereupon Lopore wriggled free, ducked out the doorway, and ran to hide in the bush, while in revenge Okware turned on the two old women and beat them severely. Their screams were heard by Lopore in his hiding place, and he said to himself: "How long will I continue to fear this man? I took my goats from the enemy." And emerging from the bush, he found two strong sticks, returned to the court, and clubbed Okware twice so heavily over the brow that Okware dropped sideways and lay as if dead. When Okware's other wives saw him quiet on the ground, they ran weeping to Kaabong for a policeman.

While the women were gone, Okware came to his senses and went into his house to get his spear. Lopore also got a spear, and in the fight that followed, Lopore was wounded on the arm with a long, deep gash that left a scar visible to this day. When the women returned with the two Dodoth askaris, as the police are called, they found Okware being restrained by several people and Lopore lying bleeding on the ground.

Then as now, the duties of askaris included the prevention of raiding and the investigation of crimes. When the askaris began the usual police investigation into the causes of the fight, their questioning revealed that Okware had claimed possession of the goats Lopore had taken during the raid. As it happened, the askaris were off duty at the time the raiding party had gone out. That day they had removed their khaki uniforms and joined the raiders, and as witnesses to everything, were able to vouch for Lopore.

In that instance, the askaris were both judge and jury. Their decision was respected, Lopore was given back his goats, and feeling a confidence in himself that he hadn't known before, he took a club and visited the two distant relatives to reclaim his cows.

"Perhaps people thought I was an animal," Lopore once said of that period of his life. "But they found then that I was a Dodoth. Then people feared me. When a third man tried to take my cattle, I beat him too, and from then on, I was like a wild animal. Before, no one noticed me. They

wanted me to die. After, people avoided me. But I reminded myself that if I were kind and generous, people
would try again to take my property.

"From that time, I knew all about trouble. But if you
want to know everything, you must first become bad. If I
was not feared, I wouldn't have my cattle. If I had no
cattle, I wouldn't have my wives. Yet I was feared, and I
kept my cattle. If my father could rise from the dead, he
would see that there are people in my dwelling now."

Mora and Uri lived in Kaabong before Lopore came
there. Mora was born in the Kaabong hills. When he was
very young, his parents died of a disease, and his father's
brother raised him. Uri came to Kaabong later, the head of
his family, though still an adolescent. With him came his
widowed mother and his three sisters, Remi, Nabilo, and
Iruata. Iruata grew up to marry Mora, bear his children, and
die. But they met when he was a boy and she an infant,
perhaps as brown and thin and delicate as her own little
girl is now.

Uri, kind and generous and also fatherless, befriended
Mora, a lonely child, and a close relationship began which
lasted more than fifty years. Lopore's friendship with Uri
must also date from the time they lived together in
Kaabong, for Lopore still sings a song that refers to the
scarification of his first ox in remembrance of the Turkana
warrior whom Lopore killed.

> Tattered ears
> The ear of Longurakori
> Who wears Uri's bell.

It seemed characteristic of Lopore that Kaabong after
the turn of the century was not an important part of his
memories. The influx of foreigners and the advent of the

Protectorate government came at that time; changes which were to influence Kaabong and which will one day affect the entire country began then, but Lopore was involved with his own affairs and more or less ignored the changes.

Uri, on the other hand, remembered very well. He remembered hearing of the first European ever to enter Dodoth, a Britisher named Macdonald. In an effort to secure the country against the French, Macdonald arrived with an immense safari in 1891. He made treaties with the Dodoth elders, leaving thumbprinted copies of the treaties and Union Jacks with the elders as a sign of change to come.

The first foreigner whom Uri remembered personally was a man whose nation was called *Choat Aberika*. This could be an adaption of the words *South America*. He was an elephant hunter, one of hundreds who roamed East Africa in those days, though most never got to Dodoth. He came, shot a few elephants, took the tusks, and went away, and as he went he also took a girl named Adupa. Why he took her and what happened to her is not known, but she has not come back yet, the Dodoth say.

Later, a group of Abyssinian hunters established themselves in a large camp by the Kaabong River. They lived in harmony with the Dodoth, trading bullets for grain and rifles for oxen and helping the Dodoth against their enemies the Jie. Uri and Mora tracked elephants for the Abyssinians. The Abyssinians dug a deep pit by the river in which to store the tusks. Like a natural hollow full of weeds, the pit is still there.

In 1911 the administration came to Dodoth. It came with a column of soldiers, the King's African Rifles, who fought a battle with the Abyssinians for possession of Kaabong. Mora and Uri heard the sounds of the battle, when the rifles went didip, didip, and hoped the Abyssinians would win. When the Abyssinians were routed, the soldiers built a camp by the river. The camp became a station in a patrol they established which went east to Lake Rudolf and west to the Nile. With the soldiers came a tall European with fair hair and pale eyes. He is remembered as Tupona, which may be an adaption of the English word "governor," or of his name, Tufnell.

The purpose of Tupona among the Dodoth was to pacify them and to start taxation, which in those days was a grain tax, and which has climbed in fifty years from grain in baskets, collected from a few people, to a few shillings collected from many people, to 23 shillings each collected from most of the 6,045 people on the tax roster, who pay a total of about £6,000 a year. Uri was one of the first to pay the tax. He brought Tupona a bit of grain. The pacification was more stringent in those days, less stringent now, fifty years later. Tupona confiscated all the Dodoth rifles and burned them in a pyre which those who witnessed remember still. He caused his Jie interpreter to say this to the Dodoth: "Don't be my enemy, because I am your brother. If I hear of anyone killing others, I will kill him."

Of his own accord, the Jie said to his traditional enemies: "Don't kill Tupona and his soldiers, or they will kill us."

Tupona was not long in Dodoth. His responsibilities, reaching as they did from the Nile to Lake Rudolf, soon took him elsewhere, and his reforms subsided for a time. But his advent marked the advent of the government and to this day that time is called Lokijuka, deriving from the word *akijukare*, "push."

In the early 1920's another man became the administrator of the entire Karamoja District, and he, too, visited Kaabong. That he was also called Tupona, which was possibly an adaption of *his* name, Turpin, may show that people saw no special reason to distinguish between him and his predecessor, Tufnell. The second Tupona built himself a large mud house with ten doors and windows, and stayed for some time. Uri said: "He came as a hunter, and was against people. He burned dwellings and killed many people, and we took him for our enemy. But later on, he came to sacrifices and he got used to eating elders' portions, humps and tongues."

To link Dodoth with the district center in Moroto, Tupona began the building of the north-south road. The work was done under a Swahili foreman, a man named Juma who was so famous for his cruelty that he dared not arm his workers with tools such as picks and shovels. The roadbed was cleared by plumed elders and naked warriors crouching to pull up stones and bushes with their fingers. No one volunteered to work under Juma, so roadwork became mandatory, and Mora and Uri, being residents of Kaabong and therefore available, were among those forced to build the road. Mora was beaten by Juma with a cat-o'-nine-tails. Uri was also beaten by Juma, who to hold Uri down made one man stand on his neck and another on his feet. Later Juma beat a relative of Mora's so badly that his back never healed. Maggots infested his wounds, and he died of infection. Mora, Uri, and many other people take pleasure in the thought that, as Juma was a grown man in those days, he too must now be dead.

The soldiers of the K.A.R. moved their camp from the riverbank to a grove of shady trees, where the government campsite stands today. When the K.A.R. were not on patrol, the grove would swarm with handsome, loud-voiced soldiers who at night would sing the songs of their own lands, Tanganyika, Kenya, southern Uganda, and the

Sudan, and Dodoth girls found the soldiers fascinating. Uri's two sisters, Remi and Nabilo, were among the girls who would visit the soldiers. Many Dodoth families preferred that their girls not visit the soldiers, who by and large were not eligible husbands because they had no cattle, but whereas a father could forbid his daughter, it was hard for Uri to forbid his sisters, especially Remi, who was older than he. Though Uri was very much opposed to it, Remi married a Baganda soldier and was taken by her husband to Kampala, industrial center of Uganda, where she bore him three children. A few years after the birth of her last child she died, and the children are now lost to the Dodoth branch of the family. Uri heard of their birth, and thinks that if they are still living, they are somewhere near Kampala, but he has no way of finding them now.

Against Uri's wishes, Nabilo also married a soldier, a Moslem Swahili corporal named Mustafa Bin Jaddin, who, having no cattle, gave Uri a hundred shillings when he took Nabilo as his bride. This must have represented a large amount of a soldier's wages, yet it is nothing to a Dodoth; even in those days it was but the value of three or four cows. Many thousand shillings would be the value of a woman, if the value could be reckoned in cash instead of kind.

Mustafa's regiment was transferred to Acholi, at the western border of Dodoth, and of course Nabilo went too. The Dodoth are great travelers; men are always going back and forth across the country, so it was not long before Uri received a message from Nabilo, asking him to visit her. There was a mission school in Acholi, which Mustafa and Nabilo wished Uri to attend. He went, taking Mora with him. They walked across Dodoth and over the hills to

Acholi, and when they found Nabilo they found her a Moslem, swathed in white fabric, veiled to the eyes. She was living in a square house with a door and windows and a bed with blankets. Uri and Mora stayed with her for most of a year, during which time Mustafa sent Uri to the school, where he learned to read. Mustafa put Mora to work as a servant to Nabilo. When Mustafa was in, Mora would carry wood and water and wash the cooking pots. When Mustafa was out, Nabilo and her servant would sit on the floor and talk about their country. Uri and Mora learned to speak a little Acholi and to this day use it as a private language, which very much annoys Lopore.

But Uri did not like school and refused baptism. "There is no need for a religion like that," said he of Christianity. Mora was homesick in Acholi. Uri found the teachers harsh, both Uri and Mora found the language difficult and the country hostile, and one day the two set out together and walked back to Kaabong. Shortly after, Mustafa's regiment was transferred to Buganda. Uri and Mora never saw Mustafa again, and a generation passed before they saw Nabilo.

Meanwhile, Lopore was working for the K.A.R. Wishing to leave Okware's house, he had allowed himself to be pressed into service as a porter. Those were the days of the famous foot safaris of East Africa, when, as in tales of travel and exploration, long columns of porters with bundles on their heads followed some European to some place which no European had ever visited before. Along the file of porters who helped explore Dodoth walked Lopore, carrying on his head a bag of millet. "Your father carried millet from Kaabong to Kitgum in Acholi," Lopore once remarked to one of his sons while telling us the story. "We

were the motorcars of those days. We were the donkeys."
His young son laughed at the image, but Lopore looked at
him severely. "Don't laugh at millet," he said.

This was in 1914, at the outbreak of the war. An eclipse
of the sun, called "When the Sun Died," came at the time.
Because of the need for soldiers, Uri, Lopore, and Mora
were drafted into the K.A.R. Mora was recruited by force
from the roadside, as workers for important road-building
projects are taken today. He was taken to Moroto, where
his headdress was cut off and his necklace and earrings
stored for him. He was issued a uniform, a soldier's felt hat,
shoes "held together with nails," and a rifle.

His regiment was sent to the southern Sudan to pacify
the Didinga. The Didinga are a pastoral people who had
been raiding back and forth with the Dodoth for years.
Mora calls the expedition "the K.A.R. raid on the Didinga,"
for the soldiers shot men, women, and children; the
Didinga were decimated; their dwellings, large round
thatched houses without encircling walls, Mora remembers, were leveled; and for a long time after, the Didinga
were pacified. If Mora had shot a Didinga, he could have
taken an enemy-name, for a victory over an enemy is signi-
ficant even if the warrior is in the army at the time. This
practice, established during the First World War, still
exists today.

Mora was later transferred to Kenya, where he saw
cities, a train—which seemed to him to be carrying a string
of houses—and a prisoner-of-war camp, which he visited
out of curiosity. Sure enough, in the barred windows of the
prison, faces would appear from time to time. Mora
watched the faces for a while, then said: "Stay well," and
went on his way. But he saw no more action, and when the

Armistice came, he was returned to Moroto. There he turned in his uniform, his shoes, and his rifle; he put his cloth cape over his back, his earrings in the holes of his ears, and buying a spear to defend himself with on the trip through Jie, he walked 140 miles home. There he found Uri and Lopore, who had spent the war in southern Uganda and Tanganyika and had returned before him. He had a few cattle, and married Iruata, sister of his life-long friend, for the bride price of ten cows. Then everyone who had dispersed and seen the world was home again, except Uri's sister Remi, who died in Kampala, and Nabilo.

Nabilo's youth and middle age were spent in an odyssey with Mustafa. She bore him three children, a boy Abibu, a girl Miriam, and another boy, Assuman. She lived in rooms in city slums in Tanganyika, Kenya, and Uganda; she learned Swahili; and because Mustafa's earnings were low, she worked as a servant to white people, saying *Bwana* and *Memsahib,* and assuming a deprecating manner never found in Dodoth. And all the while she was a Moslem, responding to the muezzin's calls to prayer from atop the towers of the little city mosques.

She did her best. She even took the Moslem name of Manumiss to please her husband. But for all that is written in the Koran, there is a lingering contempt, a disrespect felt by a person such as Mustafa toward a person such as Nabilo, of a backward people. Disparaging references are made regarding dirt and pagan ignorance, and it is possible that Nabilo felt contempt from him.

Also, she was all alone. She had no relatives, no clan, no family to be her supporters—she never met Mustafa's family, who lived in Tanganyika—and she had only her children to fill her life.

In 1953 Mustafa moved to Jinja at the source of the Nile. Nabilo's sons, Assuman and Abibu, died of meningitis in Jinja, and when they were gone, Nabilo felt such an agony of loneliness that she could no longer live with Mustafa. She asked him to divorce her. This he did, on condition that he keep Miriam, their daughter. There was no property to be returned, no relatives to consult or visit, and with the divorce Nabilo was suddenly five hundred miles from home, and suddenly as free, as unattached as a spirit in the air.

There was then no one who knew her but her brother. She had nowhere to go but back to her brother; so she returned to her country, an elderly lady in a cotton dress, walking to Dodoth alone.

She became the fourth wife of Lopore. Having given a sister to his friend Mora for only ten cows, Uri asked only ten from Lopore. Mora was a closer friend to Uri than was Lopore, but Nabilo was too old to bear children. These factors formed a balance when the men assessed her value. But when Lopore had paid two cows, Nabilo had the payment stop. "I am an old woman," she said to her brother, "not worth more."

When we first met her at Lopore's rocks, she touched her lips and forehead in the gesture of salaam and addressed us in Swahili. Lopore looked down at her with respect and surprise. Perhaps he had not known how she would act with Europeans.

Of all his wives, she was his favorite. Her travels and her experiences had enlarged her character, and her stories, foreign recipes, and foreign ways intrigued him. She was a handsome woman, with a broad, wrinkled face and a pleasing manner, and she was sensible and witty. But most women have their children with them, and Nabilo was lonely. She would work in her green fields alone, and while she was there she would think too much, for there was nothing to distract her. She would go alone to the river and in the sandy riverbed, under the huge trees, she would scrape a hole, then sit and think while the hole filled with water. Then she would fill her jar and all by herself would carry the water home.

When I knew Nabilo, seven years had passed since her return to Dodoth. She had been away from home for more than forty. Because I came from afar, because I too had seen other countries and had been in places she had been in, she liked to have me visit her. This I did. It relieved her loneliness to talk of the past and of her children. Abibu was born "as bald as a knee," she said. When he was older, his hair came in like fringe. Her descriptions were physical, as if her eyes ran over her children again. Miriam had been four and a half feet tall when Nabilo had last seen her, with breasts no larger than fists.

I used to visit Nabilo in her fields by day, to sit in the shade of her sod platform, where the light was green, filtering through her crops, or in her courtyards in the evening as the sun went down, making the tiered thatch of her sleeping house pink and casting the neat, swept floor of the courtyard in shadow. In nearby courts, people would be chopping and churning and talking, but nothing would move in Nabilo's court except the flames of her fire amid the three round stones which supported the pot. The air was cold in the evenings. She would sweep the fire ashes with a blackbird's wing, then would sit wrapped in her cape, her hands idle, for there was nothing to do and nothing to see except the high, bare poles of her courtyard walls and the sky, where at that time of evening birds like larks would be spiraling above the dwelling, their cries faintly audible as they climbed. When we talked, many subjects led to the subject of the past. Sometimes she would be reminded of it by a baby crying in a nearby court, or the news of someone going on a trip, or the subject of husbands, sisters, foreign languages—once it was mushrooms, which she discovered growing in the straw of her thatch, after a rain. "These are eaten in Buganda," she said, "but the Dodoth throw them away." She knocked them over and threw them away.

Once she said she had enjoyed her former life at first, "and thanked God for it." Another time she said: "Uri knew more than I did at the time of my marriage."

Sometimes she spoke of foreign customs. She would have liked to buy herself a cotton dress, but Lopore wouldn't give her the money. "The men here are stingy," she once said, as if in amusement. "And when they talk, it's cow, cow, cow."

She found relief in jokes, but none in weeping. Many women in Dodoth cry easily, but weeping would creep up on Nabilo when she didn't expect it. Sometimes when she spoke of her sister Remi's children in Kampala, she would find her voice unsteady and her eyes filled with tears. "I love them very much. I don't know why they won't come here to live with me," she once said. "I have none."

And once she asked me: "Do you think I was bad to come back?"

"Oh no," I said.

"Do you know why I did it? I was very angry when God killed my sons."

For Uri, Mora, and Lopore, the past and foreign travel were something else again. When either subject arose Uri, with his concern about the changing times, usually spoke of the mission in Acholi, for which he felt contempt. When once I asked him about Dodoth beliefs in the afterlife, he obliged me with the Christian interpretation. "Do you believe it?" I asked him. "If I did, I don't now. Do you?" he said.

Mora, who was desperately in need of cattle to relieve his poverty, remembered the use of firearms. He would sometimes pick up our shotgun, expertly open the breach and squint inside, then close it and sight along the barrel at a distant tree. Once a neighbor dreamed of the Dodoth with rifles, and because some dreams have meaning, I asked Mora what he thought. "Don't we all dream that?" said he.

Lopore was uninterested in the past and foreign travel. Like most Dodoth soldiers who had gone away from home and had seen the swarming cities of Kampala and Nairobi, the markets of Buganda, the villages, the schoolchildren in uniform, the bicycle riders on the paved streets, where only the bright birds at roost on the telegraph wires could remind a Dodoth soldier of his home, he had not been greatly affected by any of this. He had absorbed it all the way one might absorb a lecture, for he had always known that things were different elsewhere. When I would ask him about his travels, he would say merely that he had been to Uganda. I would persist with questions, and once told him that my father had been in the same war. "Perhaps he was," said Lopore. "I didn't know him." He then recalled a few other soldiers whom he had met, long-forgotten friends, but the subject bored him and he turned the conversation by speaking of contemporary affairs. My questions started him thinking, though, and eventually he recalled that he and Uri had seen the German ship which the British exploded on Lake Tanganyika. The ship seemed to stay on the surface after it was bombed. Lopore and Uri

discussed it often after they remembered, and eventually
they quarreled about what happened to the ship; for at the
time, apparently they hadn't bothered to find out. Uri now
thinks the British sank it. Lopore thinks it may be floating
still.

CHAPTER THREE

Kaabong

Some lives are affected by the changing world; some lives are not. But the increasing pressure from the West to modify life in Dodoth is making inroads in three of the most fundamental aspects of the culture, families, age sets, and clans.

Hundreds of years ago, before Dodoth existed as a nation, age sets and clans evolved from families, and today these ancient institutions, with their authority, their complexity, and their perpetual order, serve to unify and govern people. In families, the origins of these institutions can still be seen.

Like living things, like plants with rhizomes, the patriarchal households grow. The owner marries, the sons of each court grow up and marry, until the members of the house are many, and when the owner dies and the household fractures, the courts become new compound households, groups of brothers who live together until their cattle are many, whereupon the compound dwellings may fracture too and the brothers disperse to found single dwellings of their own.

The fragmenting of households along court lines reflects Dodoth kinship. A person calls his full brothers and sisters *lokato* and *nakato*, he and she of the place of the mother, which is the court. But all his father's other children, and the children of his father's brothers, he calls *lokapa* and *nakapa*, he and she of the place of the father, which is the dwelling itself.

From the concept of a man, his brothers, their sons, their sons' sons, and the ever-growing pyramid of male descendants, developed the concept of clans. There are at least sixteen clans in Dodoth today, perhaps more. Once clans were exogamous and men built their dwellings on their own clan lands. Today, it is said, some men have married their clanswomen and though the clan lands still exist, people build their dwellings anywhere, so clans are diminishing in importance. This diminishing is evolutionary and indigenous, a phenomenon that occurs throughout the world. But Dodoth clans are still descent groups. Though a woman joins her husband's clan shortly after her marriage, a man belongs forever to the clan of his father, his father's father, his father's grandfather, as the male line of the family is traced back into time.

There is a strong hierarchy within each family. As long as a man lives, he has authority over his sons and over the family cattle. Because of the cattle, which will be used to bring wives to the family and will one day be inherited, the members of the family are ranked by a logical system to determine right of access to the property. The man's daughters are not considered in the system, as they will be wives of other families. The man's wives are ranked in order of their marriage, and the man's sons are ranked according to order of birth and the rank of the mother. Hence, the first wife's elder son outranks the second wife's elder son, who in turn outranks the first wife's younger son, and unless extreme age differences prevent it, the three boys will marry in that order.

From the hierarchy within the family, the authority that a father has over his sons, the order of birth among the sons, and the rights a boy has over his younger brothers, there developed the foundation of government, the age-set system.

The age sets are nationwide. A man as an adult is initiated into an age set and remains in it all his life. As age sets below his are formed, and as age sets above are terminated because of the death of members, his own set advances in seniority and authority until, in time, he may become an elder, one of the most senior men. There are no chiefs or kings in Dodoth, or persons born to rule. The govenment of the country is traditionally in the hands of the elders, whose control has a religious basis, being achieved through intercession with God. When elders pray in their reedy voices, they call God's blessing down upon the people, and ask for the increase of cattle, and for rain. Elders can also pray to God to punish; such a prayer is like a curse. "Important men," these seniors are called, or sometimes "holy elders," and people on one side and God on the other side take advice from them.

As the structure of the age-set system takes shape from the structure of families, the elders are like the fathers of families. The family in each dwelling is divided into fathers (or a father) and sons; so the age sets are divided into two generations, a senior and a junior. A man must join the generation group below that of his father, as the senior gen-

eration has authority over the junior generation and it
would never do for a son to have authority approximating
that of his father.

Here and there in Africa, age sets are composed of men
of the same age. A tribe will initiate all the youngsters from
ten to fifteen into one age set, then wait five years and
initiate the next group of ten- to fifteen-year-olds into the
next age set. But in Dodoth, because initiation follows family structure, the actual age set a man joins is determined
with regard to his father's age set. A man in the first age set
of the senior generation will have his son in the first age set
of the junior generation.

The age sets are subdivided into what might be called ox-
classes because they are named for oxen. The ox-classes
within the age sets provide a hierarchy sufficiently complex
to accommodate the small differences in rank among
brothers and half brothers.

Each age set takes in initiates for many years. Several ox-
classes are open at all times. Thus, when the time comes for
a group of brothers to be initiated, the first wife's eldest son
will join an ox-class above that of the second wife's eldest
son. The system is perfectly logical. But the actual, biologi-
cal ages of the men in each age set vary greatly.

If you ask a new initiate to what group he belongs, he
will give the name of his ox-class. If you ask a man who has
been initiated for many years, he will give you the name of
his age set. But if you ask the group of an elder, or of a man
long dead, you will be given the name of his generation
group, for as time passes, as families disperse, and as the
members of the senior age sets die, the small gradations
lose importance.

Once every forty or fifty years, a great ceremony is held
in Dodoth, in which the senior generation retires. The

elders lose their power, and become as uninitiated men. The junior generation becomes the senior, the members of its upper sets become the elders, and a new generation is opened to take the junior place. Such a transfer has not happened in Dodoth for so many years that hundreds of middle-aged men, including Mora, Uri, and Lopore, are still uninitiated and still waiting.

Thus, not all old men become elders, and not all elders are old men. To become an elder a man must be initiated into a set whose seniority is fairly well advanced. If it is not advanced, other men will fill it when it becomes senior and the original members have died, for the timespan of the age-set system is not geared to an individual life. The system slowly turns in time like a waterwheel in water. Like blades on the wheel, the sets appear, then rise, decline, and vanish. Yet the system turns forever, and a man who is old, near the end of his life, whose set is about to vanish, will know that sometime within a century the place he holds in the system will come back to the world again.

Clans and the age-set system are the order and the immortality of the nation. They are joined, in Dodoth, through the sacred groves, the ancient trees in whose crowns Akuj comes down to settle, for each of the sacred groves in the country is the property of a clan. Men sacrifice oxen at the sacred groves when holding initiations and performing other public ceremonies, to induce good, such as rain, or to ward off evil, such as raiders, and at each of the sacrifices, the seniormost members of the age-set system, who are also members of the clan that owns the sacred place, perform the services and lead the prayers.

The Dodoth have a phrase which means "clan, sacred place," which could date from a time when only the

clansmen on clan lands would attend the clan sacrifice.
Nowadays, and dating into the distant past, the sacrifices
are public. Anyone may attend. And an initiated man who
is not a clansman may perform services and offer prayers
if he joins the sacred grove by sacrificing an ox. But the
clansmen of a sacred grove do not have to join by sacrifice
—their membership is assured by birth, and it may even be
that this membership lasts after death. Certain very important elders, a few people said, return from the dead in the
form of snakes, wearing on their heads white plumes like
the plumes of a headdress, to visit once again the sacred
places of their clans.

Systems such as these cannot exist within the framework
of Western culture. Huge families cannot live together in a
money economy, and clans will disappear when households do. Moreover, the authority of elders is directly opposed to the authority of outside government. The elders
are the most conservative people in the country. They have
heard of the outside government, the shops, and the missions, but they tend to forget what they heard. Seeing the
land as it was when they were younger, they ignore even
the roads, planned with such care by the government. If a
car rounds a bend and surprises an elder, he may run down
the road ahead of the car to escape it, his knobby legs
flying, his cape and plumes in disarray, but most elders do
not use the roads at all, viewing them as meaningless
scratches, as we might view a gully washed by rain. In
their absolute indifference to the West, the conservative
elders exhort their people to guard their cattle, to go raiding, to keep the customs of the sacred places; and people
obey. But elders are blamed for the raiding, and arrested,
and convicted, and serve long sentences in the Jie or the
Moroto jail.

Once we rounded a bend in the road near the Jie border and came upon nine Dodoth elders squatting in the grass, guarded by two askaris with rifles. The askaris flagged us down, we stopped, and the askaris asked up to drive the elders to jail. We asked what was wrong. The askaris told us that the Dodoth had raided the Jie two days before, that some of the captured cattle had been tracked to the district of the nine old men, and that the police had found the old men taking part in a sacrifice. One askari produced the scalp of the sacrificed ox to prove it.

The elders, all frail old men, sat in the grass passing a snuffbox. They looked blandly this way and that, not understanding a word, not realizing that they would soon be in jail, not deigning to notice the askaris. We considered the possibility that they might be rescued if they walked to jail, weighed this against the hot day and the extreme distance, thought that rescue seemed unlikely, and asked them to choose. They chose the car, thanked us with great dignity, and got inside. When we last saw them, they were standing in the sun beside the concrete jail in Jie, while the askaris made arrangements for their cells. Afterwards, we asked here and there what had happened to them, but their case was only one in many, and no one remembered them.

"Our religion is dying," Uri once said to me. He had been telling my fortune with his pair of sandals, on top of Morukore hill. He would throw down the sandals, notice their position, and interpret the meaning in their fall. There was a hum, and a tiny airplane flew over, the police plane looking for raiders. But Uri thought the police were looking for sacrifices. People attending sacrifices have been spotted from the air and then arrested, for the government believed sacrifices were preludes to raids. This is not true. The plane flew on, growing smaller and smaller over the hills until it was like a bee droning in the distance, and Uri watched it go. "Our religion is dying," he said again, "and the government wants it to."

It is ironic that Kaabong, as county seat of Dodoth, has become the seat of change, for Kaabong is the site of the primary sacred grove of one of the largest Dodoth clans. The site is slightly west of present-day Kaabong, and the grove is lovely. Long sweet grass grows under the trees, where cattle graze, and during the rainy season flowers bloom there, red flowers like Indian paintbrush and little wild petunias that wilt in the sun. Beside the grove is the sacred tree, a great wild fig with orchids in its branches. Below the tree a fence has been built by the Dodoth to enclose the actual, most sacred spot, a spot determined many years ago when a fire swept the grove, sparing only the wild fig and the enclosed area, thus demonstrating the power of these things to withstand harm. Subsequently, it is said that at times of danger, at times of attack, people who can run within the fence are never harmed, and that the fence expands miraculously to include all those who reach it. It is an old and very famous sacred place where in spring black bulls are sacrified to induce the rain.

There has always been a large population centered around Kaabong, which stands beside a river. The sacred place, and the fluvial, green plains whose soil is excellent for gardens, may explain this, and the presence of a large population may be why Tupona, representing the Protectorate government, chose Kaabong as its capital. When Tupona found that dealing with the Dodoth and other Ugandan members of the Cluster involved dealing not with a chief or king or central figure of authority but with the elders, hundreds of conservative, opinionated old men, he created a system of chiefs based on the system evolved by the Baganda. Each nation, such as Jie and Dodoth, became a county, and for each county a high chief was appointed. His title was Ekapolon, which, according to Dr. Dyson-Hudson, may have been adapted by the early administrators from *ekile apolon,* "important man," a title for an elder. The Ekapolon of Dodoth, when we were there, was not untypical: a pleasant, moderate man of forty-five who always wore a khaki uniform of shorts and bush jacket, hat and polished boots. He drove a Land-Rover, was conscientious, and unfailingly polite to Europeans, but it is not people such as he who pray to God with spears and arms raised and who, after death, their plumes asway, slip through the grass on their bellies to see the sacred places of their clans.

Below the chiefs, subchiefs were appointed for certain districts. The districts are not Dodoth districts, but vague, Protectorate ones. The title of the subchief is Jackait. This word, says Dr. Dyson-Hudson, is derived from *ajakait,* and because the office originated in Karamoja, was possibly suggested as a title by a Karamojong prankster, for the work *ajakait* is a respectful word for a woman, the wife of a very rich man. As a woman is the satellite of her rich husband, so is a Jackait a satellite of the government, to do as the government sees fit. Below the Jackaits are the third-degree chiefs, the Mkungus. A Mkungu has as his province a very small area, as did Uri's son-in-law, who was Mkungu of Kalapata. For this, the pranksters had run out of terms: *mkungu* is the Baganda word for the office.

The chiefs, the Jackaits and the Mkungus of Dodoth, have as their function to collect taxes, to prevent raids, to judge any cases that the Dodoth householders see fit to bring to trial, and to act as intermediaries between their people and the government. But the Dodoth are a volatile nation, and the appointed offices have their risks. The Mkungus are men of the people; they herd their cattle and mind their own business, unless pressed. The Jackaits are more vulnerable to criticism, but can usually pass any blame that accrues to them on to the chief. So it is the chief's office that is most dangerous. Some chiefs, held to account for unpopular decisions of the government, have been murdered. One was openly assassinated by an armed crowd. And a former chief of Dodoth was poisoned while drinking the beer of people whom he believed to be his friends.

At the time of Tupona, Kaabong became the headquarters of Dodoth county. Today the Ekapolon has his round dwelling there, as does the Jackait of Kaabong District. And by the road is the anthill plaster, boxlike county office, where, for instance, mail is brought by passersby, to be handed on to a Swahili-speaking mail carrier, who can occasionally be found in his home among the rocks of the Kaabong hills.

The road gangs that Tupona instituted are still there, small groups of sullen Dodoth youngsters who today are working for their fathers. Rather than sell cattle, the fathers send their sons to earn money for the tax. Because these young men leave their clothes and ornaments in the bushes to keep clean, the passing vehicles find them absolutely naked, leaning on their shovels or very reluctantly carrying basins full of dirt which is slowly packed into the gullys in the road. Rain cuts new gullys and reopens old ones. The road improvement advances a few feet each day, and there is always ready money awaiting any father who cares to send a son.

Along the road, some years ago, came Somali traders to

build mud dhukas and missionaries to build churches in Kaabong. There is now a line of dhukas with galvanized tin roofs east of the road, and a Protestant mission as well as a Catholic mission, the two (by Protectorate law) at opposite ends of town. The Protestant mission at the south of town was run by a Karamojong minister for a time while we were there. But he was murdered in Karamoja by his own people for his daughter's bridal cattle, which he was driving to Kaabong, and after his death the Protestant church stood empty. Its fence of living euphorbia, a spiny soft cactus with poisonous milk, grew wild; the white stones lining the driveway to the church door—a driveway over which, I think, no car had ever traveled—were kicked aside, and the wooden cross atop the church's thatch was tipped by the weather so that it tilted like the cross atop St. Stephen's crown.

The Catholic mission was more active. It was at the northern end of town and was run by a Father Superior, a young father, and a lay brother of the Verona Fathers of Italy, who in a very few years had built a series of barracks-like classrooms and dormitories, a village of houses for the African schoolteachers and their families, a house for the fathers and the brother, a house for sisters who had never come, and a mission church, of plaster painted to look like brick, with paneled wooden doors, stained-glass windows, and a beautiful altar with small chapels at its sides. The interior of the church, with its lamps and paintings, and the interiors of the houses—the dining room in the fathers' house, with its curtained windows and heavy white plates upside down on the tablecloth—were for all the world like interiors in Italy. It was almost a shock to step from the church or dining room into the wild landscape under the

equatorial sun. On Sunday morning, church bells would peal out over the Kaabong hills, a recording of the bells of St. Peter's, played on a public-address system.

In addition, the fathers and the brother ran a farm which, with crops and cattle, fed their Dodoth students, and with the help of the students had cleared a playing field, where the young father in his white robes would play soccer with the uniformed, barefoot scholars. The game was scored in the manner of an indigenous Dodoth game in which two teams of boys throw sticks like spears at a rolling hoop. The Dodoth game could be said to be educational; the spearing is good practice and the points as they are scored are called *calves* if the hoop is speared at a distance, presenting a small target, and *bulls* if the hoop is near. The long sticks whiz in the air and the Dodoth boys shout as they accumulate cattle. They accumulate cattle in soccer too, where points are also called *calves*. After the game, the boys would dance their leaping Dodoth dances and sing their ox songs.

There was a third religious group living in Kaabong. These were the traders, the Moslem Somali storekeepers, who preached no sermons, taught no school, and keeping to themselves had very little to do with the town. Now and then they would convert a young Dodoth to Islam, but this was because they could not eat meat slaughtered by an infidel and needed a butcher.

Their shops, made of mud plaster on the outside, were dark and cool within, for the walls were thick and the barred, shuttered windows were tiny. Air wafted under the vaults of the tin roofs, moving the curtains the modest Somali women had hung to divide the public stores from the private homes in the backs of the shops, and wafted the smells of cloth and candy, cornmeal dust, and the spicy

The pastoral landscape. By the dwellings are the crops in their round fields, scattered herds, footpaths, and in the foreground, tiny figures drying grain. The Dodoth favor circles. Everything they make is round.

In the dry season, water is found in deep holes in the river bed.

Cows in Dodoth are gentle. Heat radiates from their fragrant bodies even on a rainy day.

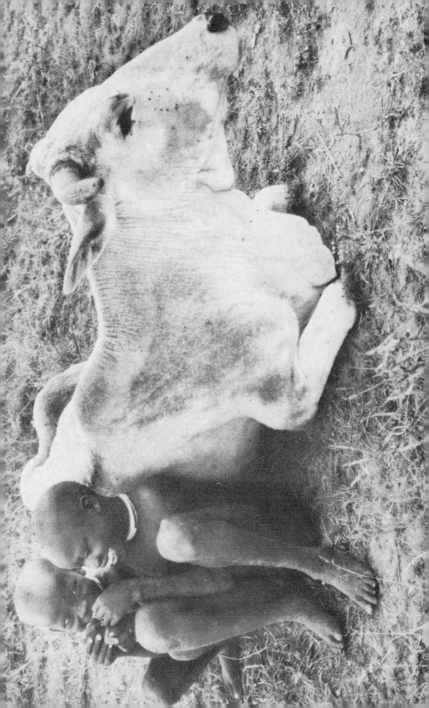

Uri, with a hive of his captive bees.

This is Mora

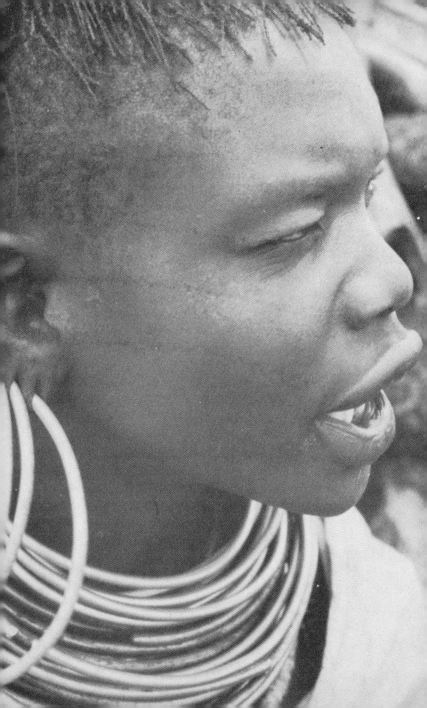

Nabilo longed for children. Her court became a haven for the children of the house.

Chuchu was tall and brilliant, with her mother's sharp tongue.

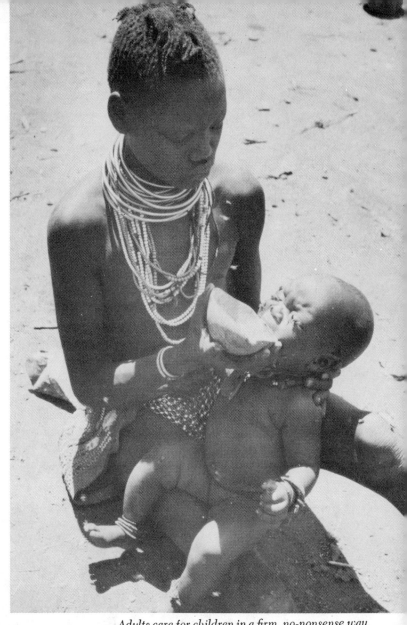

Adults care for children in a firm, no-nonsense way.

*Little girls, some of whom have just had their teeth
pulled, relieve their feelings by dancing.*

After the two boys were killed by Turkanas, Bilo's family became silent and withdrawn and like ants went about the business of building their new home.

In the harsh world, children are often very tender with each other.

To avert raids, the Dodoth hold sacrifices.

Black spots on the integument meant a raiding party of Turkanas entering, and small, thread-like capillaries showed people whom the Turkanas would kill.

Young men, in their forest of spears, watch two older men demonstrate the weaving, dodging motion of the Dodoth in battle.

At the sacrifice, Lopore advises other men to join him in risking his life for the district's defense.

From his high etem, Lopore could watch the plain. In the distance, under the clouds, is the slope of Mt. Lotim, where he was born.

In this pastoral game, sticks are thrown to spear a rolling hoop. The points, as they are scored, are called "bulls" and "calves."

little cornmeal cakes the storekeepers had for sale. The floors of the shops were of rough boards that creaked when stepped on, and the counters were oiled and darkened by the pressure of many hands. Most of the time the stores were packed with naked Dodoth, who stared solemnly at the objects on the shelves and fingered the cloth and tried on the capes. But if the dhukas, with their pocket knives and costume jewelry and bolts of bright prints ranged on the shelves, had an exotic quality for the Dodoth, to the storekeepers, Kaabong was a frontier town, a dust bowl, to be endured until enough money was put aside to support the storekeepers and their families in comfort at home.

Most storekeepers prospered. The men bought themselves turbans or fezzes, well-tailored white shirts and slacks or handsome, sarong-like garments that wrapped around the waist. Their wives wore yards and yards of white muslin, under which their jewelry sounded, and veiled themselves to the eyes, which were lengthened with kohl. Most storekeepers had cars or trucks parked beside the dhukas; most Somali children had tricycles or bicycles; and most families had refrigerators, dark, massive furniture, and radios to catch Arabic music and the news each night from Cairo or Khartoum.

When times were hard and people starving, the Somalis made money in cattle. In very hard times the Dodoth sell cattle to the Somalis to buy grain. The Somalis sell the cattle at a profit when the government cattle buyer comes to Kaabong. When times were good, however, the Somalis made money from their shops. Prosperous people bought cornmeal, capes, axes, adzes, cooking pots, and wire to make jewelry.

For the handsome Somalis, as they leaned on their counters in their dim stores or looked out of their barred windows, watching and waiting as their customers came, life was not all business. On Sunday the traders would set up tables under the trees in front of the dhukas, to play a game with a board and counters, and ignore the town.

Once the Somalis bought two young camels. These came from the Assistant District Commissioner, a European whose headquarters were in Jie. The Commissioner had come to Kaabong to investigate a raid that the Dodoth had mounted against the Turkanas, and he identified the captured cattle because the two young camels were among the herd. There are no camels in Dodoth. Only the Turkana in their desert wilderness raise them. The A.D.C. confiscated the camels and the Somali traders bought them from his office, and for a long time kept a herdboy herding them up and down the forest, and ate them at the feast of Ramadan.

To implement the government reforms and to keep order, there was a dispenser and two sets of police in Kaabong. The dispenser was an extremely nice man from Teso who maintained the dispensary, a small, concrete box of a building by the river, where he bound the wounds and did what he could to cure the illnesses of any Dodoth who cared to come. The little building was always crowded and the dispenser, who worked very hard, was always tired. He was well educated, spoke English, and wore Western clothing—white medical trousers and a doctor's high-necked tunic, blood-splashed and partially unbuttoned at the end of each busy day. One group of police was permanent—the askaris, the chiefs' police, who lived in orderly lines of huts behind the chiefs' compounds. These men, though barefoot, wore caps and cheap khaki uniforms and sometimes carried rifles, but being Dodoth, were never trusted with bullets and so, in times of need, used the rifle stocks as clubs. The second group was the Protectorate police, almost permanent in that their tours of duty in Kaabong could last for years. But they were Africans from advanced parts of Uganda, Kenya, Tanganyika, and the Sudan. They lived with their families at the police post on one of the Kaabong hills, in prefabricated round tin houses that sparkled in the sun. These men and their families, along with the dispenser and his family and the teachers at the mission school and their families, formed an enclave in Kaabong, that hardship post to which their jobs had taken them. With their Western clothes and educations, they seemed more like each other than those among them who were Nilo-Hamites seemed like the Dodoth. Their lonely wives, in the isolation of Kaabong, spent a great deal of time in their houses, where their curtains shut out the view of the raw hills, or visited each other, or stood together at the town pump installed by the government near the river, to talk while they or their daughters or servants would fill the kerosene cans in which everyone in that country carries water. Only when they had visited for a long time would the women help one another lift the heavy cans to their headrests and return home to their laundry or dishes or diapers. Any Dodoth women at the pump would fill their cans or gourds quickly and be on their way.

In their leisure hours, the men of this group would prop chairs in their doorways and lean back to read, forgetting for a time the dust and bawling cattle and throngs of people with their heavy odor and arrogant ways, people who despised the police, refused to send their children to school, and visited the dispensary only when they were at death's very door—and whom it was the work of these Westernized Africans to serve.

Day by day in Kaabong, the local governing of the Dodoth wound on. The Protectorate police, who sometimes had the use of a Land-Rover, would clatter with it into town and might unload from its truck-like back the bleeding, naked victim of a raid, speared through the leg or shoulder, whom they would heave onto the dispensary cot and interview while the dispenser sutured. When the interview, all written down on paper, was at an end, a policeman would seize the victim's hand, ink his thumb, and press his thumbprint on the paper. Relevant parts of the interview would be sent by radio to Moroto. If the victim was an aggressor in the raid, he, too, would be sent to Moroto in a truck with a back like a wire cage.

Common criminals were sometimes captured by the chief's askaris, but much more commonly by irate householders who got tired of being robbed. There were many robberies in Dodoth while we were there, often by people who had been made homeless by the Turkana raiders and, having left their gardens, turned to stealing food. We once attended the trial of a widow and her husband's brother whom Uri had had arrested. The widow stole calabashes every few days for a month from Uri's field and twice he caught her, warned her, and let her go. But the third time, when, unfortunately for her brother-in-law, he accompanied her, Uri tied them back to back and brought them, with the stolen calabashes, to the chief's court, a huge thatched roof supported by pillars, near the river in Kaabong, where trials were conducted in a Western manner. The deep shade of the thatch was filled with spectators, and the weeping prisoners crouching in the road waited a long time to be tried. Finally Uri untied the woman, but not the man. When the chief arrived in his Land-Rover, the court rose, the askaris, armed with whips and rifles, paced up and down, the prisoners were led be-

fore the bench (which was just that, a bench), and Uri
found he had to pay six shillings to accuse them. Grudg-
ingly, he paid.

The prisoners were made to stand while Uri gave evidence, while a speech was delivered by a spectator who
told the court that the man prisoner was a well-known
thief, and while yet another speech was made by a second
spectator who told the court that the man prisoner was a
thief because he had shifty eyes and all thieves have shifty
eyes, until at last the chief, becoming weary, gave the
verdict. It was "Guilty," which came as no surprise.

For helping to steal twelve calabashes, the brother-in-
law was sentenced to six months in jail. Also, he was fined
fifty shillings, a part of which would reimburse Uri. But the
widow, the habitual offender, was fined only thirty shillings, and as women are wards of their husbands' families,
the fine was to be paid by the brother-in-law, by the confiscation of his cattle, if necessary. Having aroused the pity
of the court because she had no husband, the widow was
also awarded the calabashes and then set free to go home
to the family she had so deeply wronged. She left the
courtroom looking jubilant. Uri helped her carry the
calabashes, which were too heavy for her. Her brother-in-
law was bundled off to jail.

The Protectorate government, the chiefs, the shops, the
missions and the Westernized government workers—and
the establishment of a town in a country that had never
had a town before—created a group of Dodoth unlike any
other the country had ever known. These were Dodoth
townsmen, restless and ragged, who lived in modern man-
and-wife families in back of dhukas or in ramshackle huts
in the bush around Kaabong. Most townsmen were Chris-

tians. Most had been to mission schools and thus were partly educated. And as a group, the townsmen were oriented to the West.

This was no wonder. Over the altar of the Kaabong Catholic church was a picture of God, a white man. I don't know whether the Protestant church had a picture of God, but both schools practiced fundamentalist teaching of the Bible, without modern interpretation. Thus the Book of Genesis, with the story of Adam and Eve to explain creation, and the story of Shem, Ham, and Noah to explain race, is presented as fact, not as legend, by the missionaries and mission teachers, representatives of the outside world.

Africans are not aggrandized in the Bible, nor were they in the nonreligious education offered them, which was thoroughly Western in focus. The texts were written by Britishers in England; those who organized the material were, at the Protestant church (with its main branch in Moroto) also English, and at the Catholic church, Italian, and it was not surprising that to be educated in Dodoth was to be Westernized.

Nothing was taught about the students' own people, perhaps because almost nothing was known. One group of missionaries did not know that an immense tree that grew near their classrooms was a sacred tree, and chopped it down. Elders visited the missionaries to ask that they sacrifice an ox to forestall the damage, which might take the form of a deluge of rain. But the missionaries could not do this, and a theological argument ensued. The missionaries did not believe that the tree was sacred, and could not, therefore, hold a sacrifice because to do so would be as much as admitting that the elders were right. Seeing the point of this, the elders departed. The huge tree lay on its side, and presently it rained for days and nights and the

Kaabong river rose between its banks and roared like a train.

While all this happened, the students in the classrooms were learning to speak English, reading books about Europeans, learning European history—which is valuable to know but which is not the only history—and learning science, which included hygiene by European standards. Students learned that they should wash daily, which the Dodoth do anyway. They learned to "open a window at night," though in Dodoth there are no windows in the round houses, only the tiny doors. If a person sleeps with the door open, he may wake at night to see the moonlit space darkened by the head and shoulders of a leopard which has come quietly over the dwelling wall. The students are told to eat a balanced diet of meat, fish or poultry, milk and eggs, butter and cheese, bread, fresh fruit, and vegetables. No such foods were available to the schoolboys, who lived on beans and cornmeal, with occasional meat, and the concept of diet were not taught, at least not to the students I met, who did not know that their diets of milk and blood, lightly cooked fresh vegetables in season and cereal grain may have been balanced enough. Some requirements seemed so remote from the lives of the students as to have an unreal, eerie quality. I read a composition written by a student whose parents lived near Kaabong. The composition had an assigned theme: "What I Did Last Summer." "We boys went hunting last summer," the student had written, "while the men had to go on a raid. They went to Jie and around a village [as the round dwellings are called] and set a fire to the village. The people had to escape from the fire so our men speared them while they came out."

From the same student, I borrowed a book about technology around the world. This showed what was perhaps the damaging aspect of education, for in the book "the white man" was very favorably compared to the "lowly hunting and fishing tribes." Some "negroes" had learned technology from the whites and now were fishermen in the Bahamas. These Negroes braved storms through childlike faith. "We's safe," say the Negroes, "sure till de time comes, an' when dat day come not'ing can save us. You doner have to be scared: we's all in de Lord's hands, and you can't drownd till your time comes."[1]

I asked to buy the book from the student, thinking he might be glad to get rid of it. But he did not want to sell it; he absorbed it without questioning its implications, and was learning everything it had to teach. The printed word has extraordinary power in Dodoth.

Once in a Kaabong classroom I saw this sentence written on a blackboard: "Before we sing a song we better tell you that your well come."

The teacher was not present; something possessed me to point out the mistakes. The students, all boys of about eighteen, became extremely uncomfortable. "Are you sure?" asked one. I said I was positive. "The teacher wrote it," said another. Even so, said I, it's wrong. "But we don't have to worry about it," said the third, the oldest student. "Because we're only in technical school."

What the missionaries and teachers tell the students also has extraordinary power, though one might not think so, seeing a riotous student body for the first time. But once, one evening at our camp, two students brought a bush baby as a present for our children. The students had injured the bush baby when they caught it, and as they

---

[1] P. R. Rayner: *Hunters and Fishers, The Kingsway Social Geographies,* Book I, Ernest Young, ed. (London: Montague House).

presented it, with blood smeared on its tiny hands and dripping from its nose, it had a convulsion and died. "To think," said I, to make everyone feel better, "that human beings came from creatures such as these." The students were shocked by this remark, and looked at me with horror. "How can that be?" asked one. "You are calling God a liar," said the other. I tried to explain, but the two were shaken, and presently they left together to walk home in the dark. One was a Protestant, the other a Catholic. As they left, I heard them singing to reaffirm their faith. First, for the Protestant, they sang *Turn Back Oh Man* and later, far in the distance, they sang some of the Mass.

Fundamentalism is a high price to pay for learning to read. So is the acceptance of Western standards, which by nature place Europeans and their ways in a high position, and Africans and their ways near the bottom. It is surely better for the new nations in Africa not to be broken into enclaves of tribes, and the coming changes surely will benefit the people, but it might be better for students to study the West as Westerners study anthropology. As it is, Dodoth students become underprivileged Westerners, because the advantage possessed by Westerners is the subject of their education. No Western student has ever been told that it would be wise for him to adopt some customs from, say, Dodoth.

Men who distrusted Westernization did not even allow their children to visit Kaabong, much less send them to school. The students came mostly from families who had been deeply exposed to the West to begin with, families who lived near Kaabong or who worked for the government, or families of chiefs or Jackaits. In school most youngsters learned enough to feel inferior to other people, to discard some of the values of their nation but not enough to pass the nationwide, competitive exams that qualify people for the higher government jobs. The higher-level jobs in Kaabong were held by people from afar, and the lower-level jobs by the Dodoth townsmen, who after graduation became clerks in the chiefs' adobe offices, or askaris marching barefoot with unloaded rifles, or servants to dhuka-keepers, scraping the pots and pans of the Somali women behind their husbands' stores.

The salaries of the townsmen were low and their families were poor. Westernization did not enrich them. Some owned a few head of livestock, some had wives who grew gardens, but most townsmen spent part of their salaries for food. The Westernized townsmen regarded nakedness as backwardness and spent a large portion of their money on shoes and clothing. The shoes were cheap ones, and cloth garments, unlike leather capes, wear out quickly, fall into rags, disintegrate, and must be replaced often. Very few items of Western dress are made in Dodoth. The shirts and trousers, underwear and jackets, socks and shoes must all be imported from cities hundreds or even thousands of miles away, the last few hundred miles by the dhuka-keeper's lorry. Hence, high prices are charged even for items of poor quality. Most of the rest of the money goes for gadgets. Job holders in a money economy look with longing on the things that money can buy, and pay for china dishes, pocket knives, neckties, and alarm clocks. Also, the West was stylish. A second-hand object once owned by a European cost more and gave its owner more prestige than a similar object once owned by an African. Uhuru ball-point pens, made in New Jersey, were sold for high prices in Kaabong, where people who could neither write nor draw wore them in their pockets.

It takes a strong person, an exceptional person, to over-

come poverty and Westernization. Some young men overcame the difficulties brilliantly. One such man, the son of
a well-known Dodoth family, went to the Kaabong mission
school, graduated, received a higher education near
Moroto, graduated, and returned to Dodoth to become his
country's representative in the Legislative Council of
Uganda. When the council was not in session, he managed
his own successful store in Kaabong, and owned a Bedford
truck (called Fetford Motoca by the Dodoth), in which he
transported his merchandise.

Some graduates, mostly those from the countryside, not
the town, went home to assume their responsibilities, guard
their cattle, and forget that they had ever been to school.
But most of the schoolboys grew up to be townsmen, and
remained near Kaabong. One group had formed a little
town of their own, not far from Kaabong. The first time
we passed it, it was noon and not a soul was in sight in the
hot sun by the tiny mud houses except a donkey, tethered
to a tree. The second time we passed the town it was evening, rain was coming, and people were milling in the road.
Two bruised, bleeding men and a boy were surrounded by
a small, angry crowd, which surged around the car when
we stopped. We opened the door and called to the three.
The boy reached the car, climbed in, and weeping, begged
the two men to come to him. They tried, edging carefully
toward us, but a man in the crowd caught one by the hair,
twisting his head painfully, and the crowd enclosed the
second and when they began to encircle the car, we drove
away—we being myself and our interpreter, who thought
we might be dragged out and stoned, which does happen—
and when we tried to ask the boy what had happened, and
who the men were, he was crying too hard to say.

On Sunday, Christian Kaabong came into its own. The

townsmen worked at their jobs six days a week, but most had Sunday free. Early in the morning, when the land was still, a drum would begin to sound in the middle of town. It summoned the Protestants, who would form a double line of men in clean shirts and shorts, women in clean dresses, and with tiny ragged children dancing at their feet they would march behind the drummer to the Protestant church. As they marched, they would sing an antiphonal hymn with Bantu music and a marked, insistent beat: *It is He that was Jesus, He that was Jesus.* And though in Dodoth there are no drums and no such music, the pagan people, as non-Christian Dodoth are sometimes called, would gather by the road to hear the song.

Meanwhile, in the Catholic church across the river, where the congregation knelt, washed in the pale light from the stained-glass windows, the Dodoth choir boys would sing *Ora Pro Nobis,* and the music would float out over the town, to mix with the Protestant drum. After church, the congregations would mix around the dhukas to drink a raw, fierce liquor which can be brewed from garbage and which makes people wild.

By afternoon, the respectable people would be locked in their houses; the Somali men, who neither sell liquor nor drink it, would be aloof beneath their shade trees, playing the game with board and counters, but ready at a moment's notice to go inside their stores, and the drinkers, eyes red and tempers blazing, would roam the town.

On Monday, they would visit the dispenser for aspirins, for bromides, for poultices for swollen, blackened eyes, and for mouthwashes, which they would spit, bloody red, in the dirt by the dispensary door. Our cook, who drank, was nearly killed by a group of such people. He was not from Uganda and detested the Dodoth, whom he considered backward, and one Sunday, when he was drunk, he called his drinking companions "fucking Karamojong." Though the townsmen did not speak much English, they knew these words well enough. The askaris, the clerks, the chief of the Dodoth police, and the servants of the dhuka-keepers formed a ring around him as the Dodoth do in warfare. Luckily for him, we arrived in the Land-Rover just as the ring was getting smaller. For his sake, we risked the crowd, and though people shouted and shoved us and spat in our faces, we squeezed through the ring and dragged him, still swearing, to the Land-Rover, pushed him in, and slammed the door just as the first stones struck the car.

CHAPTER FOUR

Families

THE TRADITIONAL AMUSEMENT for people in Dodoth is dancing. Dances took place in the daytime, and on brilliant, moon-washed nights when the earth, the grass, and flowers after the day's heat gave up a fragrance, and the landscape with its tumbled boulders on the hills was no longer brown and green but black and white with moonlight and deep shadow. A young man in love would want a dance held where the girl he admired could join it, perhaps somewhere near her home. His friends would see to it, and after dark, when the moon rose into the trees, the young people would go toward the dancing place in small groups, two or three brothers together, or a brother accompanying several of his little sisters, he armed with a spear to protect them against the leopards which, not infrequently, one meets at night on the paths. The young men would bellow for their friends as they passed various dwellings, but the brothers accompanying sisters were more quiet, and would stride along grimly, sometimes almost herding the group of little girls, for a young man prefers to go to a dance with his friends, and to leave with his lover.

Sometimes the chosen place was beside a dwelling. In this case the little children and some of the older people of the dwelling might come out to join the dancers. The householder might dance with some of his wives. But usually dances were held on flat land somewhat away from dwellings, for young people in Dodoth, as elsewhere, prefer to be by themselves.

At a dance, the young men form a crescent not unlike the crescent formed by the trained horns of an ox. The young men stand with their shoulders touching and their cattle clubs under their arms. The moonlight shines on their handsome backs as they lean inwards, all together, and with their hands up, muffling their voices, sing together as a chorus. Presently one young man sings rapidly, a few lines, then all sing the slow, bellowing chorus, for all the world like the voices of cattle, and suddenly the leader steps to the center of the crescent and leaps straight up in the air. Two or three girls, who have been waiting with the other girls where the horns of the crescent almost touch, rush forward and leap also, two small leaps to the young man's one. The young man leaps again, higher and higher, the young men in the crescent sing the slow bellow, clapping the rhythm, and the girls, who leap so that their skirts snap up twice to the left, then twice to the right, begin to scream.

Angaiyeya, Lopeta, a song might say, *I speared a man at noon. Angaiyeya, Lopeta,* the chorus would repeat, as the singer whose ox was Lopeta leaped and the jumping girls, their neckrings chiming and their skirts asway, danced and screamed before him. Presently the song would change.

*Cholokol's horn is a barrier in the midst of cows, in the
midst of milking cows,* a new song would begin, and
Cholokol's owner would burst into the center of the crescent to leap with the girls. The singing, the clapping, the
sharp staccato of the feet striking hard against the earth,
and the shrill, rippling screaming can be heard afar, tempt-
ing more young people to come and join the dancers, the
young men from miles away, the girls from nearby—even
with their brothers to guard them, girls cannot go roaming
after dark—and the dust rises, making the air thick and
casting a haze over the moon.

Dodoth dances are not considered as art, but as excitement. In the lulls the girls provoke the young men to tussle
with them. A young man may seize a girl by the arm and
pretend to be about to slap her, but she will laugh, and he
will release her. After the dances, people make love. Sometimes as a dance is ending, a girl entices her lover by chal-
lenging and teasing, taunting and jeering, until he follows
her home in a passion, crawls through her private gate
after her, into her little domed night house, and bangs the
door. He leaves in the morning, his feelings vented, when
the gray light in the east begins to show.

Some young people fall in love, and some of these get
married. Some are prevented from marrying by one or another set of parents, usually the girl's. It is an excellent
thing that young people in Dodoth are allowed to have
affairs before marriage, for marriage is so complex a matter,
it involves so many people, so much property, and is such a
vital function of society, that to have it entered lightly, at
the whim of young people, would be a dangerous thing.

A wedding itself is composed of so many stages, phases,
and ceremonies that it lasts most of a year. After it, two
families are united, and a person and her descendants are

replaced by a herd. The herd is gathered from among the bridegroom's relatives and friends, each of whom contributes stock, and then it is taken to the bride's father and distributed not only to the bride's father, but among his relatives, and his wives' relatives, and his sons. A web of property is cast over the families: they are enmeshed.

An affair is a personal matter, a woman in her lover's arms. A marriage is a public matter, and a married couple are a segment of a larger whole. In a Dodoth marriage, usually the bride does not leave her mother's court until she has raised two children who can walk. Meanwhile, she goes to dances and is visited by her husband, who lives at home. Afterwards, she takes her two children and a cow accompanied by its calf, a present from her father to her husband, and goes to join her husband's clan in a ceremony, becoming a member of his family for life.

There is no such thing, in traditional Dodoth marriages, as a man and his wife and children alone against the world. A man, it could almost be said, is only partly a single entity; he is also one of his group of brothers. But for a woman, it is different. Each girl alone, without her sisters, will join her father to her husband. Each married woman alone, without her co-wives, will raise her family in her courts. Of course, a woman is considered as one of the group of her husband's wives, and co-wives often like and help each other. However, in Dodoth a man and his wives do not function as one entity; they constitute a series of distinct marriages, and the relationship of a man with each particular wife has its own particular nature. If a man is happy with his first wife but not with his second, the children of both marriages reflect it.

The family of Lopore, whom we met when we first arrived in Morukore, was an example of this. It is said in

Dodoth that a man should marry women of different physical types and characters, to give variety to his life. Some men's wives seem homogeneous, but Lopore's were not. His four wives were very different, he married them for different reasons, and his family was complex.

His first wife, who was named Rengen, was a reserved and austere woman, almost the same age as he. Her skin was soft and wrinkled, so delicate and thin it looked like crumpled silk. She was not tall but she looked tall, so straight did she carry herself. She smoked a delicate, long-stemmed clay pipe, wore an aluminum lip plug, and owned and wore a handsome leather cape that swept the ground. She was the bride of Lopore's youth, the girl he had courted at dances, and for whom, at the most difficult time of his life, he had paid a hundred cattle to her father, Thonal.

Rengen was sharp and sometimes hostile: she had great strength of character and a forbidding, brilliant mind. Father of the Tall White Sorghum, she was called—women have father-names for grain the way men have for oxen— and Akimat, which derives from the word for fire, and Thonal's Daughter, both of which are terms of respect.

Lopore had a deep affection for Rengen, and a respect sometimes tinged with awe. She could hurt his feelings and was not afraid of him; in this she was different from some of his other wives. Some Dodoth husbands consult their senior wives about their business; Lopore often consulted Rengen.

His children by her were his favorites. Lopore and Rengen had had six children, three of whom had died. The oldest living son was Akikar. Lopore was very fond of him. Akikar did not resemble either of his parents. He had none of Lopore's temper and impatience, none of his mother's cold brilliance, and must have taken after a gentle grand-parent now dead, for he was a dreaming, thoughtful person who, now too old to be a herdboy, spent a great deal of time in the shadowy green gardens of his father's wives. He would lie on his back and watch the sky for rain clouds, and talk with his little sisters, or carve objects for the family, or improve the garden fences. He was very kind to us and undertook to teach me the language. He would sit patiently in a garden house or by the river for hours, repeating words. "What is that?" he would ask carefully.

"An ox," I would reply.

"Yes, very good. An ox. But you should say 'a brindle.' What is that?"

"Little stones," I would say.

"Yes, very good. It is little stones. But learn to call them 'sand.'"

Lopore was protective of Akikar; he had, for instance, never allowed Akikar to go on a raid. Akikar would not have been a good warrior; Lopore was wise.

The second child of Rengen and Lopore was a daughter, Chuchu, who was in her early twenties. She was alert and brilliant like her mother, and also very beautiful, with a soft, pretty mouth, a clear voice, and wide eyes. She lived in a little court within her mother's section, and had built herself a sleeping house for all the world like a huge, thatched jar. It was entered through a narrow passage, and was hot and dark inside, for the walls, floor, and ceiling all were plastered. It was built this way for privacy, a girl's or a bride's house. Chuchu was married. Her husband, chosen for her by Lopore, was one of his dearest friends, therefore much older than Chuchu, and was not in the least good-looking. But he was amiable and kind, a very fine person, and Chuchu loved him dearly; the whole family was devoted to him. He and Chuchu had had two little girls who had died, and then two more girls, a sprite of a three-year-old and a rose of a baby whom Lopore and Rengen had had named Iloshabiet, for me.

Perhaps, of all the people in the family, Rengen most loved Chuchu. Rengen and Chuchu spent their days together in Rengen's garden, and went to the river together, and in the evening sat together in Rengen's court. One day Chuchu would have to leave Rengen to live with her husband, whose dwelling was very far, but to replace Chuchu in Rengen's affections, when Chuchu was gone, it was said that Rengen would keep Iloshabiet to raise as her own.

Perhaps Lopore's favorite child was his third child by Rengen, the fourteen- or fifteen-year-old herdboy of the family, his son Akral. Akral was tall and still growing, and had an untroubled, pleasant face and a forthright manner. He had Lopore's courage, his fondness for harsh jokes, his lack of subtlety, and his directness; he was, I think, the sort of boy Lopore was once, long ago.

Like Akikar, Akral enjoyed teaching. He taught us all about the personalities of his father's cows, which he took every day into the forest. He asked us many questions about life in America, but made fun of the answers, because he was impish and too exuberant to be polite. He tried to teach me how to braid ten grass blades into a toy animal, but such teaching took a lot of patience. Finally he made the animal himself and capered around with it. "Yah! it eats people," he cried. Once he gave me a spray of berries to eat. I did. They were like dumb cane, which burns so strongly that it is temporarily blinding and takes away the power of speech. Akral laughed loudly and said: "But you mustn't eat the seeds!" He once made me a grass earring like his own, and asked, as I inserted it, if my ear-piercing had been painful. I said it had not. "Mine was terrible," said he with pride, "almost unbearable. But the lip is worse." He removed his lip plug. "You don't do that, do you?" I said we did not. "That is cowardly of you," said he.

Akral was deepy attached to his father. Together, Akral and Lopore had charge of the cattle, Lopore as the owner, Akral as the herdboy, and every evening the two would discuss the herd. One evening Lopore criticized Akral for neglecting the cattle. Akral made excuses, increasing Lopore's anger. Lopore shouted, and grown up as he was, Akral burst into tears.

Rengen, as the chief wife, had the largest courts in the dwelling. Entering her section from the corridor that bordered the cattle pens, one walked along a high-walled passageway that gave into a bare, round kitchen containing only fire ashes amid three round stones which were to support her cooking pot. Beyond the kitchen to the left was Chuchu's little court. Rengen's own night court was at the right of the passage, and her sleeping house, which was larger than Chuchu's, had plaster walls, but only the inside of the thatch for a ceiling. Older married women build houses this way, as they do not need the same privacy younger women need. The plaster walls were red, the straw ceiling black with soot and smoke. On the far side of the night court was Rengen's day court. This, in a Dodoth home, is the work court, where the woman keeps her churn, her cooking utensils, and her grindstone, and where, on heavy wooden legs, stand her thatched granary baskets, in which throughout the year she stores her harvested, winnowed grain. In the center of Rengen's day court was her day house, a circle of small poles two or three feet high supporting a thatch, where Rengen could work if it rained. Most of the important activity of the dwelling took place in this court. If a calf was sick, it spent its illness tethered to the leg of a granary basket. If one of the children of the house was sick, it might lie in the shade of the day house. When Chuchu went for the day to visit her husband, she left her baby there for Rengen to mind; Rengen would play with her and trundle her until she was hungry, and then would offer her water in place of Chuchu's milk. By the end of the day the baby's crying could be heard for miles. Rengen blamed me for the crying, which put her nerves on edge, and whenever I would visit her in the evening before Chuchu came home, she would look with great annoyance from the shrieking baby in her arms to me. A baby takes on the character of the person it is named for—obviously, said Rengen, as a baby I had cried a great deal. Rengen once let the baby suck at her dry breast; the baby tried, then wailed with disappointment. Rengen was very angry with me. "This is your fault. You hold her," she said.

When the family spontaneously decided to extract the lower teeth of all the little girls in the dwelling (except the baby, whose milk teeth had already been extracted), the operation was performed in Rengen's court. Her son Akral sat in her day house with one of his weeping little half-sisters between his knees. Her twenty-three-year-old son Akikar, mild and impassive, placed a stick as a bit in the girl's mouth, and while Akral held the girl tightly, Akikar expertly hooked out the lower teeth with an awl. They were second teeth, deeply rooted, and as they came, cracked loudly, and the smell of blood filled the air. The little girl screamed that she was dying, and vomited red foam.

She was released, to wash away her tears and rinse her mouth, and her sister, begging and crying, her hands pressed over her mouth, was captured by Rengen, who firmly handed her over the heads of all the seated people to Kubal, who gripped her with his knees. The weeping little girl began to scream: "Akikar, help me!" Akikar dispassionately pried open her jaw and forced the bit into her mouth. He worked carefully, the extraction took only a moment, but she struggled so much he nearly pierced her palate with the awl. She moaned hysterically when it was over and her teeth lay on the ground.

There were three girls in all, and splashes and trails of blood covered the court from their spitting and bleeding. Oddly, all three girls, including the only girl who had been brave, who had seated herself between her half-brother's knees and of her own accord had placed the bit in her mouth, were teased for complaining by Chuchu, who long ago had suffered the same fate. The extraction is done for beauty. Girls "don't have to have it done if they don't want to," say the Dodoth. But for a baby, it is different. Rengen had decided when the baby's teeth should be extracted, which is done by a specialist, an old woman in Kalapata who knows how. The baby's teeth were cut from her tiny gum a few weeks after she was born, the gum slit and the little buds hooked out, because their presence, say the Dodoth, threatens a baby's life.

Lopore kept his shield and spear in Rengen's night house, but he seldom slept there. She had given her night house, with its thick mud walls and blackened thatch, to the young men of the household; they slept inside with the door shut, the smoke from the fire making them keep their heads near the floor. But years ago, Rengen had had enough of stuffy houses and of coughing at night. She slept alone in her day house, between two leather mats. At night the fresh wind blew through the poles and foggy air beaded her eyelashes; the little bats that hung in the thatch flew over her and on wet nights the rain drifted down on her sleeping face.

The marriage of Lopore and Rengen had been a long one. When we knew them, their marriage had evolved an aura of mutual respect. In their attention to their children, Lopore and Rengen were like partners, for Rengen had as much to say as he.

One day the cattle buyer came to Kaabong. Many people sent their sons, usually their oldest sons, to earn tax money by being herdsmen for the buyer. Akikar was not feeling very well at the time, but because the pay was good and because Lopore and Rengen wanted someone in their family to be sure of a job with the buyer, they sent Akral.

During the sale, an ox which had been purchased by the buyer died of an injury. An older man, a resident of Kaabong, suggested to Akral and another youngster that they cook some of the ox's meat and eat it. An alert policeman smelled the roasting meat and arrested the three for eating what belonged to the buyer. The three were taken to the Jackait's round, tin jail.

News of Akral's arrest reached Lopore a day later. He put on his Western clothes, a pair of shorts, an army overcoat, an army hat, and a pair of heavy, rubber-tire sandals, and went to Kaabong to beg for his son's release. Though many women would have left such a matter entirely up to their husbands, Rengen accompanied Lopore, her head high, her face expressionless, and a bowl of cooked pumpkin in her arms so that Akral would have enough to eat. We drove them in the Land-Rover.

The jail must have been fearful, without air or windows. Sunlight winked and danced from its eight galvanized sides, and no one inside made a sound. Lopore stood looking at it as if he could not believe that it contained his son.

Rengen, the bowl in her arms, stood looking at Lopore. A guard appeared, and Lopore spoke with him, explaining that his son was young and could have made a mistake. The guard said Akral would have to stand trial. Lopore asked that Akral be released to his custody. "Give him to me," he said. "He will not escape." The guard said indifferently that Lopore should have explained the matter to the Jackait. While Lopore went to see the Jackait, Thamal gave the guard the cooked pumpkin, then waited to see that the guard opened the jail door a crack and pushed the pumpkin inside.

Lopore returned, very discouraged. The Jackait had offered to try Akral in the morning; he would have to stay in jail another night. "We can go," said Lopore. Rengen said that she for one would not go home, but would stay at the dwelling of a relative to be near her son and to bring him more food early in the morning. So we left her standing by the jail, her arms folded, and we went home.

In the morning we returned to Kaabong to attend the trial. But either Lopore or the Jackait had been mistaken. We found the courthouse empty and learned that the Jackait had left Dodoth the previous evening on a long trip. If we had not happened to meet the Ekapolon that morning —and he, to please us, the Europeans, offered us any or all of the prisoners in the jail—Akral might have been there indefinitely. As it was, the three prisoners were brought out so that we might choose the ones we wanted. Akral came blinking into the sun, followed by the boy his age and the older man, who was wearing a ragged cloth garment, voluminous and brown. Akral came straight to his father, who hugged him against his side. Dazed by his experience, Akral leaned on his father, and when asked how he was, said mechanically: "I have eaten an ox." Lopore held the

boy tightly as he promised the Ekapolon to bring his son
to trial. The other boy noticed Lopore and looked hopeful.
Lopore asked for him too, and the Ekapolon assented. The
boy was Remi, it turned out, the son of one of Lopore's in-
laws. Lopore flung his arm around Remi's shoulders too,
and pulled the two boys toward the car. He pushed them
in, got in behind them, and slammed the door. The Ekapolon waved, Lopore thanked him, and the man in brown
was taken back to jail. I often wondered how long he
stayed there, for in all the time we were in Uganda, the
case of Akral and Remi never came to trial.

We found Rengen at the roadside, and when she saw
Akral, she looked him over quickly to see that he was all
right. She then climbed in the back seat respectfully, as
men were present, and said nothing. When we came to our
camp, Remi dashed home, Akral dashed home, and Rengen
walked quickly after him. But Lopore paused to thank us
before strolling home after Akral. Later we visited Lopore's
house. Almost the entire family was gathered at the cattle
pen, for it was just the time when the cattle were coming in.
Akral sat on the fence. Several of the cattle came over to
see him, their herdboy, and blew him with their breath. He
pushed them affectionately with his foot and said: "They
are wondering where I have been."

To thank us for our part in redeeming her son, Rengen
came out of her court and gave us a little teapot full of
milk, a green calabash, a bowl of ripe tomatoes, a bowl of
string beans, and an egg. This done, she stood smoking her
pipe, looking at Akral with satisfaction.

"He was in jail two days," said someone.

"Three days," remarked Rengen.

Nothing was required of Akral that evening. He watched
his sisters getting ready to feed the calves, he took deep

breaths of the clear air, and basked in the pleasure his family took in having him home again. On an impulse, he dropped from the fence and milked a cow onto his palm. He crouched beside her, milking and drinking, with Lopore watching, and I wondered how often the family let him do this, as the milk from each cow in the household herd is assigned.

"Whose cow is that?" I asked Lopore.

Lopore smiled down at his son, to whom at that moment he would have given anything, and softly, his voice alive with pride and pleasure, be answered with another question: "Isn't it mine?"

That evening, just as we were going home, the shadowy figure of a woman we had never seen slipped through the cattle gate, and skirting the wall, went silently around the cow pen and over the fence, and disappeared through the low gate of a courtyard. The conversation stopped as she went by, and Lopore glanced at her. She passed with her eyes cast down, she said nothing to anyone, and no sound of greeting or talking came from the court she entered.

Her name was Ngira. She was Lopore's second wife, who had caused him deep unhappiness. Yet from her appearance, now that she was middle-aged, it was hard to see how she could cause anyone pain, for she was as thin as a stick, with spindly arms, long spidery legs, and a gaunt, emaciated face with huge eyes. Like soft cows' eyes, like dark mirrors, her eyes looked as if a landscape could reflect in them. Only those eyes and her straight body showed what must have been her beauty as a girl.

She had been courted by Lopore while his marriage with Rengen was new, and she had entered his house as a bride within four years after Rengen had been established. Ngira's son Torori was born the same year as Akikar. Ngira

was shy compared to Rengen, abstract and silent where
Rengen was expressive. Perhaps Lopore wanted a change
from dominant, assertive women when he married Ngira.
He married her for love; he chose her for herself, not for
the alliance with her family, who fell on hard times and
were never very helpful to him. Perhaps her quietness ap-
pealed to him, or perhaps her huge eyes, but after a few
years it became clear that this remote woman was no wife
for him. Perhaps he lost his temper with her. Perhaps he
beat her. (He did not hesitate to do this if one of his wives
annoyed him.) His quick-witted wives could dissuade him,
but silent Ngira probably could not. After four years of
marriage, she left him. She was pregnant with her daughter
Alaina at the time, and followed by her little son Torori,
she walked all the way along the plain and up to the slopes
of Morunyang, where her father had his dwelling.

Lopore had paid her father forty cattle for her. He could
have had them back, but did not, first because in the heat
of the moment, when he might have demanded them, her
family had very few to give—raids and the marriages of
her brothers had taken most of them—and second because
Lopore did not want to part with his children. I believe he
never saw his daughter Alaina until she was almost
grown.

But in Dodoth ties from children to their fathers are
strong. When Torori was thirteen, he decided to visit
Lopore. He walked alone from Morunyang and presented
himself at his father's dwelling. He must have remembered
his father exactly, for he was exactly like him. He had the
same large frame, the same strong body and deep eyes, but
more than that, he had copied Lopore's personality. He had
Lopore's gestures, tempers, and spells of sudden tenderness
too. Lopore was so glad to see Torori that Torori decided to

live forever with his father, and Rengen took him into her courts, where he sleeps to this day.

Not long after he came, his sister Alaina followed. She was shy, like her mother, but like her brother she resembled Lopore. This was unfortunate, for his heavy face and jaw are better suited to a man than to a woman. Also, Alaina was short, not willowy like her mother, but rather stumpy, and had an incurable sore beneath her arm. When she came she brought her father an offering, a gourd filled with butter.

Meanwhile, in his dwelling in the mountains, Ngira's father died. Ngira's mother was old and senile, and when the household fractured, Ngira was helpless, hungry, without a protector, and alone. Her children visited her, and begged her to rejoin Lopore. Finally they persuaded her to return. Her coming was rather touching. Her children preceded her, to announce her to their father. Lopore made her welcome and helped her to build a court. Even so, there was no real reconciliation. She had returned for economic reasons, and though she lived within his walls, the two were never again as husband and wife. She had very little contact with the people of his house, but slipped in and out without being noticed; like a little dog, she would step hastily and quietly along the curved shadow of the wall, through the doorway and be gone. If she met someone on her way, she might give a greeting, a wan smile. She might come back in the evening, or she might not. While we were there she vanished for three weeks, almost without notice. Rengen had overheard her tell her daughter she was off to visit someone in her family. Otherwise, Lopore would not have known.

Hearing of Ngira's good fortune, a part of her family had also come to live with Lopore. They built a rather

shoddy dwelling adjoining Ngira's court and demanded
many things from Lopore. He usually refused.

The family consisted of Ngira's widowed sister, the
widowed sister's married daughters and their children, the
widowed sister's son Sokot, titular head of the family, who
dressed himself in a ragged, frayed coat and a pair of
shorts, and was not above visiting Lopore's dwelling in the
middle of the day when no one was there, to help himself
to something. He once stole money from Torori, money
which Torori had earned by working on the roads and
which he had planned to give to Lopore in order to please
him. Torori found it difficult to believe that his own cousin
would wrong him so deeply.

But it was in the treatment accorded Ngira's mother that
the harshness of this family showed most plainly. Though
Ngira had courts and houses, though her widowed sister
and her sister's daughters all had courts and houses, no one
had built anything for the old woman, who was blind. All
she had was a wretched hut resembling a garden shelter:
four posts, open walls, and a flat, sod roof that absorbed
rain. The old woman had used her clothing to stuff the
walls, and wore only a filthy rag as an apron. Ngira's sister
had taken the old woman's jewelry, as it was just a question
of time before the old woman died. I used to wonder what
sort of a mother she had been to her children, to reap such
treatment from them. She may have been harsh, like
Ngira's widowed sister; she may have been remote, like
Ngira.

The first time we visited the old woman we found her
squatting in her shed. Her bones seemed covered only by
her dry skin, which was covered with sores and gray ashes,
for nobody had troubled to clear her fireplace in many
days. Everything in the hut—the walls, the floor, the few

utensils, the rag that was her bed—was gray with ashes, and the old woman, whose eyes were white balls in their sockets, was fingering the largest pile of ashes for the remnants of roasted pumpkin seeds. Perhaps she had overlooked a few from last night's cooking. Her fingers moved with desperate quickness but she found none. Not six feet away, on the other side of the dwelling wall in which there was no door, Ngira could be seen through chinks in the wall grinding sorghum without as much as glancing at her mother. I gave the old woman some cigarettes. She seized them, then let them fall. "This is tobacco!" she cried. "Not food!"

We came back shortly with a basin of cornmeal. We found her crawling in the dust outside her hut. Because she was so starved and weak, and also blind, she almost always crawled, as she was afraid of falling. She was groping for a stick of firewood which she felt sure was there, but if there had once been a stick, someone else had used it, for the space was empty. We brought her a few sticks from elsewhere. Taking them one at a time, she crawled with them into her hut, thinking that at last she had found them. We gave her the basin of cornmeal. Like an animal, she became alert and trembling. She sat up, took the basin in her lap, and let the cornmeal run between her fingers. When she knew what it was, she asked to feel me. I gave her my hands. She held them with a solid grip and spat four times in my face. This, as is all sprinkling of water, is a blessing. She asked to feel the interpreter, David. He gave her his hands. She spat her blessing over him and said: "Is that your wife?"

"No," he said, "but a European woman who lives on the hill."

"You will marry a nice woman," she said. "You will have

nice children. You will get rich. You will grow old, and when you do, someone will help you when no one else will, as you have helped me."

Later that day I met her widowed daughter in Ngira's court. Ngira, as usual, was silent. But the widow came up to me. "You gave our mother cornmeal today? I'll ask her for some," she said.

Lopore did not consider his second wife a part of himself. She had preferred extreme deprivation to being his wife and she spent her time within the sphere of her widowed sister, whose family made Lopore uneasy with their poverty and strife. Whereas he was warmly loyal to his other wives as far as outsiders were concerned, he often spoke of Ngira with bitterness. Once he said this of her escape: "Some women run away because they think other men are richer. But when no one wants them, they come back to their homes."

His distance from her had affected his relationship with her children, who were not his favorites, no matter how submissive Alaina was, no matter how carefully Torori copied him. Lopore once told me that by leaving him Ngira had forfeited her position as his second wife, therefore Torori would marry after all the other boys of the household had married. He added: "Torori is like a porter here. If he does his work well, I will give him enough cattle to marry." While it is true that young men marry in part according to the seniority of their mothers, Lopore didn't mean a word of what he said. But Torori, who had been sitting near his father listening, got up and left, injured, believing that his father did mean it. Lopore's feelings vacillated quickly. When Torori had gone, I asked Lopore if I had heard him rightly. "Of course not," he said. "Did you think Torori would marry after Botia?" Botia was his third wife's five-year-old boy. "Torori marry after Botia? Why would I do that to Torori, my second son?" But Torori didn't hear these words, with their ring of loyalty and affection. The harshness of the first remarks had driven him away.

In his pursuit of his father, Torori matched Lopore's harshness. Once I asked Torori why nobody had built his grandmother a house and in his reply he was exactly like his father. "What for?" he said.

As for Alaina, Lopore had married her to a very elderly man whose name was Nathigiria and who was almost senile. He had knock-knees, a frowsy headdress, a doddering manner, and an upper lip perpetually stained with snuff. Remi, the boy we had rescued with Akral from the Kaabong jail, was his son by his first wife. In all his years of marriage, Nathigiria had married no other woman. Alaina was to fill the gap.

From Lopore's point of view, the marriage had an advantage: Nathigiria belonged to the family of some of Lopore's closest friends. Lopore was allied in one way or another with most of the neighborhood, but so far he was not united with this dear friend because the friend was a newcomer to Morukore. The friend also desired the alliance, but he had four wives already and didn't seem to want Alaina. The friend's brother had two wives and was courting several other women—he more or less offered me two hundred cattle and some small stock for my four-year-old daughter, but nothing for Alaina—so the lot fell to Nathigiria, an impoverished, dependent half-brother. Lopore's friend was willing to gather sixty cattle to form the alliance, a bargain was struck, and the two friends were at last united when Alaina became a bride.

If a girl's family has chosen a husband for her but her

heart is set on another man, she has at least a chance to win. There is a well-known song that a girl once sang to her parents about a young man:

> If you drive him off
> I will not leave him.

But poor Alaina had no lover. Having no cause for strife, no special person she preferred to Nathigiria, she found herself married to him. After the wedding, he used to beg things fron Lopore; "He begs like a woman," someone said of him. We would see him in Lopore's etem, fingering Lopore's black cape, asking for it. Lopore always made excuses and did not give it, yet was always polite to his new son-in-law.

All that can be said for Alaina in her plight is that she was at least escaping from the sphere of Sokot and her mother's family, who at her wedding behaved very badly and insulted many people, as they felt that too small a share of the marriage cattle had fallen to them. I suppose they had reason. They had brought Alaina up, yet at the wedding received but one heifer, who in time committed the only crime a cow can in that paradise of livestock—she refused to nurse her calf. Even then, public opinion had it that this was not the cow's fault, but somehow accrued to the family. Sokot complained bitterly, and tried to have the heifer exchanged, but his efforts were unsuccessful.

Once, at a party attended by several of Lopore's close friends and neighbors and their wives in Rengen's court (Rengen had wanted a roof moved, the neighbors had come in to help and were repaid in beer), Sokot's efforts came under discussion. People were sitting very close together, crowding the courtyard, the sun beat down, and everyone drank a great deal of the foamy, sour beer. People grew emotional and banded together against Sokot.

"He wants to be above me. He is taking himself as Alaina's father," said Lopore hotly.

"He wants Alaina to marry someone richer," said Uri.

"When I opened my cattle gate this morning, Sokot was standing there," said Lopore's friend, head of Nathigiria's family. "He said he wanted me to visit him about the heifer. But I said: 'If you want to see me, you come here.'"

"He came to me," said Rengen, "to ask me to speak with Lopore. I refused. He said he was going to slap me. I told him: 'If you do that, I'll tell Lopore and you will meet a spear!'"

"If he troubles us again about this matter," said Lopore, "I will beat him on the head until he is bloody!'"

So in the end, Sokot fumed about the cow in silence. Lopore and his friend, in-laws at last, had triumphed, and Alaina had at least four years, or the time it takes to raise two children to the age when they can walk, to get used to the idiosyncrasies of the elderly man. And if he died soon, which was not unlikely, she might become the wife of one of his half-brothers. The half-brothers were witty, strong, and handsome, quite another matter than Nathigiria.

The next of Lopore's wives in age, though not in seniority, was his fourth wife, Nabilo. His marriage to her was his happiest, I think, and he spent many of his waking hours within her tidy courts, many of his nights in her thatched house beside her, and ate most of his meals sitting by her fire, for she was an excellent cook. Dodoth cooking is always delicious, but Nabilo's was even better than most. If there was meat, she made aromatic stews flavored with tomatoes and red, spicy peppers from the pepper tree outside the wall. If there was no meat, she made vegetable dishes of pumpkin, calabash, roasted corn, or beans. She cooked the hyraxes that Lopore trapped in the rocks by the dwelling, a delicate meal, and she made marvelous beer, excellent sweet butter, sour milk, and cheese.

As a wife, she was perfect. She was grateful to Lopore; she was tender with him, a quality which one might not expect in the wife of so volatile a man. Once, when he sold an ox to the government buyer and gave 100 shillings from the profits to each of his wives, she used her share to buy him an overcoat, because, she said, he was not getting younger and the coat would protect him from the wind and the rain.

Once, at Lopore's etem, she had an argument with our cook, who learned that Nabilo had lived in Jinja. They argued in Swahili, which Lopore didn't understand. But seeing Nabilo in adversity, he came to stand towering beside her, glaring at our cook with great hostility. The cook was too aroused to stop the argument, however, and as it turned out, Nabilo defended herself alone, with wit, and very well.

The argument began because the cook could not believe that a woman who had lived in Jinja would ever return to Dodoth. "Did you wear skins in Jinja?" he asked derisively.

"Would anyone?" Nabilo asked in return.

"You mean you left your husband there and came here?"

"Lopore is my husband," she said. Lopore frowned deeply when he heard his name.

"And put on skins?"

She spread the folds of her beautiful fluted skirt and smiled pleasantly. "That's exactly what I did," said Nabilo.

"So you work in your fields and wear skins and speak Dodoth language," said our cook.

"It took me several months to learn Ngadodotho again," said she.

Of all his wives, Lopore was most protective of Nabilo. He understood her very well, I think, and understood her loneliness. He had not married her expecting children, and was especially protective of her with regard to this. When I first met him and was asking the names of his wives and children, he said of her: "As we are recently married, we have no children yet."

Nabilo had a way with children, as do all women who long for them. The children of the household loved her, and would creep away to her court. Feeling her affection, my children would climb into her arms. When sorghum was in season, she almost always had a sweet, green sorghum cane for a visiting child to suck.

Of the women in the family, Nabilo's best friend was Rengen. They were like sisters, really, and complemented each other very well. Together, they could turn away Ngira's begging relatives so adroitly that the relatives were hardly aware they had been refused. "What is your hurry?" Nabilo or Rengen would ask when the beggars finally gave up asking for whatever it was they wanted and started to go.

One night, a leopard jumped over Lopore's wall and bit a heifer through the nape of the neck, almost killing her before Lopore's sons woke up and chased the leopard away. The heifer lay in the cow pen for a day and a night, smoothing the rough earth with her convulsions, before she died. The family then began to cook and eat her. She weighed almost 400 pounds, and to consume the meat took a very long time. Rengen boiled the last of the meat early one morning in her garden house, with Nabilo sitting beside her, and when I arrived, Nabilo covered the stew.

Rengen was not as sophisticated as Nabilo with regard to Europeans, and took the cover off. I saw that there were maggots on the meat. Nabilo said defensively: "Here, we are not rich people." Rengen then realized why the stew had been covered, and looked at me angrily. Nabilo added: "Here, we have to eat what we find."

The only person in the family who did not like Nabilo was Adwong, Lopore's third and youngest wife. Adwong, who was young and pretty, must have resented Lopore's devotion to his older, childless bride. One day Adwong and Nabilo had a quarrel, then a fight. The two women scratched and struck each other, weeping and shrieking until Lopore had arrived to slap Adwong. Though Lopore had taken Nabilo's side, Nabilo never forgot the quarrel, and never forgave her co-wife, and when she was depressed, she would feel once again the bruises and bites Adwong had given her. Once while speaking with Rengen, Nabilo said bitterly; "Why can't Adwong be sent to kill the enemies?"

"Because she is a woman," said Rengen.

Adwong did not forgive Nabilo either, and smoldered because of what Lopore had done. But Adwong was much younger than Lopore. She never knew, I think, and never perceived the source of his devotion to her rival. Adwong was in her late thirties, and had been married to Lopore about eighteen years. Their first child, a daughter, was twelve years old, and their last child, the boy named Botia after Lopore's father, was five. Adwong was unimaginative and rather simple, thus reflecting a deviation in Lopore's preference in wives. Perhaps by the time he married her he had had enough of Rengen's strong character and of Ngira's difficulties and had turned, for once, from interesting women and taken refuge in the unimaginativeness and

obedience of Adwong. His later choice of Nabilo was per-
fection; he learned something from Adwong.

Physical attraction had influenced Lopore, for Adwong
was excessively pretty. She had a round, smooth face with
small eyes, a round and pretty body with straight arms and
legs, and very pretty clothes. She often wore a brown
furred back skirt, the hem of which was fluted with six
large inset gores of white fur, on which were appliquéd
brown and black furred circles, the actual spots cut from a
spotted hide. Around her neck she wore metal rings, one
of which had a tab that showed that she was married; it
was a wedding ring. She wore bracelets and anklets and
two strings of red beads crossed between her breasts. She
used to beg me to give her a cloth dress, but when Lopore
found out he said he wouldn't let her have one. Most
Dodoth men are too conservative to let their wives dress up
like foreigners. Adwong cried. But often his relationship
with her was one of jokes. If she had been smarter, he
might have liked her more, but then, he had three intelligent wives and one brilliant daughter, perhaps enough.

One day Rengen and Nabilo, those close friends, asked
Lopore to trap a hyrax and use its chyme to spray their
gardens against pink caterpillars that were eating the
crops. The chyme of a hyrax, cast in a circle, is a magic
insecticide. Lopore trapped the hyrax and gave it to
Adwong to prepare. She skinned it so clumsily that he had
to finish himself, but as he bent to do this he pointed out to
her the L-shaped penis of the hyrax and whispered in her
ear. It must have been funny; she laughed. Then Lopore
turned the hyrax belly down for modesty; Adwong laughed
until she cried and had to hold Lopore's arm. Pleased with
his joke, he smiled at her fondly. He sprayed the gardens,
in the evening, using a cowtail whisk that he would dip in

the bowlful of chyme and water Adwong had prepared. He strode in a circle around Rengen's garden, then around Nabilo's, shouting "Ahrr" at the caterpillars as he flung the drops about. But when the bowl was almost empty, he carried it to Adwong's garden and simply dumped it, though Adwong had as many caterpillars as the other wives. When Lopore got home he tossed the bowl to her and said, good-naturedly: "Wash it."

The relationship carried over to his son Botia. The little boy would visit Lopore in his etem, stand on a boulder so he would be eye to eye with his father, and talk man to man. Once, when Botia was visiting Lopore, Adwong called him to come and help her. "Say you're not coming," said Lopore, which he knew would annoy Adwong. Adwong called again. "Tell her," said Lopore. But Botia neither went nor told her, and by disobeying both his parents in that difficult situation, he extricated himself, for both parents forgot.

"You will have to have your teeth pulled someday," said Lopore to Botia one morning.

"Not I," said Botia confidently.

"Then the girls will not consent," said Lopore. But Botia was too young for that sort of joke, and looked at his father darkly.

Botia used to chase his older sisters and half-sisters around with a cornstalk. They would lead him on, pretending to be frightened, then turn on him, push him over, and take the cornstalk away. He would lie on the ground, crying and defeated, and his father would tell him to get up. To tease Botia further, his sisters would ask him to dance with them. This embarrassed him, and he would refuse. Presently the girls would tire of their game, turn their backs and leave, and Botia, if Lopore was there, would fling dirt or a stone after them when they were far enough away.

Botia got along better with grownups. He never saw me but that he would walk up boldly and ask for something. He got this trait from his mother, who would stand outside our gate and beg in a soft voice for a bottle of the orange soda Marinda. At first, not speaking the language, I didn't understand her. That there was any other language never occurred to Adwong; she would persist in her soft begging. One day, at last, I realized what it was she wanted and I gave her some. It was our last bottle. She was very happy and was just sitting down to enjoy it when along came Lopore. Her face fell, and she looked up at him sulkily as he stood above her holding out his hand. But she gave him the bottle, and he drank it, making no attempt to soothe her, knowing that if she was upset or disappointed, she would get over it soon.

When something similar happened with Rengen, who asked for and received a bottle of Marinda, only to have it taken from her and almost emptied by Lopore, no one would think, to look at her stern face, that she cared in the least. Presently she went home, went into her court, and began speaking with Chuchu, her daughter, all the time keeping an ear cocked for sounds outside the fence. When she heard Lopore approaching she began telling Chuchu in a casual voice about the Marinda, and as if it were a habitual remark she said: "He is a very selfish man, your father. He is so greedy that people make fun of him."

Hearing himself mentioned, Lopore became curious and tiptoed to the fence to eavesdrop. What he heard wounded him deeply. He shouted in a loud voice in which his injury sounded: "Is this what you say about me? Am I to hear things said against me inside my own house?"

The note of injury was what Rengen had wanted. Her

voice became agreeable. "Ask for Marinda of your own,"
she said.

Adwong was unable to wound Lopore. She would never
have been able to devise such a plan. If she had tried,
Lopore would have seen through it, the thought that she
was trying to hurt his feelings would have angered him,
and she might have risked a beating. The relationship
seemed simple between Lopore and Adwong. She did as
she was told, she seldom argued, and if, at night, the mood
would strike Lopore to enter her court, he almost always
found food cooked for him, a sleeping mat spread in the
stuffy house for him to lie on, and a little fire kindled to
keep him warm.

But if Adwong was obedient, she was also stubborn, and
if she was dull, her desires were very strong. She used to
visit me to beg me for a sheet. Sheets, which are sold in the
dhukas, are often used for capes, and come in three colors,
black, white, and brown. She wanted a white one and daily
she would ask me for it, in a slow, repetitive voice that
began to irritate me with its dullness. She would even follow me from place to place, begging: "A sheet. A sheet.
Give me a sheet," until one day Lopore heard her, scolded
her, and said to her, as if he were speaking to an animal:
"Go home." After that, she came when Lopore was away.
My refusals never seemed to hurt her feelings; she would
not be deterred. When part of her harvest failed, she
begged not for food but for the sheet. When we would be
about to drive a sick or injured person to the dispensary, she
would delay our departure while the sick person groaned,
to beg me to buy her a sheet in a dhuka. One day I found I
was no longer annoyed but sorry for her, and I went to
Kaabong and bought her a sheet, a fine white one, made in
India. Her pleasure, when she unfolded it, was very mov-

ing. Her eyes brightened and her face shone. She shook out the sheet, examined it, and put it on, and with her anklets ringing and the sheet billowing behind her, she ran home. She kept the sheet only half an hour. Lopore saw it and held out his hand, and she had to take it off and give it to him. He put it on himself. This depressed her so much that she wept for a time before returning to our camp, her face streaked with tears, her dull expression resumed, to begin the long task of begging for another.

I asked Lopore why he had done it. He looked down benignly and asked: "If your husband wanted something you had, wouldn't you give it to him?" But he must have felt guilty. Adwong was standing near him, listening as he said this, her face stupid, her arms dangling. He turned toward her angrily and said: "Go home."

Little Botia made special visits to us for the purpose of begging. I was very fond of him and often gave him what he asked for, but Lopore objected. If he caught Botia begging for candy or sugar or tobacco, he would scold him and send him home. Botia would vanish for a time, only to return and beg again, relying on his father's affection and knowing exactly how many times he could reappear before his father became angry. Once I asked Lopore why he objected, and he told me that although to him I was not a stranger or an outsider, children might not be able to make the distinction and should not get accustomed to begging from outsiders, for foreign objects such as candy create desires that children should not have, desires that cannot be gratified, and ungratified desires lead children into stealing.

Adwong had no objection to Botia's begging. Far from it; she encouraged him to do so, and if he received something, she sometimes begged it from him. This made him return for more. Lopore couldn't watch Botia all the time, so matters slid, Lopore more or less forgot about it, and Botia came several times a day to stretch out his little hand.

Lopore had reason to worry about Botia's begging and his desire for other people's things, for Botia's uncle, Adwong's brother, was a thief. He and Adwong came from a large family who lived near Kalapata. Their father was dead, and the family had lost their wealth. They often visited Adwong, coming in groups of two's and three's in single file along one of the paths, leading Adwong's mother at the end of a stick. Like Lopore's other mother-in-law, she was totally blind. Their visits displeased Lopore, partly because they stayed in Adwong's courts, which meant he couldn't go there, as it is forbidden to a Dodoth man to have close contact with his mother-in-law, and partly because Adwong's brother usually stole something. He stole pumpkins from Nabilo's pumpkin field, which upset her so much that she took a stick and slashed all the vines, crying that it was useless to raise plants that someone else harvested. At night he stole from the grain fields of Lopore's wives.

One night my husband and I were hunting guinea fowl in Lopore's grain, and when Lopore's children heard us rustling, they told their father, thinking we were the thief. Lopore came out with his spear. He heard us speaking English and assumed that the thief was trying to deceive him by pretending to speak English. We saw Lopore loom from the dark, wet grass with his spear raised, and identified ourselves just in time.

News of the episode circulated, and reached the ears of Adwong's brother, who then robbed several fields with impunity, for as he stole and rustled, he pretended to speak

English. He sounded so much like two Europeans having a conversation that it was a long time before he was suspected, whereupon he gave up the enterprise.

Lopore's wives knew all the time that the thief was Adwong's brother. When Lopore found out about it, he became so angry that he took a spear and hid beside a path that his brother-in-law often followed. But the brother-in-law took another path that day. This gave Lopore time to calm down. He went home and told Adwong that she was very lucky, her brother had almost been killed.

The first time we saw Adwong's brother, he was sitting in her court, doing nothing. He was a handsome, heavy young man just past adolescence. His naked body shone with health, and he had decorated his hair and arms carefully with bead ornaments, for he was at the age when young men look for lovers and pay great attention to themselves. Near him sat his mother, in the shade of Adwong's granary basket. The mother kept her head covered with her cape because, we learned later, she had just been told that her son had taken Nabilo's pumpkins and she was ashamed. Her son pretended not to notice. His face was set and sullen; his mother was embarrassing him.

The second time we saw him he was dead. He had been robbing a granary outside a cattle camp near Kalapata the night before, the camp owner had heard him and had speared him through the fence. Terribly wounded, he had run zigzagging down a path, had fallen, gotten up, and fallen again on his back in a patch of bushes. When we heard of his death we went to look for him and we saw him there. It had been raining and the ground and leaves were wet. Water had wrinkled his skin and washed his scent into the ground, so hyenas had not noticed him. Not even birds, but only the white ants that make the sugarloaf towers in the forest, had discovered him. The ants had started to build around him; along his arms and neck and sides and between his legs stood their little, inch-high earthen structure. He must have died hard. Coils of intestine bulged from the spear wound in his belly and he had clawed up grass, which he still held in his fingers. Fresh leaves were clutched by his toes. But his face was impassive, pale and drained of blood. He must have died looking up at the bushes, for his eyes were still fixed there, wide open and full of rain.

His death caused trouble. The camp owner who had speared him reported himself immediately to Uri's son-in-law, the Mkungu of Kalapata District, saying that he had mistaken the boy for a Turkana. The police arrested the householder and took him to the Kaabong jail, where he awaited transport to Moroto for trial. Murder cases go to Moroto; only thieves are tried in Kaabong. But as it had been raining, the roads could not be traveled. The camp owner's wives were left alone, with instructions from the police to guard the corpse as evidence against their husband, until the corpse too could go to Moroto as a sort of exhibit at the trial. After the corpse had been three days in the rain, the police asked us to convey it but luckily the roads were still impassable, so we were able to refuse. Meanwhile, people from Adwong's family had begun to visit the cattle camp at night, encircling it and whispering threats to the people within. The camp owner was temporarily out of their reach, but his family was not, and it was generally felt that someone from Adwong's family sooner or later would claim a victim in revenge.

Adwong had almost nothing to say about the death of her brother. Neither she nor Lopore had seen his body and neither asked about it. She was depressed and very quiet for a few days, but it was not long before she came again to beg for things.

Lopore, who was not directly involved either with the murder or with the revenge, seemed to feel as everyone else felt, that thieves take chances if they come at night, and deserve what happens to them. "Let him die," said Lopore. "I once almost killed him myself." But the matter troubled Lopore. The day he discussed the death of his brother-in-law, he was in our camp drinking a cup of tea. He talked for some time about the undesirability of thieves, but as he spoke, he kept pausing and turning his head as if he heard a whisper. He did hear a whisper. It was his own son Botia, hiding in our fence. Botia was whispering to me: "Candy, Iloshabiet. Candy! Candy!" And suddenly Lopore, who for weeks and months had forgotten Botia's begging, scrambled to his feet, ran like a charging bull to the other side of the fence, seized Botia by the neck, and ripping a branch from a tree, struck Botia with the full strength of his arm, once, twice, five times, roaring at him while Botia screamed and struggled and finally broke away. Even then, Lopore did not forgive him, but ran after him, slashing at him every chance he had, as his hysterically screaming, terror-stricken child ran dodging down the path toward their home.

CHAPTER FIVE

Raiding

Looking at the wide, pastoral scene upon the grassy hills by Morukore, where the land like a green tapestry was dotted white with flocks of sheep and the green plain under its orchard trees was grazed by herds of cows; looking at the round fields by the dwellings, with the tiny kneeling figures of women pulling weeds; or looking at the distant figures of men, one by one or two together striding the paths that crossed the fields and crossed ravines and passed the deep shadows of immense old trees—the scene so pleasant, the landscape so peaceful—no one would think the country was in a state of siege.

But only in June, a month before, a party of Turkana warriors had swept the valley, costing the district hundreds of cattle and many human lives. In the valley below Morukore, there are still skeletons of people who died that day.

For Morukore, it had been the worst of a series of raids that began in January. Before January the Turkana and Dodoth had been at peace for a very long time. Many Turkana families had moved into the northern hills of Dodoth, settling there to escape a severe drought that had overcome Turkanaland. Relations between the two peoples seemed good. Many Dodoth men knew the names and families of many Turkana men with whom they shared the grazing. Some families intermarried.

But in January the fighting was resumed. The Dodoth began it—a great mistake, it soon appeared. The Turkana families withdrew to Turkanaland; Turkana women married to Dodoth men were sent home lest they should spy. The allies of the Turkana, the Jie, began raiding Dodoth from the south, and there was a series of raids and counter-raids which, once started, were difficult to stop.

There are at least three possible explanations for the ending of the long peace. The first, which I heard from a policeman, was that the Dodoth were tempted too strongly by the presence of the Turkana cattle, resented the intrusion on Dodoth grazing grounds, and raided their guests. The second, which if true was not the whole story but was at any rate generally believed, concerned a group of Dodoth warriors who came upon the daughter of one of the appointed Turkana chiefs as she was bathing in a river, and murdered her there. The resumption of raiding was her father's revenge. A point which might bear out this version is that warriors in the uniform of the appointed Turkana chiefs' police—rifles, ammunition belts, and all—were seen taking part in raids. But some of those government servants, the chiefs, were not above using everything at their disposal against their enemies. A Jackait of Jie was said to go raiding himself, with his askaris as his warriors, arriving in Dodoth in a Land-Rover, to fire out the window of the car.

The third explanation was suggested by an anthropologist and was possibly the most likely of all, though the person who offered it was merely making a guess. This was that the fighting in Katanga and the Congo (this was just before Hammarskjöld died), or the uneasiness in Kenya stirred by the move for independence, may have started a wave of unrest that moved from tribe to tribe. In the case of the raiding in northern Uganda, colonialism was not an issue. The coming of independence was not, I think, an issue as such, though some of the younger people in Dodoth may have supposed that independence would mean an end of most restrictions. Rather, the raiding wars in northern Uganda were for the cattle, so passionately owned, so fiercely defended, and it may be that the unrest of surrounding people, like a breath over ash-covered embers, revived the old desires for cattle by conquest and set the herds of little cattle patiently jogging through the bush between Dodoth and Jie or Turkanaland, lashed on by their mud-streaked captors fighting and shouting at their sides.

At first, the heaviest raiding by the Turkana was directed against the very Dodoth neighborhoods where the Turkana and Dodoth had shared grazing; because those neighborhoods were nearest to Turkanaland. Before long, Dodoth families in the extreme north began abandoning their homes and their newly planted crops to move south for the relative safety of more heavily populated areas. The families which stayed behind became the more exposed, and soon had to move also.

This left empty the dwellings in the tumbled hills at the

top of the Escarpment, the straw roofs sagged and weeds grew in the manure of the cattle pens. The tobacco plants growing in the courtyards matured, grew older and older until they were like fat little trees, for no one gathered them, and tomato plants and squash vines grew up the walls where baboons with their gray hands picked over the fruit. No one chased them away.

The Turkanas sent spies to learn where the cattle were living, and finding them dispersed, sent raiding parties farther and farther south, to Morukore, to the mountains across the valley, to the plains beyond. By July, the raiding parties could be found anywhere. They mounted large raids, clearing entire districts of cattle; they mounted small raids in which a few warriors would ambush and kill a herdboy in the forest and be gone with the herd. One night a group of spies came to Lopore's house to assess his cattle through the cracks in the wall. He heard the Turkanas whispering and saying: "The Dodoth are women, the Dodoth are dogs." Lopore seized his spear and shouted a challenge, but the Turkanas did not come in.

Neither did he go out, for the Turkana are formidable enemies and very much feared. There are almost 85,000 of them in Turkanaland, against 20,000 Dodoth. Not only that, the Turkana have rifles. The Kenya government cannot prevent the Turkana, in their vast desert wilderness, from going to Ethiopia, where the exchange of cattle for firearms still goes on. The Uganda government has stopped the Dodoth from having rifles. While the long spears are good enough for raiding, if the Dodoth raid a Turkana neighborhood known not to have a rifle, a Turkana raiding party is almost sure to have one or more rifles, against which spears are inadequate defense. So the Dodoth cannot stop the Turkana. Neither can the police. The Turkana have a reputation for an extreme, rapacious bravery; and the police, in their small groups, are afraid. A Turkana raiding party almost succeeded in killing an Assistant District Commissioner accompanied by his armed police and in a Land-Rover. He was pursuing the raiding party, which doubled back through the bushes and had almost encircled him when he saw the trap and, spinning the car around, escaped in the nick of time. Once a police plane tried to rout a group of Turkana raiders by dropping explosives on them, but the Turkanas fired on the plane, thus routing it, something a pilot might not have expected from plumed and naked warriors running in the bush below.

By July, the raiding had created an almost desperate situation in Dodoth. Many families had lost their cattle; many families from isolated areas had moved their cattle to heavily populated areas, causing overgrazing where the cattle competed for the grass. Refugee families, without cattle and without growing crops, did not have enough to eat, and a famine had begun in the country. People whose energy was spent by hunger fell ill with dysentery or with a viral pneumonia; people in a weakened condition, especially children, died very quickly; and many people—men, women, and children—became thieves. Hundreds of refugees, without homes or cattle, came to Kaabong and the town was swarming with people, ill and emaciated, who made camps near the missions, or lean-to shelters in the woods near the police post, in hopes of getting food from the foreigners; and a state of famine was declared. A program was instituted by the government to give free food to widows and to provide jobs for men, but with the shifting throngs of people, it was not easy for the government to reach everyone. I met a refugee woman who in desperation had gone to the Catholic mission, pretending an interest in religion, to try to get food for her three daughters, who were ill with dysentery and starvation. Sometimes, passing the mission's classroom, I would hear her voice as she pretended to recite the catechism, a low voice beneath the little girl students' waspish hum. But her efforts were for nothing: her daughters died.

There are many customs involved in raids and raiding, most of which are used to escape vengeance and death. A man who is recently married, for instance, should stay at home while others go raiding; otherwise, he may be killed. After a raider kills a victim, he must purify the spear by licking the blood from the spear blade or by jabbing the spear blade into the ground, and later he must dismember the spear, to use the foreshaft as a knife, and perhaps the balancing tail as a hoe, but never as a spear again. The whole spear may be given away to someone else, but if the original owner uses it again, its taint will cause his death.

After a man has killed an enemy, he must free himself of the stain of death through the sacrifice of a goat. He eats the goat and cuts the goatskin into strips, which he wears to show that the "enemy blood has been washed away," and until the allotted time has passed and the goatskin strips can be removed, he will not go raiding because the enemies would notice the strips and single him out to kill him.

These rules do not apply for other murders. If a man kills a thief, he need not purify himself because "a thief is nothing." If he murders a person in a fight, it will not help him to try to purify himself. God will know his crime and kill him in revenge.

But when a man has killed an enemy, after he is purified he may kill an ox to feast the elders and take the honorary name ending in *moe*. The name describes the victory. Such a name might be Lokuwaremoe—from *lo*, the prefix for "he"; *akuware*, "night"; and *moe*, derivative of *emoit*, "enemy"—to show that the owner has killed an enemy at night. And later the man will have his shoulder decorated with a pattern of tiny scars, some so fine and delicate that only when the sun shines on them obliquely, in the early morning or in the evening, can they be seen. A man waits, and has his shoulders scarified during peacetime. If he should be rash enough to have the scars made during wartime and he should have to take part in his neighborhood's defense, the enemies would notice the fresh scars and kill him first, before doing anything else.

The formations used by the Dodoth and the Turkanas are very old, maybe older than the nations themselves. The basic formation, that of surrounding, was known more than a century ago. It is sometimes described as the two horns and the bony mass between the horns of a bull or an ox. But in East Africa the formation may derive from a time before pastoralism and could have been originally used in hunting. The method is like the hunting method used today: an area where animals are grazing is encircled and the animals are driven with beaters toward nets or people with spears or a safarist with a rifle. The "horns" of the formation are in Dodoth two long columns, each called *ekichot*, which is a hunting term. The bony mass between the horns is in Dodoth a mass of men called the *abuthia*, a wide-mouthed gourd. The columns straggle through the hills, each column extending perhaps a mile on either side of a valley, with a leader in charge of each. An advance is stealthy; no one speaks. The attack is more effective if it is totally by surprise. When the leader decides the time is right, the columns burst from cover, the men, shouting the

names of their oxen, form a huge ring which tightens gradually, drawing cattle and people close to the abuthia.
People trying to run from a column find themselves
trapped, the abuthia moves forward, the circle is complete,
the people inside are killed, and the raiding party reverses
itself for the escape. This time the columns move side by
side, forking open only at the forward tip, where the captured cattle run. The abuthia, with its experienced fighters,
guards the columns from the rear.

Riflemen are strategically incorporated in the basic formation. If there are only a few, they are interspersed in the
columns during battle. During escape, some will cover the
party from the rear. During advance, the riflemen may
kneel or lie flat to shoot over the heads of the spearmen.
Turkana attacks used to take place only at dawn or in the
evening, but because of the riflemen, they take place these
days at any time.

To counter a raiding formation, the defending forces
sometimes surround it. Usually, the defense is only able to
surround part of it, and this part, if possible, is the forward
tip of the columns, where the cattle are. If the raiding
party has riflemen, the riflemen during escape will be with
the cattle. If the defense surrounds the cattle, the raiders'
two columns will separate, advance, and surround the defense. Defense is a dangerous business requiring many
men, more men than are usually prepared for battle in any
group of neighborhoods at any given time. The advantages
are with the raiders. For defense against a raiding party
armed with rifles, the Dodoth use guerrilla tactics, ambush
and harassment, as did the people of Morukore on the day
of the June raid.

Everyone in northeastern Dodoth knew that a raid was
coming. The aspect of surprise in a raid involves only the

time and place, not its advent, for the tracks of hundreds
of men had been found leading toward the hills west of
Morukore, where the raiding party massed. The prints of
Turkana sandals differ from those of the Dodoth, but even
if the men went barefoot, as most of them did, there is only
one reason for so large a group to gather without being
seen. It took several days for the raiders to mass. They had
come from different parts of Turkanaland in small groups,
passing through settled areas of Dodoth at night. They
brought food, and because they had rifles, they took their
time getting organized. The Dodoth did not try to surprise
them or to rout them out. As far as I know, the only action
taken against a massing raiding party is by courageous
young men, of which there are plenty in Dodoth, spying
and listening at night near the Turkana encampment to
overhear the plans. Sometimes, it is said, the Turkanas
purposely discuss false plans, and sometimes, if their camp
is well placed, for instance on a wooded hill, and guarded,
it is not possible for spies to come near, so sometimes, as
was the case on that fresh June morning when the Turkanas, organized at last, came out of the hills to form in
mile-long, straggling columns on either side of Lokoki's valley, the Dodoth are not well prepared.

The raid began near Kalapata, about five miles north of
Morukore. The people of Morukore heard shouts and rifle
fire and alarm cries and ran out of their dwellings to fight
or hide—a man who lived near Kalapata came dashing
down the main pathway, running for his life—and presently, thirty Turkana appeared, all armed with spears, all
under the cover of two naked riflemen who knelt on a hillside behind them and guarded the advance through their
sights. The spearmen dispersed in small groups to capture
cattle. Uri, who upon hearing the alarm had concealed his

wives, old aunts, and children in a thicket of euphorbia
that grew atop Morukore hill, took two spears and stood
with his sons beside the thicket, defending the hilltop all
that morning, spearing two of the Turkana raiders who
tried to attack them there.

Three Turkanas went into the valley below the hill,
where they found the cattle camp of Bilo, a frail, small,
elderly man who was married to the sister of the eldest of
Lopore's wives. Bilo, a very brave man, had run from his
camp to confront the dispersing Turkanas and the riflemen.
His two little sons, ages three and five, hid in the thorn
fence of the camp behind the cattle. But even in Dodoth,
little children cannot keep still. When the three raiders
found the camp, they noticed the boys immediately, knew
they had time and nothing to fear from the children, and
rested themselves, even sharing a gourd of milk that stood
under the fence, before getting ready to leave. Then one
drove out the cattle, one blocked the gate, and the third
pulled the children from the fence and one by one slaughtered them with his spear. All this was seen and recounted
by Bilo's ten-year-old nephew, who had been on his way to
join his little cousins when he saw the Turkanas coming
and hid in a tree.

Lopore, that June morning, had joined himself and his
two grown sons with a neighbor and a house guest of the
neighbor, a rich, burly man who came from afar. These five
watched the riflemen, and knowing the rough hillsides and
the tactics of the Turkanas, hid themselves in what they
felt was a logical place for a rifleman to pass, a clump of
flowering bushes at the mouth of a ravine. They were quite
right. When the Turkana came cautiously through, the five
Dodoth men fell on him and held him down while the
house guest clubbed him to death with the stock of his

own rifle. They then divided his ornaments, cut off his
ears to get his earrings, cut off his hair to get his headdress,
a cap of red feathers, which fell to Lopore. He wore it
through July and August, and it earned him a nickname.
"Hey, Turkana," people would call. The house guest got
the rifle. There must be several rifles in Uganda, useless
without bullets, acquired in this way.

From the start of the raiding in January, until the end of
November, when we left, there were, according to the police census, 125 raids involving the Dodoth. Of these, the
Dodoth mounted twelve against the Turkana and twenty-
eight against the Jie. Against the Dodoth, the Turkana
retaliated with forty-nine raids, and the Jie with thirty. Six
times, the Jie and the Turkana joined forces to raid Dodoth
together. During these raids, according to police reports,
more than 150 people were killed and 25,000 head of cattle
changed hands. In some respects, I think, the police figures
are inaccurate, especially with regard to the numbers of
people killed. Eyewitness accounts of specific raids, such as
the June raid on Morukore, would bring the toll of the dead
very much higher. The police files have no record of the
five people killed on Morukore that June day. And in my
rendition of the police census, I am not counting as raids
the murders, on April 28 and 30, in Kaabong and Morulem,
of two Turkana women by vengeful Dodoth; or a hand-to-
hand combat between a Dodoth and a Jie whom he met
near the border, and by whom he was killed; or the time,
on the eighth of March, when the Turkanas burned down
the roadworkers' camp up in the north, near an ancient
sacred tree called Pirre. The police files do not report as a
hostility an attempt by the Turkana to blind the Dodoth.
The crafty Turkana, at the end of August, led an old blind
woman to the border and abandoned her there, hoping that

she would wander into Dodoth, to be found and killed by Dodoth warriors. If she was killed, it is believed, her infirmity would pass to her assassins, who would go blind too. The plot failed; the old woman was found and taken to Kaabong.

But if the police figures may in some ways be inaccurate, they show one thing on such an enormous scale that small discrepancies make no difference; this is the amount of cattle lost to the Dodoth. In their forty raids against their enemies, the Dodoth captured 6,400 cattle, of which 3,400 were recovered at the time of the raids, by the police or the owners, leaving 3,000 in Dodoth hands. But in the eighty-five raids against Dodoth, 18,000 cattle were captured from them, of which 8,5000 were recovered; in other words, about 6,500 cattle left the country and were never returned.

The bad effects of this, of course, devolved on individuals. In raiding, one man loses his entire herd and becomes a pauper in an hour, while his neighbor's herd, not found by the raiders, remains intact. In Morukore during the June raid, Bilo lost all his cattle. For all his courage, he was left with nothing, and when we met him in July, he had accepted six head of cattle and asylum from Lopore, and was building a dwelling adjoining Lopore's northern wall.

The people of Morukore were able to take care of their own. No refugees left the area to become famine victims begging in Kaabong. But when we arrived in July the population of the district had begun shifting, a bad sign. Remi, the owner of the cattle camp on Morukore, had withdrawn to his dwelling in Lokoki's western section; the camps in the forest had been abandoned; and of the neighborhood just north of Morukore, the three easternmost families moved away. The eastern line of habitation was thus brought to

Uri's, Mora's, and Lothimidik's doors, and Lopore was furious. Remi had been the first to give way to his nerves; Lopore talked of denying him the right to water in the river, since he would not stay to defend it, and publicly called him a very cowardly man.

Almost every day, news would come that a raid had taken place nearby or that a raid was massing. Once, on a hazy bright day at Lopore's etem, where eight men were gathered to talk and whittle, everyone suddenly jumped to his feet, listening and looking, silent and intent. Presently everyone relaxed and, smiling, sat down again. The road-workers, who had rebuilt their camp south of Pirre, had set off a blast in the extreme distance which had sounded like a shot.

The raiding and the number of people dislodged from their homes brought on an outbreak of stealing, and almost every morning someone in Morukore would find that during the night his gardens had been robbed. A thief caught near Kathile, some miles to the south, was speared through the throat. The thief lived to visit the dispenser, who sewed him up. One hot afternoon a boy caught stealing in Kaabong walked into the dispensary with his throat slit from ear to ear. He spoke hoarsely and painfully to say that he had cut himself falling on a stick, which made all the Dodoth patients who were waiting in the flyblown anteroom laugh heartily.

Throughout the troubled times, the work of the countryside went on. The cattle had to graze and drink daily, even though reports came to the neighborhoods that the Turkanas had moved to occupy the forest beyond the river. Sometimes early in the morning or just at dusk a plume of smoke would be noticed rising from the depths of the woods, the morning or evening fire of whoever waited there

—the Turkanas were as bold as brass and perfectly certain that the Dodoth, without rifles, would never seek them out. Adwong, Lopore's third wife, often came to our camp in terror to beg us to give her water. The Turkanas were by the river, she would say, and she was afraid to go there. Sometimes we gave her water. Sometimes Lopore would catch her begging and would scold her fiercely for it. So sometimes she was made to go to the river anyway. But sometimes, if her fear overcame her entirely, she would send her daughter. The little girl, affected by her mother's terror, would set off alone, walking slowly, almost numbly, the water jar atop her head.

The Dodoth are not protective of their children. In that country, the most dangerous work is done by the children, by the eight- to fifteen-year-old boys who tend the cattle. Every day these youngsters take the herds into the wild pastures and every day at the river between noon and two or three o'clock there are ten or fifteen herds waiting in an orderly file that reaches almost a mile up the roadlike riverbed. As each herd is given water at the permanent water hole—the water is handed up from the shadowy well in calabashes by the herdboys and splashed into the community trough, a hollow log. The cattle drink and blow, the herd moves slowly up the bank, and the waiting herds move forward each one place. Now and then a group of armed Dodoth stand guard above the cattle and the herdboys on a rockslide at the top of the bank, but usually there are hundreds of cattle, all together, guarded by children who come regularly, all at the same time every day.

It is hard to say why life is lived this way. When people do lose their children they feel the loss no less than people who protect their children more. Bilo and his wife, after their little boys were killed by the Turkana, became silent and withdrawn and like two ants went about the business of building their new dwelling. Bilo would go methodically into the bush and return with a log, his wife would go slowly in another direction and return with branches, again and again, time after time, day after day, as the round wall grew, but the only person one would hear speaking when one passed the new wall was their grown daughter's fiancé. He was a pleasant, personable young man, polite and kindly, helpful to Bilo, and would sometimes try to introduce a note of gaiety into the new home. But the family was like a hand with two fingers amputated, unable to close itself because of its wounds. No one would respond to him.

One morning very early, when rain clouds were settled on the ridges so that the air was cold and heavy and the light was gray, an alarm began sounding in the distance. It was an unearthly, high-pitched, rising cry, a lulululu, plainly audible though far away, which in a moment was repeated from a hill nearby, then from a third hill, then a fourth, then spread west out over the plain. Then came whistles, then a word shouted faintly and repeatedly— possibly "enemies," *ngimoe*—and a little dog on Morukore began to bark and then howl eerily after the cry. We had never heard such a cry in our lives, but we knew what it was. It is a sound to make you stiffen and set your skin crawling under your clothes. The sound slowly faded into the distance opposite the direction from which it came, until we could no longer hear it, and in the intense silence that followed we went partway down the hill. The light was faint and dim and in the gloom we saw Lopore crawling through his doorway, dragging his shield and spear. He stood up, shouldered his spear, turned his shield so that its black ostrich-feather ball was at the top, instead of at the bottom, as it would have been had his quarry been an animal, and walked quickly toward the north, through the foggy hollow between the ridges, in the direction from which the alarm first came.

Then came a sound of someone running and crashing in the bushes, and a woman appeared. She was a wife of the rich young Lothimidik whose dwelling was just north of our camp, and she was going toward the euphorbia thicket on top of the hill. Lopore called out to her: "They'll kill you if they find you there." She stopped for a moment, looked around, and then ran on, having nowhere else to go. After a time, Lopore came quickly back, ducked into his doorway, and emerged again with an oxhorn, which he blew. It gave a blast like a muted ram's-horn trumpet, and it told the people on the far side of the hill to gather, for a raid was on the way. Already, on the paths below the hill, men from the district were walking quickly, almost running, their spears in hand. Men were passing our fence in two's and three's, all with their long spears on their shoulders and their little shields on their arms, little squares of buffalo or oxhide leather made not to hide the body but to swing, deflecting blows, catching and deflecting spears.

The men were gathering in a grove beside our camp. Soon almost thirty had assembled, a formidable company, I thought, for they are such large people, and if any of them felt uneasy, they didn't show it, but spoke and acted in a quick, businesslike manner. They had assembled like this many times before, and everyone knew what to do. Some men had already begun to strip from their spear blades the small, grooved leather thongs that sheathe the edges, and the sharp rims gleamed. Some men, rather than carry their spears, stacked them against the trees the way soldiers stack rifles. Most men were waiting for Lopore, who

presently strode up and said angrily that the raiders had
been seen near Kalapata, and that Dodoth should go to
meet them there. It was the first definite news of the morning. Three of the younger men backed away from the
group and began to run in and out of the bushes, ducking
and rising, twisting and feinting, in an eerie, stylized
movement, a deadly dance. It was the movement of
Dodoth in battle, quite formal and planned, designed to
present a weaving target to enemy spears.

Lopore was scanning the crowd. "Someone is not here,"
he said loudly. We noticed that several people who could
have rallied for defense were absent, Remi among them.
The courage necessary to seek out a raiding party armed
with at least one rifle is not found in everyone, a lack which
Lopore despised. Uri was nearby. He had removed his
cape and sandals, as these catch in the bush to detain a
warrior, and he stood with his wise face serene to say: "We
are needed elsewhere, perhaps others will join us. Let us
not wait here." Most of the thirty men set off with long,
rapid strides to Kalapata. One of them, a householder, was
empty-handed; his sons had borrowed his weapons and had
gone on ahead. "My spears have gone before me," he said,
causing a burst of laughter in the procession as it hurried
through the trees. The other men climbed into the Land-
Rover. My husband had returned a few days before to the
United States. "Hurry, Mother of John," they said to me,
and without having planned to, I found myself driving in
the wet, dim morning, the back of the Land-Rover looking
like a hedgehog, bristling with spears.

Kalapata was a clearing that the road passed through, a
tiny place, a shallow basin of hard, red earth amid the
bushes and trees. There were no Dodoth dwellings in the
town itself; these stood on the hills around, but at one side

of the basin were five or six red earth dhukas with gleaming, galvanized tin roofs, the shops of several Westernized storekeepers, Uri's son among them, whose families lived in courtyards at the backs of the stores. Usually these courts were noisy, but not that morning. The storekeepers had gone after the raiders, and the families were hiding, keeping very still. At the edge of the basin, where the road went in, there was a blue and yellow sign that read: NILE BEER, and below, in smaller letters, the name KALAPATA, a public service provided for Dodoth by the company. Groups of naked warriors were trotting past the sign and disappearing in the bush beyond the town. Drizzling rain began to fall. We waited in the Land-Rover for something definite to happen, while the spearmen in the back climbed out. As they did, they were met by the men from Morukore who had come on foot, the long striding pace of the Dodoth being just as fast as a vehicle grinding along the rough road. Then everyone waited by the Land-Rover, for the men who had vanished in the bush were beginning to come back. No one had found the Turkanas. A rumor had it that they had retreated into the hills and might be planning to attack elsewhere, the surprise having been spoiled. Lopore summoned his oldest sons and sent them home to guard his cattle. Other men were doing the same; an air of haste and determination had entered the gathering. Soon every household had sent a few of its members back to guard its cattle, while those who remained regrouped for an alternate plan. It is like the Dodoth to have no formal leader, no general to tell people what to do. A hasty conference took place, then most of the men from Kalapata fanned out and disappeared among the trees. The men from eastern Lokoki, however, did not join them. The concerted effort that would have carried a combined attack, had the raiders been engaged at Kalapata, could not be sustained while the raid was only in the offing. Each group wanted to make sure of its own ground. The men from eastern Lokoki wanted to go to the hill where the raiders were first seen, to travel in a half circle north of Lokoki, perhaps even to look down into the district from the high hills. Too, if the raiders were seen taking cattle from the district, the Dodoth could ambush them and cut off their escape. The group seemed suddenly a small one, setting out, as it was, into the remote expanse of hills.

Just then, from behind one of the dhukas, six strangers appeared. They were not Dodoth, but shorter people dressed in undershirts and khaki trousers. "Don't worry, Madam," said one of them with contempt in English. "These people always think there'll be a raid."

They were the Kaabong policemen, posted in Kalapata to forestall the raids. "We're just going now to have a look," said the sergeant, whereupon the six went back behind the dhuka to put on the rest of their clothes. Many minutes later they emerged in full uniform, each with a helmet, boots, and rifle, to ask if they could use my car. Not liking to refuse, I said they could, though Lopore seemed angry, and they all got in. Lopore got in too. I didn't know why until much later, when he told me that he not only had wanted to search the hillside but had promised my husband to look after me. That day, and many times after, though I seldom knew it, he was as good as his word.

The highest-ranking policeman sat in front. The lowest-ranking, least experienced, sat in back in the open, experience and exposure being in opposite proportions. Lopore sat on the tail gate, with his long legs hanging down. At first the police were unwilling to have him come at all, but I, not realizing why he joined us, told the sergeant that if

Lopore wanted to come he would come, or I wouldn't drive. Then everyone was angry, and when we drove on, no one spoke. The policemen, some fresh from police school, perhaps in Jinja, could see no advantage in having a Dodoth come along; to the developed, landed agriculturalists of Uganda, the Dodoth are heathen tribesmen, disorganized, naked, and wild.

Inside the vehicle was the military smell of leather and the grease that lubricated the automatic rifles; the men's voices, when they began to speak to one another in Swahili, had a harsh, military sound, and I thought the carload must seem formidable. But as we left Kalapata, with its red-earth clearing empty except for chickens, we saw one wrinkled elder, with a pattern of scars all up and down his arms, laughing wryly to himself to see the foreigners about to give chase.

The hill was much farther than I had supposed. The rain came down in the silent bush and the car made its grinding sounds and soon we seemed exposed and very far away. At one time, in a valley, we stopped while the sergeant sent the youngest corporal to look at a herd of goats on a remote hill. The corporal was gone for almost half an hour, and I asked what was happening. "The corporal is going to get a goat from the herder," said the sergeant. "Or buy one," he added vaguely. I asked if we couldn't go on to our destination and pick the corporal up on our way back—only then, in the distance, had he encountered the herdboy, an eight- or nine-year-old—but the sergeant said: "We are now keeping watch over him. These herders cause trouble. We will see if he comes back safe, and if he does, so much the better." I noticed that the corporal had left his rifle in the car, perhaps for fear it would be wrested away. The herdboy's father, spear in hand, ran down from his lookout when he saw the police, and a rapid discussion between the father and the young corporal followed. Presently the corporal began the long hike back to the car alone. "The goats were all sick," he said when he joined us. He subsided behind the sergeant and an older, larger corporal, and we drove on.

When we came to the hill, the police got out, and except for the youngest corporal, who stayed with me to guard the car, they walked all bunched together, their rifles at an informal parade rest, to the windswept summit, perhaps a quarter of a mile away, where they stood uncertainly, looking around. Lopore, however, set off alone, with only his shield and spear, and no group behind him. But as if he were hunting for an animal, a dangerous one perhaps, or for a valuable lost object, he watched the ground and poked intently in the bushes, climbed the hill to look over the land, and as his search expanded over a wider area, he disappeared from sight. The policemen sat down in a cluster on top of the hill. Though the hilltop was bare, the road was in a dense bush that went on for miles to the south. The policemen may have been right not to wait by the car, a decoy plainly visible among the leaves, and while we waited by the car in the silence I began to realize how unwise it had been to go there, and how frightened I was. Thunder was rolling in the hills behind us, the only sound. The young corporal stood by the fender, straight and tall, with his face expressionless, and showed his fear only in that he could not keep his hands from shaking. I think he was fifteen or sixteen, but not more.

All at once, not far away, a branch cracked sharply. "What was that?" cried the young guard, leveling his rifle at the sound. We then heard the clack of a cowbell, the noise of trampling, and more branches moving, then no more, as the herd which was afoot beyond us was made to stop. The profound silence that followed was broken by a whistle, not that of a bird, and then a rustle, which we saw was caused by the bushes swaying, nearer and nearer, as something made its way toward the road. It was very frightening. "Let us get in and drive on," whispered the corporal. I was very glad to go. We went forward until we came to a place where the car could turn around, only to find that the police on the hill had caught up with us, perhaps afraid that we would leave them behind.

"Did you find anything?" I asked the sergeant.

"Absolutely nothing," said he.

"We heard cattle being driven by, over there," said the young corporal.

"Oh?" said the sergeant.

"We can return to Kalapata," said the older corporal.

But we couldn't leave without Lopore. "What to do?" I asked him when, shining with rain, he finally appeared.

"Drive back to Kalapata," said the sergeant with contempt. "Nothing here." And so we did, as fast as possible through the hollow where we had heard the sounds.

On the way back we overtook a group of twelve young men from eastern Lokoki. They were walking casually, spear tails dragging, and parted ranks in two columns to let us by. Lopore wanted to speak with them. They told him that, in fact, the raid had come and gone. A group of Turkanas had attacked three dwellings in the northern Kalapata section and had escaped with three whole herds. A large group of Dodoth had followed them and so far had not returned. As for the twelve, their part was over; having made the scouting foray, they were going home. Not one of

them so much as glanced at the police, who had turned
their backs on them and had begun to speak together in
Swahili.

I knew one of the young men rather well. "What do you
think of the police?" I asked him when the chance came.

"Nothing. Where were they?" was his reply.

To this day, I don't know all that happened that rainy
morning. I can't, for instance, think who whistled and
stirred the bushes by the road. That it was a Dodoth man
herding in a place like that during a raid seems quite unlikely—besides, the herd was in the bushes and cattle don't
browse. Yet, if the report of the twelve men was accurate,
it seems equally unlikely that it was a party of Turkanas.
The Turkanas would have been farther on their way toward
their country. So it seems to me now that the person who
whistled and shook the branches was a child, a Dodoth
child there by accident and hiding, or perhaps a few Turkana youngsters, separated by confusion from the main
party, in charge of a captive herd.

Also, I can't say for certain why the twelve young men
from eastern Lokoki had not joined the pursuers. My guess
is that the obligation to defend nearby neighborhoods or
districts does not extend to the retrieving of cattle raided
from those neighborhoods. This is not to say that any of the
twelve, granted the courage, would not have joined the
pursuit if a close friend or relative had been robbed. But I
think in this case it was none of their business. The Dodoth
do not risk their lives simply because a robbed householder
is a fellow tribesman, and I think that because the cattle
were stolen from Kalapata, it remained for Kalapata people
to get them back again. This they did. They engaged the
Turkanas early in the afternoon, defeated them, and
brought home the three herds all before dark that night. In

the fighting, one of the Dodoth and two of the Turkanas
were killed.

Two days later, the people of eastern Lokoki heard that
they were going to be raided again. This they learned from
the Teutho in the forest, from, in particular, a young
Teutho named Toperi-peri who occasionally did odd jobs
for Lopore, gathering wood and helping to repair the
fences in exchange for food. Lopore caught him stealing
once and fired him, but their relationship was not totally
destroyed, and now and then Toperi-peri would come with
a report. The Teutho spy for the Dodoth. They do this not
only for reward but because the Dodoth occasionally punish them severely if they fail to inform. For the same reasons, the Teutho spy for the Turkana. The Teutho are a
poor tribe, few in number, and their position is not an envi-
able one. The result of the ambiguous loyalty is that the
Teutho tell the Turkana where the Dodoth are grazing
their cattle, assist the Turkanas to hide in the forest and to
get food while the raiding party masses, then announce
to the Dodoth that a raid is on the way. It takes courage to
live as the Teutho live—not that there is a choice. Toperi-
peri was rashly courageous, even for a Teutho, and once, to
amuse himself at the expense of the warring parties, he
played the exceedingly dangerous game of scaring a Dodoth householder by speaking in Turkana outside the
householder's walls at night.

According to Lopore, Toperi-peri was a vagabond. This
in itself makes a person untrustworthy to the substantial
Dodoth, who have two terms of insult, "bush" and "dog,"
for unestablished people, the dog because it begs and wan-
ders, and the bush because it lives in the woods without a
home. The fact that the Teutho spy for both sides makes
them doubly suspect. It would, for instance, be perfectly

possible for a Teutho to win himself a meal by inventing a raid, or to oblige the Turkana by diverting a defending force from the actual scene of the raid by giving misleading information—and when Toperi-peri came to Morukore to say that the previous night he had learned from the Turkana that a raid was to come between Kalapata and Morukore sometime the following morning, no one knew whether to believe him.

Several men from the district gathered at Lopore's etem to sit on the boulders and look out over the valley below. The site mentioned by Toperi-peri was a likely one, a well-worn pass between the hills which the Turkanas used so often for escape with captured cattle that something like a road was trampled there.

The men were talking about the Teutho. "You can't trust them," said one.

"If they hear our plans for defense, they will tell the Turkanas," said another.

"If they try to pass here, they will not pass easily," said Lopore.

But the raids had been so many, and the sense of risk and tension in Dodoth so great, that the men decided to hold a sacrifice to rally themselves, foresee the future, and avert the raid, if it was coming, before it began. At midmorning, men began to gather at the ceremonial ground. This was on a high bluff above a bend in the river, where stood the sacred trees, an old wild fig like the fig named Pirre and like the sacred fig tree in Kaabong, and an enormous, hollow, sausage tree, with yellow, club-like fruit and a cavity in its trunk so spacious that eight or ten men, at rainy sacrifices, could take shelter within. The trees were near the permanent water hole in the river—sacred trees are usually found at least within sight of permanent water.

Perhaps this is only because such trees have lived for centuries and could not have survived so long had their roots
not been able to reach a permanent water table somewhere
below. But perhaps there is another explanation. Holy elders, say the Dodoth, founded the sacred places of the sixteen Dodoth clans as the Dodoth first moved north through
their country. Today, like ancient churches, the sacred
places are not always in logical sites. But though the population shifts because of tsetse fly or raiding, and though
even the riverbeds move and change, perhaps the Dodoth,
who with their need for firewood and fence posts have
chopped so much that they have affected their forests (almost all the trees are young or skimpy), have spared the
same ancient sacred trees for hundreds of years.

The ceremony was a long time beginning. I asked
Lopore if I could attend it. He said that women never came
to sacrifices; I said I only wanted to see it from afar. He
was busy that morning, trying to make people go to the
ceremony. It is felt that many people should attend, but
people are often reluctant. As is the case with meetings in
this country, everyone believes that others will fill them.
Presently he agreed absentmindedly, and I followed after
him, Uri, and other men of the area, along the path to the
river.

The rock slide above the river was dark with the crouching figures of many men. There must have been sixty or
seventy, in a thicket of spears, and people kept arriving in
two's and three's over the hills all through the morning and
the afternoon. In the riverbed below, the herds were taking
turns at the trough and the men were looking at the cattle,
waiting for an ox suitable for sacrifice to appear. It was to
be a red ox, its coloring foreseen in the intestines of a previous sacrifice. When the red ox was killed, its intestines in

turn would reveal the coloring of the next sacrifice, in a chain of divination that reaches back through time.

Around the bend of the river came a large herd numbering a red ox. The men on the rocks merely glanced at it, and a discussion began with the owner—really the owner's father, for the ox belonged to the herdboy. When a man's ox is sacrificed, he is reimbursed with a heifer. The heifer is paid by the man (or by the father of the young man) who kills the ox. To kill an ox brings respect and the honor of being a public benefactor—something, I think, that people more or less take turns doing—but that morning no one could be found. The owner's father didn't want to give the ox, fearing that too much time would pass before he was repaid. There was a great deal of discussion. People were shouting.

"There is a man who never kills an ox at a sacred place," someone said loudly, "but he always comes to eat."

"Someone takes meat home to his wife," said a voice, perhaps that of the man in question, "which spoils the sacred place."

Meanwhile the herds moved to the water, then up the bank, until at last even the red ox had finished drinking, whereupon the men on the bank called down to the herdboy to let the herd go but to keep the red ox and a few of its compainions in the riverbed. An ox will not let itself be driven alone. The herd grazed at the top of the bank, and the little boy, with his red ox and one of its companions, a white ox, looked up at the men and began to cry. The talk continued. No one paid the slightest attention to the boy. Men began to leave the gathering, lest they be asked to pay a heifer, then came back when someone finally volunteered. Then a few young men in a rather businesslike way got up, stretched, took up their spears and scrambled down the rocks to the riverbed. There they drove the red ox away from the white ox and threw a spear into its side. The white companion was startled as the red ox bellowed and ran, blood streaming, into a cover of dense bushes from which it looked out at its pursuers with its gentle, alarmed, ox eyes. It was routed by the young men, who tried to spear it again but missed, then hit it at last and chased it farther as it ran bellowing and bucking, the waving spear caught in its side. Sixteen or twenty people were chasing it now. Among them ran the little owner, choking with his tears, catching his breath at the sight of his name ox, still wearing its bell and braided necklace, but doomed to die. Trying to rejoin the herd and at the same time escape its pursuers, the ox ran more than a mile in a huge circle north of the river, and all the while the little owner tried to keep up with it, calling its name and crying. But when at last the ox, trembling and bleeding, stopped near the top of the bank, the child had fallen far behind and could not catch up in time. The ox wanted its white companion. It was supposed to die under the sacred trees, but it wouldn't go alone. Someone drove the white companion to it, it leaned its head against the white ox's side, the white ox supported it until it was under the fig tree, where it groaned, knelt, and rolled over, dead. "The owner didn't want to give it," said Lopore. "That's why it was so wild."

Its death began the ceremony. Now the mood changed from the arguments of the old men and the dispatch of the young, and took on a formal, passionless quality like that of an important church service here. The men, ninety or a hundred of them by now, divided according to their age sets and sat down under the trees. The dark ranks bristled with plumes and spears. There it was, the core of polity in eastern Lokoki: the young, uninitiated men on one side, the

initiated men on the other, these ranked by seniority, all
having abandoned their two- and three-legged stools, to sit,
as the ceremony demands, flat on the ground. The large
group of householders who were not but should have been
initiated took places with the lower age sets, or performed
the services provided by the lower age sets, called "waiting
on the old men," such as the overseeing of wood-gathering
(the youngest men actually fetch and carry) or butchering
the ox. This is done by a member of the clan that owns the
sacred place, who on that occasion was Lopore.

Sacrifices in Dodoth are not devotional or worshipful in
tenor, but somewhat mechanical; the rituals are both intricate and precise, with an almost infinite number of requirements and prohibitions, like the casting of a spell. The
ox must not be skinned; it must not be cut with a knife or
ax, but only with a spear; its front leg and the adjoining
ribs must first be lifted from the chest to make bowls of the
chest and abdomen into which the blood wells; the shining white integument and rumen must be carried to a bed
of leaves. The sacred part, the joined hind legs and hips
must be severed from the body, and then the sacred flesh,
the fatty fold that hangs between the anus and the with-
ered testes, removed to be eaten by the old men. The joined
hind legs must be divided, a special duty—the age groups
are designated by who is and who is not dividing the legs
—not with an ax but with a spear, and with the severed
front leg used as a club to batter them apart. And the meat
must all be eaten, and all be cooked, never boiled, always
roasted on a fire prepared in a special way with all the
wood that is used to feed the fire first carried in a circle
around the ox.

As Lopore worked, hair and blood stuck to him, and flies

made a silver mantle over his back. When the ribs and front leg were removed, and blood had welled into the cavities, the elders came, one by one, to kneel at the abdomen like elders at a pool, putting their lips to the blood's surface to drink. As each finished, he wiped his lips on the hairy hump, because, the Dodoth say, "there is fighting there." The younger men drank after, not at the same place, but from the chest cavity. The men talked, even joked, as they waited their turn, for blood is very much enjoyed and gives men courage and strength.

The integument, spread like a tablecloth over the distended rumen, had begun to dry. Its iridescent shine was vanishing, and along its fluted edge, where the intestine ran, it was constricting. Uri called for a calabash of water, which he poured over the white mass so that the translucence and the gloss returned and many small details that the drying had hidden sprang to view again. A horde of flies leaped up to escape the water. Uri waved his hands to chase them away, then squatted down. The integument is read "like a page in a book (*abuk*)," the Dodoth say. Any one can do it, there is nothing special about it, except that everyone near must crouch down. Those who were curious to see what it said came to squat beside it while Uri looked and looked, and ran his fingers over the spots, the irregularities and mounds, and saw the land of the Dodoth, a fire on Dodoth soil, a streak, the path of a bullet, and a mottled brown ox, the next sacrifice. Like tiny hieroglyphs, or pictures, or figures on a map, it was all there; in a hollow between two lumps, a pass between two mountains, were tiny black dots that meant a raiding party of Turkanas was entering, and beyond the dots, tiny, threadlike capillaries showed the people whom the Turkanas killed. The men discussed these matters for a long time, then folded the integument in half, carefully but quickly, as one closes a book, and returned to the sacrifice.

The young, uninitiated men, who cannot partake of a sacrifice, were roasting the meat for the older men, both initiated and uninitiated. The ribs and other parts were flung upon the burning branches, and when the meat was cooked, hot chunks of it like softballs flew threw the air as the young men distributed it around. Little brown hawks flew low over the gathering, stooping to try to catch the meat that flew below, and far above the hawks were vultures, a wide, slowly wheeling column of them looking down.

A piece of meat was the size of a four- or five-pound rolled roast. It was black and charred outside, dripping, tough and giving off a fresh, sweet smell within. But it was excellent. As it was served, a hush fell over the gathering, and people ate. Spear blades flashed at people's faces, for the Dodoth bite first, then cut the morsel, and nine feet away from each man's mouth the spear tail swung around.

Presently a short, middle-aged man in a plumed head-dress swallowed his mouthful and stood up, brushing his hands on his bare thighs. Picking up his spear, he began to pace up and down. Suddenly he stopped, and turning around to face the crowd, he cried: "The Turkanas! We may ignore them, but if we do, it is our fault if they come!" He paced up and down. "We have let the Turkanas and the Jie come into our land. We said we were friends. But they caused trouble here. Let us do as our fathers did. You are always dancing. Let us forget the dancing and see what comes from there." He pointed east, paused as if he had finished, then walked and said: "There was a man who lived here, but he moved. And we agreed that no one was to leave here! Some people need the protection of others but will not protect others in return. Hi! They will not! When we heard the alarm, we went to Kalapata. That was good!" His voice was hoarse now, and rising, and he walked and cried: "But even so, the Turkanas marry with Dodoth cattle! Why do we let them! They kill us! But we let them! They have blood too! If they come now, let us fight them! They will meet a spear!"

There came a brief, sharp hum. The old man had sent his spear flying over the heads of the crowd. "My people are here!" the old man cried.

"They are," said a deep, harsh roar, the voice of the crowd responding from its forest of spears, and before the sound had died, the old man said:

> Our cattle will drink in peace
> They will
> The disease of cattle will go
> It will
> The disease of calves will go
> It will
> The disease that weakens their legs will go
> It will
> It will
> It will
> And all bad things will be destroyed
> They will

It was invocation and response of a short, sharp prayer, after the fiery sermon, and the first of many said that afternoon. When the speaker was done, Lopore got up and walked and said: "We are many. The enemies who come to kill us will be fewer than we. What's wrong with us? They kill us. Why do we let them? We have ears to understand.

We have legs. We have eyes. All this. Why do we let them?" No prayer followed; Lopore was not initiated, and, as far as I know, only an initiated person leads a prayer. He sat down.

The previous speaker, whose name I learned was Nakade, then called for the young men to stand. Thirty or forty of them stood, spears at their sides, formed two columns, and, led by Nakade, sang the somber, almost tuneless, rolling hymn, *Yabulia,* "The Bellowing of Calves." At a signal from the speaker, the song broke in the middle as the men broke ranks and charged, spears brandished, straight at the crowd. It was a show of force. Afterwards they formed their lines again and sang: "A Man is a Man in Cattle," and then were sent by Nakade to wait for the Turkanas at the pass. The young men went in a body, with their ground-covering, businesslike strides.

When the defense force was dispatched, the tone of the speeches changed. Uri began walking and speaking; he was known for his judgment, not for his ability to arouse a crowd, and he said to the older men: "These days we find young children herding. It used to be that we took care of our children, and grown men such as you looked after cattle. But these days people think only of milk and beer, only of food, not cattle. People steal pumpkins instead. It is good for grown men to look after cattle. This way they protect their children, also their cattle, and can spy on the camps and pathways of the enemy besides."

After this speech a lull came, broken only by the sound of throngs of people chewing. It was the time of the ceremony when, metaphysical protection having been cast by the ritual, and physical protection having been provided by the dispatch of the young men, the older men consume the sacrifice, speak their minds formally, and offer prayers.

Uri's point was well taken, and was thought over by the massive, bull-like men who sat eating. The only thing against it was that most men have several herds of cattle, also goats, sheep, and calves, all of which require different types of herding. Few men can guard all their property at once, and men who are herding are far away in the forest or on the plain, not available when they are needed for defense. No one commented, but then, the Dodoth almost never comment on the speeches made at a sacrifice.

The next man who got up to speak brought up another matter. He lived northeast of Morukore. The tension of the raid, of course, was still with him, and when he walked he said: "Are we the only people living here? Let the refugees who left come back and help us. They let us fight for them. We from the east have answered the alarm eight times, but no one from the western dwellings came." Several people from the west, Remi among them, were sitting in the crowd. "Why are you so quiet there?" the speaker said to them. "If you like, we can all leave this place so the enemies can go as far as they want. In the last raid, every one of you ran with your wife. Why did you, if you were men? You!" he said to one. "You are responsible for telling the people of the west what was said here today."

This was Lopore's sorest subject. Lopore, who often went too far, naming names instead of saying "someone," stood up and pointed straight at Remi. "Why are you hiding here?" he said. "When you want water in the dry season, where will you get it? You think yourself a man, but it is not so."

Remi seemed implacable. His household was large, his sons and affines were many, and he himself was as independent as any other Dodoth. After all, he had only stopped using his cattle camp. His dwelling stood where it had always been. He cracked a marrow bone against a rock. The marrow came out. He licked the rock.

But Lopore and the preceding speaker had raised two important subjects, two irrefutable truths: that a neighborhood cannot stand alone and needs the help of others; and that the western neighborhoods would soon become the eastern neighborhoods, if the people in the east should move or fall. Not every neighborhood has the power to force outsiders to help defend it. But in the case of the western neighborhoods of Lokoki, I hope they rallied eventually, for by now dry seasons will have come and gone and they will have needed the water.

The last prayer of the day was inflammatory. It was offered by a late-comer, a tiny, senile elder, a senior in the age-set system who wore a fur cape that was almost bald. His senility amused the gathering; they laughed behind their hands when he childishly showed, by means of his walking stick, how the enemies would fall. But his prayer neither played with thoughts nor wasted words, and the responses came roaring. He had not lost his power to control a crowd.

> They will all die! he shouted hoarsely.
> They will!
> Our spears will stop them!
> They will!
> Rain! It will come!
> It will!
> Will it stop?
> No, cried the crowd.

"Hi!" said the old man, looking around for a bite to eat, though the ceremony was over.

It was late in the afternoon when the men walked home.

I followed Lothimidik, the rich young man who lived down the hill. Lopore caught up with us, and so did our interpreter and our cook, who had come to see the ceremony. As we walked through a dusky hollow, the alarm sounded. It seemed to come from everywhere. "Run," said Lopore. But we were in a trap in the hollow; no one knew which way to go. "Run," he shouted. But still we stood rooted with indecision and fear. Lopore, in a sort of fury, tore a branch from a tree and, stripping the leaves off rushed at us with it and would have hit us if he could, but Lothimidik, me, the interpreter, and the cook were running up the path as fast as we were able, my loose-leaf notes on the ceremony vanishing one by one. Lopore chased us almost all the way home, then sprinted past us to his dwelling, to find that his fifteen-year-old son Akral was still in the forest with the herd. Catching up his shield and spear, which one of his wives held ready for him, Lopore ran for the dark woods to find Akral.

In half an hour they came back together, driving the herd before them. The alarm, they had learned, was false, started by panicky people who had seen the armed men leaving the ceremony by the river and assumed that the raid had begun.

But the rumors of the raid were true. During the morning, more or less as Toperi-peri had predicted, the Turkanas, avoiding the pass, which, as Toperi-peri could have told them, was sure to be guarded, entered the district between Morukore and Kalapata, and turning north instead of south, raided a neighborhood on the plain. They had burned a dwelling to drive the people out, killed a man and a woman, and escaped with the herd.

If there had been an alarm, no one would have heard it at the sacrifice, over all the noise. I wondered what people

would say. Since the sacrifice had been held to secure protection from the raid, I wondered if something had gone
wrong with it. Not so, said Lopore. In fact, far otherwise,
for the raid had not been in Morukore but elsewhere, and
the sacrifice had worked miraculously well. To begin with,
the people had bargained and argued instead of sacrificing
at once. This was providential and illustrated a phenomenon recognized in Dodoth—that if you propose to do something, then delay, there may be meaning in your delay
which you do not immediately know. If the men had
speared the ox at once, the benefits shed by the sacrifice
would have come too early. But the people delayed, and
seemingly by accident, speared the ox just as the Turkanas
were coming in.

Moreover, the ox, of its own volition, had run in a circle
for almost a mile. Its ebbing life had cast a widespread
circle of protection which had saved the dwellings of all
the people present by keeping the Turkanas from coming
near. And as for the man whose dwelling was raided, if he
had been willing to come to the sacrifice, he would be alive
today.

CHAPTER SIX

Influence

THROUGHOUT THE TIME OF RAIDING, the district of Lokoki did not become depleted of its population. Very few people became refugees, most families stood fast, and by the end of October a few refugee families from elsewhere had even moved in. The stable population was responsible for the newcomers. Men such as Mora, Uri, and Lopore, with their courage and their unwillingness to abandon each other, were responsible for the stability of certain neighborhoods, but even they would not have been able to help the district if it had not been for the protection and influence of two very important men. One was an *emuron*, a diviner of great reputation. The other was a millionaire.

Both men were members of the age-set system, but it was not through this that they achieved their power, for neither was an elder. An elder attains power formally, within the political system. But the emuron got power from God, and

the rich man gained power entirely through his own re-
sources and through people's opinions of him.

Just south of Morukore, in the neighborhood Kailele,
called for the beautiful Kailele hill that rose like a sugarloaf from the plain, stood the rich man's dwelling. The
dwelling was so large that the hill did not conceal it. From
the top of Morukore, one could see the walls of the immense structure swelling out at the side. The fields cultivated by the women of the dwelling were, in the distance,
like a pale green sea. Though I often walked around these
fields, I was unable to estimate with any exactness the acres
they covered, for the fields were round, like all Dodoth
fields, and made loops and zigzag patterns in the distance.
It is enough to say that it took most of an hour to walk all
the way around them, and that the sound the wind made in
their corn and millet was like an ocean on a distant beach.
The owner of this property had ten wives, eight of whom
were living; fifteen sons; ten sons-in-law, one of whom was
an appointed chief in Kaabong; twenty-three daughters,
nine daughters-in-law; and twenty-five grandchildren. No
one knew exactly the number of his cattle, but there were
legions of them, quartered in many camps around the
plain. He kept only thirty or forty cattle in each camp and
none in his dwelling, which not only was too small to hold
them all but had once been infested with a cattle disease.
By moving his cattle to camps, he had escaped reinfection,
and by dividing the cattle into small herds (and by having
enough sons to tend them all), he had escaped heavy losses
during the June raid, during which only two of his herds,
only sixty head, were stolen. He had lost more cattle than
some men ever have at one time, but he hardly missed
them. He was a sagacious and a very wealthy man.

Like a rock in a stream, a dam for flotsam, his dwelling was a focus. Households such as his do not move easily; neither did his neighbors want to move away, as there were few places better than Kailele so long as the rich man and his army of sons and resident sons-in-law were living there. His stable group was attracting newcomers. A cluster of ten brushwork structures sprang up during October around the slopes of his hill, the temporary homes of ten refugee families. The goats of these families climbed the trees to browse where the rich man's goats were used to browsing and the cows competed with the rich man's cows for grass. The rich man complained that in order to build the brushwork structures, the newcomers were cutting down too many trees. But he tolerated the newcomers because they increased the defense. Even so, he did not much respect them; to him, they were unfortunate but spineless people who gave way to panic too soon. He listened blandly when people spoke of evacuated dwellings. "I won't leave mine," he said.

His eight wives called him Lokiding, but to the rest of the world he was Lokorimoe, the respectful, honorary name that indicated he had killed an enemy. It meant "He of the Spotted Enemy," and derived from a time he had killed a Turkana who was wearing a brightly printed tablecloth instead of a plain cloth cape. Or else it derived from a time he killed an enemy at a place called Lokoriot. Most people insisted that the first version was the true one, but he himself gave both versions, at different times.

He was a tall man in his mid-seventies, overweight—though not by much, perhaps twenty or thirty pounds—with a large, soft body and a condition like gout or poor circulation, which made his ankles swell. He wore a lip plug the size of a pullet egg, made of precious ivory and inserted ingeniously on his lip by means of a second, concealed plug like a collar button that stuck through the hole, its thin, protruding end shaped to fit a socket in the ivory ball. Otherwise, with his thin nose and domed forehead, his balding skull, his pompousness, his evident wealth and self-important manner, he was so much the sort of person one finds seated on the terrace of a country club that it was always a surprise to find him sitting naked. He seldom stood.

At Lopore's house, the name Lokorimoe was synonymous with the word "fat." It was a family joke reflecting some of the envy with which Lokorimoe was regarded. But envy bothered Lokorimoe not at all. "I am an important person," he often said. "Even small children know Lokorimoe."

Aside from his elderly wives, the only person in his dwelling anywhere near his age was a very thin old man named Botia who lived in an abandoned section of the spacious home. The section was the farthest downhill, where the drainage ran, and contained two broken courts. Pigweed and overgrown tomato vines choked the courts, and through the gaps in the outer wall, brambles had come in. A rotted granary basket and an old, broken house with its roof caved in sagged back against the walls, but Botia had been able to use some of the straw and sticks from the house and basket to build a lean-to shelter for his wife and his tiny, emaciated son. Botia was a relative of Lokorimoe's, his lokapa (he of the place of the father). Botia's father and Lokorimoe's father were brothers who had very different fates; Lokorimoe's father became rich, Botia's father had been ruined, and when, near the end of Botia's life, extreme poverty had overtaken him, Lokorimoe had taken him in.

Botia served as Lokorimoe's retainer. In a country without servants, to possess a retainer makes a great man greater still; Botia would accompany Lokorimoe on journeys and carry his stool and his clay pipe for him. If, on the journey, Lokorimoe would want to smoke, he would take the pipe and the stool from Botia and sit down while Botia would find a dwelling, go in, beg a burning stick from someone, and return to light Lokorimoe's tobacco. These journeys were always slow; Lokorimoe with his flat feet and his buckling ankles would lean on Botia's arm. In return for his services, Botia had the place in Lokorimoe's home, also a tiny spot outside the walls where his wife could dig a garden, and milk from one or two of Lokorimoe's cows. The relationship of Lokorimoe and Botia was in contrast to the relationship between Lopore and his affine Bilo, who treated each other with dignity and respect, as friends and equals. But Lokorimoe did not get rich by giving things away or by encouraging poor relations to come and live with him. He got rich by raiding, marrying, and having daughters. Warfare and personal gain were still his favorite topics of conversation when, in the shade of his etem tree, many polite visitors would gather to listen to him. As a younger man, he had been a famous warrior. He had captured many herds of cattle and had been known for his astuteness and his ability to make rapid changes in strategy. Once, when leading a defending force against a group of raiders escaping with a herd, he had found his force outnumbered and the raiders very fierce, so he had led his men ahead of the enemy, down into the raiders' own district in Turkanaland, and raided there. When the Turkana raiders arrived with the Dodoth cattle, they found their own herds gone.

Lokorimoe had on several occasions captured not only

cattle but little Turkana girls. These he brought home and
raised as his daughters. He no longer remembers exactly
how many, perhaps five, perhaps four, nor does he exactly
remember their fates. "Some went home, some married,
and some died," he once said of them expansively. For
those who married, he received the bridal herds. One girl,
now a young matron, occasionally travels from her husband's home near the Acholi border to pay Lokorimoe a
call.

Though a capable warrior with the mind and nature of a
general, Lokorimoe was a merciful man. But to listen to
him, you wouldn't know it. "Did you ever kill a person?" he
once asked me. I said I hadn't. "Then you are nothing," he
said. Nevertheless, he often spared the lives of enemy
women and children, and once when his sons brought him
a Turkana spy discovered near his home he spared the spy's
life too. "The rest of your party is there," said Lokorimoe to
the spy, pointing to a hillside where it was believed the
Turkana raiding party was massing. "Hide with them. I
won't kill you." The spy ran. Lokorimoe had the spy reported to the Kaabong police. Two European officers came
to interview Lokorimoe, who confided to the officers where
the Turkanas could be found. But the police were unable to
intercept the Turkanas. The raid came; after the fray, the
Turkanas went home, and a year later the spy, not knowing
he had been reported, returned to thank Lokorimoe and to
have a ram sacrificed for him.

The bulk of Lokorimoe's riches were gathered when he
was older by the planning of long-range investments,
which, once started, could be expected to grow. He had
married ten times, which meant bride payments of at least
one thousand cattle. But if each wife bore two daughters
his investment for each wife would double within twenty

years or so. (If a wife is barren, she can be returned to her family.) Most of Lokorimoe's wives had several daughters apiece, which absorbed his losses for the one wife who died before bearing children. Thus, his initial investment worked out well. He had more daughters than sons, for whose brides he would dispense cattle, and of his twenty-three daughters, only ten were married. He had thirteen to go.

As a father, he seemed vague and benign rather than personal and intense in his feelings toward his family. When I first visited him, I went with Lopore, who claimed to be a friend but was really only a clansman and acquaintance. However, with the fascination for the rich and powerful which seems to prevail in the world, Lopore knew the members of Lokorimoe's family better than Lokorimoe himself. On that first visit I asked Lokorimoe the names of his wives and their children. He began to tell me but was interrupted and corrected so many times by his oldest son and by Lopore that he dropped the subject in disgust, saying crossly: "You tell her, then." They did, remembering three wives whom he had omitted and quite a few children. To make things easier while talking to me, the oldest son would refer to his father very informally—as if by his first name. This annoyed Lokorimoe, who turned stiffly on his stool to face his son and cried: "I used to fear my father!" But that he was benevolent was demonstrated by his son's reaction: the young man paused politely, then did the same thing again.

The great households of Dodoth take much of their character from the owner, and in Lokorimoe's house his impassive benevolence had given rise to an affectionate, very pleasant air. His vast house was a splendid place to stay—on its dry slope, in warm sunshine, under the sky. With the exception of the family of the retainer, Botia, hunger and want did not exist there, and most of the eighty-odd people in the dwelling were young. All the young women at work in the day courts filled the air with the sounds of their churning and grinding and with their irregular, private singing, a vibrant hum. The little children and grandchildren ducked in and out of doors and played in the passageways, and with sticks built not armies or battle formations, but miniature dwellings, their pens filled with cattle, tiny white stones.

As a husband, he may have been somewhat egocentric. This was no surprise; his eight wives were all nice women who waited on him and taught their children and grandchildren to respect him. Though it is usual in Dodoth for a man to marry his first four or five wives for love and the rest for the political connections that result from his alliance with their families, Lokorimoe's wives were all so well connected that he had begun to marry for love again, and though his first seven living wives were elderly, his eight was only twenty-five or thirty. Her name was Kapoi. Her children by him were younger than most of his grandchildren. In his fatherly, impassive way he was very kind to her.

Once when I visited him, he was sitting in her field. It was the harvest season. He was about to enjoy a calabash of beer and she was about to thresh some of her bulrush millet, picked and stored in her open field basket. She was a handsome, tall woman with a lovely figure and wide, dark eyes. Lokorimoe called to her to bring beer for his visitors, David and me. When the beer came, he recalled for me the story of his life. "Have you heard?" he asked. "Have you heard of my birth? I was a herdboy and looking after cattle. When I became a man, I started marrying my wives."

Suddenly Kapoi began to shriek and cry. Lokorimoe, who had finished his life story, turned stiffly on his stool to look in her direction. She wept and shrieked the same words over and over. "Who did it? Who did it? Why did they? Why?"

Presently Lokorimoe realized what had happened and turned back to announce to us: "Yesterday they stole bulrushes from her field. Today they have stolen from her basket." He turned to her. "You won't get it back," he said sensibly and gently. "You are crying for nothing."

"But I only now discovered it," she wept. Her little boys, perhaps two and four, having been upset by their mother, were also in tears. One of Lokorimoe's grown daughters emerged from a nearby field and flung her arms around Kapoi, and the little boys ran weeping to their father. Lokorimoe wiped their noses with his thumb and cuddled them tenderly against his side. "Yes," he said, reminiscing, "I don't know the year I was born, but it was a long time ago. Years have passed and I can't remember. Today comes and goes. Who can count the days as they go?"

Kapoi, her breathing still unsteady, brought a second calabash of beer, into which she had dropped a hot stone. The thick beer boiled from the stone and from its own fermenting and Lokorimoe, tipping his head back, drank a great deal. "Here," he said to her. "Sit down." She sat down beside him. "You drink some too, Kapoi." He was benevolence itself as he ministered to her.

Later, in a reverie, he began to sing his ox-song, a song in which the members of his family, if not considered individually, are symbolized.

> Oh Loina, the song begins, Loina being the
>   ox, everything is against your father.
> My wife says: "It is evening now and
>   Lokiding has not yet come."
> Oh Loina, everything is against your
>   father.
> My child says: "It is evening now, and
>   Lokiding has not yet come."

If, when he had finished singing, anyone had suggested that the song seemed egocentric, Lokorimoe would have been much surprised.

But in the outside world, Lokorimoe's estimation of himself was entirely accurate. He was, in his own words, a very important man. With his multitude of neighbors, affines, family, and friends, Lokorimoe had many opportunities to express his opinions, which were conservative. Since in Dodoth, as elsewhere, a rich person is credited with wisdom above and beyond the wisdom needed to accumulate wealth, his opinions took root in the minds of those who listened to him. For instance, not a few people believed, as he believed, that the Protectorate government was to blame for the raiding. To begin with, the government had disarmed the Dodoth, making them cowards. The police, armed to defend the Dodoth, failed to do so. And lastly, "the Europeans" had unwittingly encouraged the Turkanas beyond all precedent by failing to avenge the death of a young English police officer whom the Turkanas had killed. The Europeans should have mounted a savage massive raid against the Turkanas, killing hundreds in revenge.

The sacred place to which Lokorimoe belonged stood in

a grove perhaps five miles north of Kailele. If a sacrifice was to be held, he would leave to attend it very early in the morning and walk slowly and heavily as the mist rose from the earth and evaporated, and the day turned hot. His sons and neighbors, who left later, would pass him, and almost always when he arrived at last, composed but perspiring, he would find the whole congregation patiently waiting for him.

When a few years before, one of his elderly wives had died, a sacrifice was postponed indefinitely in deference to his mourning. Once, while we were there and a huge Turkana raid was massing on a forested ridge west of Kailele, when the smoke of their campfire could be seen from Kailele hill, the sacrifice to forestall the raid and protect the area was postponed a whole day because Lokorimoe was unwell.

I used to wonder why his presence was so much desired, and why he commanded so much respect. He was not the sacred place's most senior member, nor did he say anything at sacrifices that he had not said informally many times before. In fact, at a sacrifice he would get to his feet laboriously, walk up and down and address the congregation in his matter-of-fact manner, lead a brief, matter-of-fact prayer, then resume his seat and converse with the men around him while the next speech was made. Because he paid little attention, he never seemed to know what was happening, never knew what the divination had revealed, and always had to ask.

But I think his inattention did not matter to his countrymen. I think that people respected his benign self-importance. Like an elderly, fearless general, Lokorimoe was as indifferent to danger as to many other things, so that the repressed terror which the raiding caused in many people left him unmoved. Around Lokorimoe there was an air of composure. His countrymen took heart from him.

Straight up Lokoki District from Kailele, at the farthest, northern border lived the other person of enormous power, the emuron. One of his names was Lomotin. He had several honorary enemy-names which he didn't use because he didn't need to. He was not rich, not an elder. He made no use of any external symbol to enhance his prestige, but even so, his fame extended south through Jie into Karamoja, east through Turkanaland, west through Acholi and Napore, and north into the Sudan. In times of peace, people came from all these places to obtain advice from him.

There were *ngimurok* (the plural of emuron) in most of these places, and many other ngimurok in Dodoth as well. But very few were great ones. Great ngimurok appear from time to time like comets, rise to fame, change matters in Dodoth a bit and die. Long after they are gone, the world remembers them.

While we were in Dodoth, we heard of an almost mythical emuron who was sometimes called Ibongo, and sometimes Ikwaibong. Dr. Dyson-Hudson heard of him in Karamoja, where he was usually called Ikwaibong. He lived on a mountain which some said was in Dodoth, some said was in Acholi, and some said was in the Sudan. He never grew old, he could not be injured by a spear or a bullet, he could make rain with rainstones and could make sticks go into rocks.

Once he lived in Dodoth, near Lokoki, and while he was there, there was prosperity and an abundance of crops. When he returned to his own nation, which some said was Didinga, that prosperity ended. Now and then, though, a

Small boys, their spears and shields beside them, build replicas of dwellings and fill the pens with cattle, little white stones.

Lokorimoe had 10 wives, 15 sons, 10 sons-in-law, 23 daughters, 9 daughters-in-law, and 25 grandchildren. His vast dwelling was a splendid place to stay.

Mora's boys bleed an ox, shooting its neck with a blocked arrow.

Blood is cooked with millet flour into a soft pudding, airy as soufflé.

Rengen, on the right, and Nabilo, on the left, spent their leisure hours cooking by Nabilo's garden shelter.

A stuffed calf skin stands by Uri's door. The cow, not realizing that her calf has died, lets down her milk when she sees this.

Shelter from the rain.

Nabilo's fields were wild and jungly. The wind rustled in the long, green leaves.

Women thresh with solid flails. In the foreground, where a dog has be-
witched the floor by soiling it, charms are laid to turn the spell back on the
dog again.

The winnowed kernels pour like water and the chaff blows down the wind.

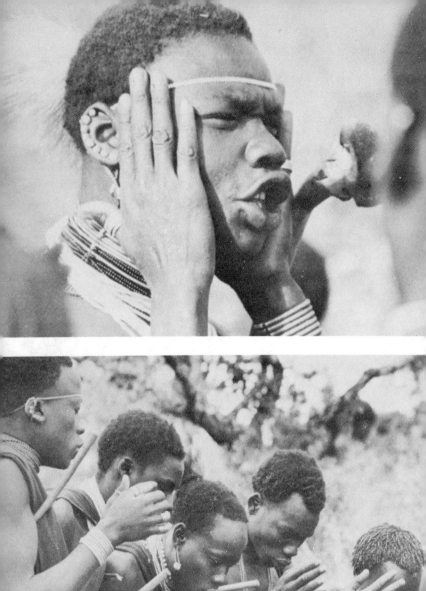

The Uganda Special Forces.

ABOVE LEFT: *Torori singing at a dance.*

BELOW LEFT: *At dances, young men stand with shoulders touching and sing their ox's songs.*

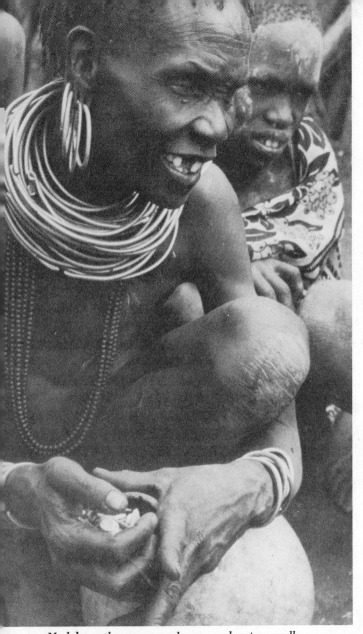

Nadolupe, the amuron, who can suck poison spells
from her patients.

Akral and his cousin protect their fathers' herd.

"A bull is father of the herd," say the Dodoth, "but an ox encourages a man."

delegation would be sent to visit him. The delegation
was said, was never received by him personally, but wo
be received at his etem by one of his sons. Because of
and because Ibongo was said to have been an old
when Lopore and Uri were youngsters, he was quite
sibly no longer a living person but an institution reta
by his sons.

But it was hard to know. After we returned to the U
States we got a letter from a friend who said that a
traordinary man had visited Karamoja. The man, who
friend saw with his own eyes, wore the dress of a vi
and had come on foot from the Sudan to Moroto, cla
to be lost. People suspected him at once, as this in i
unusual. It was then found that no matter in what lar
he was spoken to, he would use the same to answer. I
found to speak Akarimojong, the language of the
Didinga, Iteso, and Suk, also English, Italian, G
French, and Luganda—perhaps more. After this,
generally felt that he was Ibongo. He disappeared c
as mysteriously as he had come.

No great mystery surrounds the lesser ngimur
are simply doctors. One such was Lopore's only bl
tive except for his children—the woman named N
She was an *amuron*, which is the feminine form
word, and she lived in a dwelling which I often
compound dwelling near Lopore's, owned by thr
ers, with three sections, each with its own entr
cattle pen. Nadolupe lived with her younger son
court between the sections of the first and second
Her elder son was a Moslem, the Somali's b
Kaabong, who, when he came to see his moth
wear a suit of underwear. This gave rise to
among some of the older, more indifferent househ

union suits were "Moslem clothing." Nadolupe's younger
son was just a boy, and was expected some day to become an emuron, following his mother. Nadolupe herself
was a wrinkled old lady with a very sharp wit, who had
divorced her husband because she couldn't bear his second
wife. Her tiny court was untidy in a pleasant, lived-in way;
her pots and jars lay casually about, for she preferred visiting to housework. She often sat in the sunlight with her
knees up, her elbows on them, saying whatever she chose in
the most casual manner possible. "My grandfather was an
emuron," she once told me," and Lopore could have become an emuron, but he said he couldn't stand the traveling. So I said: 'Let me become an amuron.' Someone asked
me: 'Can you do it?' I said: 'Yes.' And here I am, an amuron.
    "We do the same work as a doctor," said Nadolupe. "Sick
people come to us, or else we go to them. If a child has a
sore, we can usually suck out what is causing the trouble.
Or we dream. God can slaughter you in a dream, or take
you to play in the water, where you do bad things. I get
tired of it though. I get tired of walking around to people.
Some owe me and haven't paid and I'm not getting my
harvest in because I've been so busy. I have to go all the
way to Kaabong tomorrow because a policeman wants me
to take out a spell.
    "No one wants ngimurok anyway," she went on. "Every-
one goes to the dispenser. When you had an earache, you
went to Moroto. Don't you like my medicine?"
    "I still have the earache," I said.
    She looked pleased. "I'll try to cure it," she said, "and if I
do, you can pay me later. I have a pain in the ear too, but
of course I can't treat myself."
    I asked her not to pour anything in my ear. She laughed.
"Europeans! I won't pour anything in your ear. Your trou-

ble was caused by a witch who watched you eating. Wait, and I'll be back."

She stood up, then stooped to crawl out the door. Presently she came back, followed by four wives of the household, all young women who entered reverently to watch. Nadolupe showed me a bulrush, and with a joking, mysterious expression she said: "This is what I use to cure."

She dragged up a log so she could sit in front of me, then put her hands on her knees and looked about dramatically. "Everyone is to sit while I work here," she said. "No one is to walk around." The young wives of the household sank to the ground, and Nadolupe took from her apron a sprig of *lothiru*, a plant with soft fuzzy leaves like the leaves of an African violet, tiny yellow flowers, and a pungent bittersweet smell. She first inhaled its fragrance, then rubbed it under my ear. She put her lips to my neck and sucked, removed her lips and picked from my skin a tiny, hairy pellet, not much larger than the head of a pin. "Hairs from the witch's eyebrows," she said, holding it up. She threw it in her fence. "Look at it if you like," she said, "but don't touch it." The young wives in the courtyard opened their eyes in wonder and shrank away from the fence.

"Now you have seen," one said to me.

Nadolupe put her lips to my neck and removed a second pellet, which she flung after the first. She removed another and another, six in all. She sucked a seventh time, but no pellet came, so it was clear she had taken the last. "I'll tell you this," said Nadolupe, very matter-of-fact. "You got that spell in another part of the country, or perhaps in your own country, but not here. When I throw away a spell that a Dodoth witch made, the spell flies off like a bird."

I went to the fence to see the pellets. They were like gray clay, with fine hairs imbedded in them like fine fuzz that grows on a bulrush. "Don't touch them," one of the young wives reminded me.

A few days later, I gave Nadolupe a sheet to thank her. She seemed both pleased and amused, thanked me very warmly and said as she folded it: "I think I fooled you. I got you to believe I used a bulrush in my cures."

Nadolupe, I thought, was a very nice woman. She made no pretense to greatness, but was amusingly realistic, worldly, and natural. The great ngimurok such as Lomotin are, however, supernatural. They could be called prophets, for though they too are doctors and are called night and day by the families of the sick, it is on the strength and accuracy of their prophesies that they rise to fame. Their job is not to cause wonder but to serve as God's oracles, and though they do cause wonder, it is not by contrivance. By their prophesies, great ngimurok make rain or cause dry weather, or bring health, disease, or locusts, or avert disasters to the nation such as raids.

The Protectorate government has been regarded as traditionally dangerous to prophets. During the 1920's the government hanged a famous prophet in Karamoja because he opposed the Protectorate, and just a few years ago the government imprisoned a prophet of the neighboring Suk whose name was Elijah and who had founded a movement called Dini Ya Msambwa, something like Mau Mau, based on Christianity and aimed at ridding the people of their European overlords. To this day, it is thought that Elijah passed like smoke through the stone walls of the prison and sat down outside it, where he was found by the guards, who then released him, realizing that there was no means of keeping him in jail. Some say that he was executed, but others say he is invisible, living in the mountains, waiting for the time to come appropriate for his return.

Because of the danger to prophets, and because many people confused us with the government, we were in Dodoth more than two months before we learned of Lomotin. I saw him at two sacrifices, for he usually attended the sacred place beside the river. At each sacrifice he performed the divination, and once he led a prayer, then came to wring my hand, very much as a minister might greet a newcomer to his congregation. At the time, I didn't know who he was.

Lomotin lived with two wives, two married sons, two resident married daughters and their children, and perhaps fifty cattle in a weathered, vine-covered dwelling on the slope of a windswept hill. The dwelling was old and crumbling in places and stood in the midst of the family bulrush crop, so from afar no one could see it, but only the patch of green or ocher made by the fields. He had no human neighbors. Beyond the hill was the forest, then Turkanaland; because his household was small, it did not anchor the neighborhood and all the people who had lived around him, east or north of him, had moved. This left as his only neighbors a troop of gray baboons who with the people gone roamed where they liked in the deserted neighborhood, harvesting the abandoned fields. Lomotin lived, in fact, at a gateway of Dodoth and Turkanaland. His house stood not half a mile from a pass, a roadway worn by the escaping raiding parties, and it was no wonder that he found himself alone.

He was seventy or more. His arms and legs were knobbed and sinewy, and a slight palsy caused his hands to shake. Yet when a Turkana raiding force would pass his home, to do what he could against them he would go to meet them with his shield and spear. He was fearless. His shield, a strip of buffalo leather eight inches wide, two and a half feet long, was scarred with the cuts of spears he had deflected. Scars of spears he had not deflected showed on his dull, black skin, old wounds that ached when the air was damp and cold.

His face was most impressive, broad and dark and deeply lined. The heavy bone ridge of his brow made a hollow for his eyes. He wore no ornaments but four brass earrings, his hair and beard were cut short and were gray, and even his expression was severe. He wore a black cape and a wide felt army hat, and under its brim his forehead was set in a perpetual frown, for he was a person of enormous gravity. His face showed mystery and austerity, and his voice, which trembled, was soft and slow.

He was, in short, an extraordinary man. Even Uri, an unusually self-possessed person, was in awe of him. When, with Uri, we visited Lomotin the first time, we did not approach his dwelling directly, to sit at his etem as visitors to most dwellings do. We waited in the tiny clearing by his wife's garden shelter while Uri went ahead to announce us. The dry stalks of the sorghum rustled overhead and the hot sun filtered through, and for an hour we waited but Lomotin did not come. Finally we heard a man approaching and stood up, but when the sorghum canes parted, Uri emerged alone. Lomotin was with a patient. We all sat down and waited and after a very long time the canes parted again and into the clearing stepped the gaunt figure of the famous man. His face, beneath the hatbrim, was in a deep sharp shadow, and he stopped still to look at us for a long time. He finally greeted us in European fashion, shaking hands with poise and very cordially, but afterwards he ignored us to exchange the long, formal Dodoth greeting with Uri. Uri was tense, alert, composed and most respectful.

I had brought Lomotin a present of a shirt, which I gave him. He tucked his stool under him and sat down, the shirt forgotten on his lap, to hear Uri tell of the death of an amuron's son, killed by Turkanas a few days before. The young man was wounded while running from the Turkanas, his companions deserted him, the Turkanas overtook him and speared him to death.

Lomotin then told Uri that the Turkanas had passed his hillside on the same morning that the young man was killed. One Turkana soldier had had a rifle; he had stood under a nearby tree, the top of which was visible above the sorghum, and had fired at Lomotin but had missed. Lomotin pointed to the tree with a trembling, arthritic finger and said he had tried to turn the Turkanas by approaching them from the west, but when he heard the bullet whine past him, he realized he would not be able to turn them alone.

When the two men had exchanged these stories, Lomotin stood up, said goodby very courteously, and walked off slowly, his back bent, into his field. Many times after we tried to visit him again. He was always polite, always courteous, but he never spoke with us more than fifteen minutes. One day I told him I was very anxious to talk with him. I told him that influence such as his was not understood everywhere in the world, that ideas about the supernatural varied so widely that his own would be most valuable, and that it had been suggested by everyone that I try to learn from him now that I had met him.

He asked: "Are there no spirits in your country?" The spirits in Dodoth are called the *ngipian*. I said we had none. "We have them here," he said. I asked if he would tell me more. He said he had been ready to leave on a trip when I arrived, and he could have gone almost halfway to his destination by now. So I went home. Shortly after, something happened which may have made him think of us more favorably, or made him think of us at all, for he was a man who had nothing to do with Europeans. His eldest son came to our camp one morning and sold me the narrow battle-scarred shield. I bought it because I didn't know to whom it belonged. The son kept a dhuka in Kalapata and may have regarded the selling of the shield as a way of making money. But he was also fond of his father and may have felt that it was time for Lomotin to give up the defense of the pass. When Lomotin found out about the shield, he came to see me and said, so softly and so angrily that his voice shook: "That shield was mine. I looked for it this morning and I found it was gone. I came to see for myself, because I couldn't believe my son would do such a thing." I offered to give back the shield, but he refused it. "You bought it, it is yours now. I have another. Perhaps he didn't know that. But I can't think why he did this. He must want me to hide at home when the enemies come. He must think I am a woman," said Lomotin.

The next time I visited him he thanked me for offering to return the shield. Lopore, a man undaunted even by a famous emuron, had come with me, and pointing out that Lomotin was wearing the shirt, he said: "Try asking about the ngipian." So I did. Lomotin was thinking of something else and didn't notice, but Lopore, who saw no harm in my learning of the ngipian, caught hold of the shirt and said firmly: "You were given that shirt for something, not for nothing. This woman wants to know something for that shirt. She once asked me if I was an emuron and I said 'no.' She has seen that Lomotin is a famous emuron and she wants to learn from him."

In his detachment, Lomotin listened gravely to Lopore,

then slowly took his leather doctor bag from his shoulder and showed me, object by object, everything within. As he removed each object, he explained it. There were sections of roots used for medicine; there was a special pair of eland-hide sandals. All Dodoth men use sandals for divining—a man on a journey, wanting to know what is happening at home, will sit down, remove his sandals, and drop them over and over again, to learn what he can from the positions in which they fall. Lomotin used his special sandals only for divining, never for walking. They had no toe or arch straps and had never been worn. Also in his bag was a short stick. It was the shaft of a spear which had killed an enemy, and stained as it was with death, it had been broken. The blade was removed but the wooden shaft and the balancing metal tail were still there, festooned with little bell-like duiker hooves. Lomotin had seen in a dream that these hooves would protect him. He used the dismembered spear to dig medicinal roots.

After that time, having decided to talk to me, Lomotin told me a great deal. He was as detached and as dreamlike as any person I have ever met, and like a person in a trance, he would speak with his slow voice and tell me things he never should have mentioned to a European. Physical events, raids, gossip, cattle, ngipian, and witches were all equivalent to him, and once, when he began to tell me of a raid that the Dodoth were planning against the Turkanas, I stopped him. No one else in the country had ever told me anything like that. No one else I met was as detached, and a tacit agreement existed between me and the Dodoth whom I knew that only the theory of raiding or specific attacks on the Dodoth would be discussed. It was the best arrangement. If I had learned of a Dodoth raid, I would have been expected to inform the police; but no one, no

matter how inveigled, can inadvertently reveal a secret he
or she has never heard. Before Lomotin had decided to talk
with me, he had refused to tell me even things which were
known to everyone; and perhaps his total reversal shows
one reason why great ngimurok are protected by their
people. If other great ngimurok are like Lomotin, they are
too removed from worldly matters, too deep in their spirit-
uality, to care about themselves.

Like a fanatic, Lomotin was concerned with his work as
a prophet and his protection of Dodoth. He may have taken
part in offensive measures, though I never knew of such an
episode. But often Dodoth raiding parties, before setting
out, consult an emuron to see if the plan is favorable. The
emuron then divines. Lomotin may have split a goat or
dreamed a prophetic dream for many a raiding party,
which would then set out or stay at home, according to his
recommendation. This was a service which he, like any
other emuron, might have provided, but it was not in this
capacity that he influenced Dodoth.

His influence lay in his supernatural abilities, which,
being below the surface of ordinary affairs, made people
weigh his opinions very carefully, try to do as he advised,
and show profound respect for him. Even the enemies respected him, perhaps they most of all. I used to wonder
why he was not killed in his efforts to stop the Turkanas
from coming through the pass. I could only guess that because the Turkanas are very like the Dodoth, and are said
by Dr. Gulliver to have a respect for the Dodoth ngimurok
and are said by the Dodoth to consult their ngimurok in
peacetime, perhaps the Turkanas purposely spared the
fierce old man. But then again, some prophets such as the
Suk Elijah are said to be impervious to bullets. Some
prophets are said never to grow old. Some ngimurok, with

their great and mysterious power, are said to be not only ngimurok but witches, and perhaps the raiders thought these things of Lomotin. Perhaps the raiders would steal by his house in secret so as not to engage him. Perhaps the thought of his gaunt figure rising from his door and slipping after them made them hurry on.

Lomotin's father and grandfather had been ngimurok before him, but not as famous as he. God grants the power to families; it passes from parent to child or grandparent to grandchild, a man can inherit it from a woman or a woman from a man. The family will know which young person has inherited the gift when the young person begins to receive God's messages at night, to divine in dreams. The word for God is *Akuj;* the word for dreams is *akiruj.* Some dreams are God's messages, and the ngimurok receive them. Lomotin had a stool on which he sat when he rested by day, but used as a pillow by night. The stool was beautifully carved and had a special power to make his dreams come. He dreamed of ways to heal the sick, and his cures had an eerie, dreamlike quality. He would tell a patient, for instance, to sacrifice an ox, a dog, and a bird. On the stool, he dreamed his prophesies, which, like messages, were literal. He would see it raining in a dream, then see a red ox being sacrificed, and he would know, when he awoke, that the sacrifice of such an ox would bring the rain. He was uncannily right. Whenever such a prophecy would rise from the depths of his mind to form itself into a dream, the result of the dream would leave the world astonished and increase his reputation.

Sometimes at night I thought of him in his dwelling on the hill, with the wind stirring the dry canes of his field and the tiered thatched rooftops within his walls half black, half moonlit, and I thought of him sleeping in his dark house, his dark face frowning, and I wondered what he was dreaming, for in those dreams of his he saw us all. In his sleep his mind pored over us and in the morning when the sky turned gray in his door and his cattle would get up and bellow, he would awake and might then visit someone he had dreamed of. Sometimes we saw him early in the morning, never on the road but always on one of the paths that led through the misty hollows to Morukore or Kailele, a path which he would be following slowly, leaning on the dismembered spear. His back would be bent, his leather doctor bag would be over his shoulder, and his black cape would be tucked up to keep it from the dew.

After his visit, something in the countryside would change. A woman patient might close her court to visitors or request anyone visiting to refrain from sitting on a stool. A man might hang a wooden charm above his cattle gate so that the dangling charm could streak each cow's passing back with magic, and thus protect them from an impending sickness which Lomotin had foreseen. The change might be no more than a sacrifice held in a courtyard, or it might entail an entire family's abandoning its home to move.

One day he visited us to bring a root shaped like a severed thumb. Having learned I had an earache, he told me to boil the root and pour the hot juice into my ear. I asked if he had heard of Nadolupe and the witch's eyebrows. He raised his eyebrows and asked a question of his own. "Did it help your ear?"

I asked about the sucking cure; Nadolupe had, after all, been extremely adroit. Lomotin answered diplomatically: surely Nadolupe was right, he said, but his root would "kill the witch eye where it was," as the drugs at the dispensary kill germs. I offered to pay him and the payment he took was a tube of disinfectant ointment which he had seen cure sores.

Lomotin did not fear competition from the dispenser, or from the West. The gift of being an emuron is given a person so that he can help his nation by any means—by dreams, by root broth, by charms, or by the dispensary medicine—all of which, except dreams, are called *eketoi,* the word for tree or wood, which is the source of physical medicine in Dodoth. But then, Lomotin had no competition, for anyone can handle eketoi, but very few people have important dreams.

Sometimes Lomotin saw witches in his dreams. Witches are associated with hyenas, and when hyenas give their ear-splitting, shuddering cries like laughter, one can know that witches bestride them and are riding to somone's dwelling to do harm. If cries like these came at night from the forest, the image of a person might form itself in the sleeping mind of Lomotin, and when he awoke he would visit his patient to describe, without naming, the person he had seen in the dream. The patient would then recognize that person as a witch when he saw him again. Because a witch usually intensifies his spell by visiting his victim's dwelling often, Lomotin might make a protective charm with wood, and with it encircle the dwelling, casting a spell to transfix the witch when he or she revisited, so that the patient could put the witch to death. If a dwelling were gripped with a very deep spell, causing many people to fall ill or die, Lomotin might advise the people to move. Five years before, he had so advised Lopore. Lopore, that volatile man, was a person much troubled by witches. One of them killed his daughter Chuchu's two little sons; and Lopore and his wives, following the advice which a dream gave

Lomotin, carried their dwelling, pole by pole and roof by roof, to a new site fifty feet away, where it stands now, near the huge round mark of the spellbound dwelling still visible on the ground.

Many years ago Lomotin, with his deep eyes and mystery, young but already supernatural, was courting his second bride-to-be, visiting her at night by her private doorway in her father's wall. One of her brother's children was dying, and while lying asleep in his fiancée's little night house, Lomotin dreamed that an old man witch was making the child ill. Lomotin awoke long before dawn, as young men do, and when he crawled quietly through the outer door so as not to disturb the family, he saw the old man witch, a stranger, sitting in the moonlight by the wall. Going quietly toward the stranger, Lomotin took him by the arm. Lomotin spoke to the stranger; the two supernaturals had a little conversation in soft voices, though Lomotin no longer remembers what they said; then Lomotin led the stranger to the bushes where his cries would not disturb the family, and put him to death.

To an outsider visiting Dodoth, it seemed dangerous that a person should have the power to dream the identity of a witch. But even an emuron does not harm a witch unless, as in the case of Lomotin and the elderly stranger, the witch is caught where nobody belongs, at night outside a wall. The Dodoth are very suspicious of witches, who betray themselves by extraordinary behavior, such as fixed staring or prolonged, direct pointing, or by saying shocking things. Even animals can be suspected—cows that roll their eyes and wag their tongues eerily, or dogs that drag their hind quarters to scratch their rectums along paths or over threshing floors. Though cows that act weirdly are put to death, and though charms are burned over dogs' drag marks to turn the spells back on the dogs again, people are not deeply concerned about the witchcraft of animals and the suspicion that would focus on a person who acted strangely would soon vanish if the suspicion proved a mistake. But it is no mistake and no mere suspicion that certain people know themselves to be witches, and tumble and roll at night around other people's walls to cause illness in their victims or, eventually, death. Witches are accused of worse than that, if anything can be worse, and more than spite may prompt them, for they are said to love death, disease, and corpses. It is said that witches sometimes visit the cattle pens of families known to have had recent funerals, to unearth the corpse. People claim to have seen the evidence of this—human footprints, the corpse gone, and a gaping hole. A witch would carry the body in his arms to a remote place, where he would "eat it or play with it," the Dodoth say. While we were in Dodoth, a man was seen in Timu forest with a body in his arms. Perhaps it is the fear of visits by witches which prevents the Dodoth from burying all but the most important of their dead.

The risk in being a witch is very great, for most practicing witches meet violent ends, bound hand and foot and beaten to death by householders. But the risk may almost be worth it, especially to people nearly consumed by malevolence, for the witches have power almost equal to the ngimurok.

Certain families are known to breed witches. Witches are feared, and getting in the bad graces of these families is avoided. A man from a witch family has to marry a woman from another witch family, thus magnifying the trait. As with the ngimurok, the supernatural quality passes from parent to child or grandchild. In fact, the witches are not unlike the ngimurok. They share the inheritance of a supernatural trait. Both groups cast their spells in circles around dwelling walls. Both groups cause supernatural harm: witches harm the innocent, while the ngimurok harm only wrongdoers, casting spells to transfix witches or spells to transfix thieves. But if you brought the leavings of a thief, such as a bit of partly eaten food, to a powerful emuron, he could make the thief sick without knowing who the thief was. In the same way he could make anyone sick, any wrongdoer, anyone whom he considered a wrongdoer, or any personal enemy of his. Lomotin would perhaps never do such a thing, but the fact is, if he wanted to, he could.

One could not help comparing the mystery of Lomotin and the optimistic influence of Lokorimoe, with his family and cattle and neighborhood increasing around him, his implacable personality, which was so greatly respected, and his vast holdings, so greatly envied. Just to visit Lokorimoe in a cordial mood in his etem on Kailele hill while at your feet lay the great house with its thirty or forty roofs and ten or fifteen doors, gave you a sense of confidence. But when you went to visit Lomotin, and waited outside his broken wall, on which vines and moss were growing, you might feel uneasy. He was never indoors by day. He might emerge from a field where he would have been helping one of his wives with the harvesting, and visit briefly before taking his bag and spear to be on with his affairs. He was twenty minutes by foot from his nearest neighbors, and when he was gone, the poles of his house and the millet stalks in his fields would creak and rustle in the silence. His wives were shy and seldom appeared.

I was not the only person made uneasy by Lomotin. I seldom went alone to visit him, but was usually accom-

panied by someone in the neighborhood, with whom Lomotin would become engrossed on the subject of the Turkanas. No one would ever try to change the subject, and no
matter what he said, very few people would ever openly
disagree with him. Perhaps some people were made uneasy
by his warrior's righteousness. When he spoke of the Turkanas, a surprising harsh and puritanical anger would
sound in his voice, which would shake with hatred. Perhaps others were made uneasy by the supernatural, witchlike power that lay in his deep eyes; as he listened to his
visitors, he would swing his head to look around him slowly
and intently and if his eyes met yours, your eyes would
drop.

Lopore, however, was not made uneasy by Lomotin.
Even the famous ngimurok must have friends, and Lopore
and Lomotin were cronies. Now and then Lomotin would
stay overnight at Lopore's, and Lopore would evict one of
his wives so he and Lomotin could share the night house.
Before they retired, they would drink beer together beside
Lopore's fire and talk about the raids and cattle far into the
night. Sometimes Lomotin would tell Lopore of a dream,
and Lopore would count himself honored. Many times
Lopore told me of the good works done by Lomotin, and
even once told me of a time that Lomotin dreamed of
Lopore on Mt. Morunyang, where Lopore was then living.
Lomotin saw in his dream that Lopore moved to Morukore,
where he escaped a raid that came to Morunyang, escaped
other raids, and became rich. When Lomotin told Lopore
of the dream, Lopore accepted the prophecy and moved.
The other people on Morunyang whom Lomotin told to
hold a sacrifice for protection did not take the advice, and
when the raid came and the prophecy was fulfilled, many
people on Morunyang were killed by the raiders, but Lo-

pore was safe on Morukore, where he lives today, richer than he was on Morunyang.

It was Lopore who told of Lomotin's relationship with the third group of supernaturals who live in Dodoth, the water spirits, called the ngipian. Water is so important in a pastoral country that it is no wonder that a prophet who can cause rain is associated with it. The spirits are associated with water through the masculine singular of their name, which is *ekipi*. If there were a feminine singular, it could be *akipi* which has no meaning, but the feminine plural, *ngakipi,* means water. And as Lopore described the spirits, they seemed like water, for they are transparent, iridescent creatures, human in form, with billowing, many-colored hair. "They have hair like Europeans," Lopore once told me. "Like that," he said, pointing to a rust-colored caterpillar that was making its way, its long hair flowing, across a threshing floor. The ngipian are seen in lightning and appear like mist below the clouds, for the ngipian can float in the air. Sometimes they roam the earth, following the rivers, and appear above wet places early in the morning like wraiths. They keep their cattle under the rivers, letting the cattle come to the surface at night to walk in the grass. When you hear the spirit cowbells ringing in the darkness, you know, say the Dodoth, that the little magic cattle are grazing near.

In their homes below the rivers, the ngipian have spirit wives, who bear them children who grow up, grow old and die as people do. When an ekipi dies, the ngipian family abandons its pool and moves elsewhere and the pool goes dry. The ngipian control the rain, the rainbows, the mist, the clouds, the water level in the pools, and must be treated with respect. If you displease them, they can make your cows stick in the mud or catch you in a whirlwind which will drive you mad. If you throw stones in the water, the ngipian will think you are stoning them and will want you to die.

To please the ngipian, you can throw the chyme of a goat in the water. It also pleases the ngipian to see the lips of cattle drinking far above them at the surface of the pool or to see calabashes dipping as people fill their jars with water. But as a great and witchlike emuron can cast a spell on whosoever displeases him, an angry ekipi can come like a wind to possess you. It will occupy your body and eventually kill you unless an emuron paints you with clay stripes like the stripes of a rainbow, then persuades the ekipi to enter a goat, leads the goat around a tree so the ekipi will climb the tree, and kills the goat.

Once when a plague of dysentery came to Dodoth, we saw almost daily a person striped with clay coming from the path that led to Lomotin's. Women would carry little striped babies on their backs to the dispenser, which did not seem to displease Lomotin, for here again, there was no competition. As the ngimurok are in one way like the witches, they are in another way like the ngipian. As Lomotin could cast a damaging spell, so could he, in his affinity with God, mollify an ekipi with chyme and sacrifice. The ngipian are very close to God, and great ngimurok such as Lomotin are their relations. Lomotin, the people said, could visit the ngipian in their pools. Now and then, the people said, he would be welcomed by the ngipian in their deep homes down underwater where he would talk and rest and visit, and drink milk from the little, spirit cows.

CHAPTER SEVEN

Harvest

THE MIDDLE OF OCTOBER to the middle of November in Dodoth is Lara, the next to last month of the year. The sun shines bright and in the hot dry weather the millet ripens and the sorghum becomes full of sugar, and wherever people walk they carry a supply of sorghum, for one can suck the canes for syrup, and spit out the fiber, and over every pathway in Dodoth in Lara lie these fibrous mouthfuls, brilliant white and shiny like big flakes of snow. During Lara the harvest is taken in. A woman goes to her field early in the morning and walks about among the stalks of grain. When she sees a ripe stalk, brown and hairy, she catches it as it blows in the wind, bends it down, and with a simple little dagger severs it just under the head. She lets the stalk spring back and tosses the head into the basin she has brought with her. A Dodoth woman gathering her grain is like a cat catching birds, she is so deft and stealthy;

she slips her hand quickly up a grain stalk before the wind snatches it away.

A basin full of grain heads is dumped on to an old cape spread out near the field house, and the cape, when full, is made into an immense and rustling bundle which the harvester carries home on her head. She empties the bundle in the huge, but temporary, open storage basket that stands outside the dwelling wall, and giving the cape a flap to shake the chaff off, goes back to fill it once more. She works until the sun sets and shows the Pleiades, the misty group —whose name, *ngakuliak*, is said to seem to come from the term for "poor women"—in their autumnal place above the horizon, marking the end of the year. Normally the rainy season has ended before Lara. The little thorn acacias drop their leaves and the grass disappears in patches or turns brown. And during Lara a wind from the east begins which rises up hot from the Turkana plains, and during the day pours warm and steady over Dodoth. It dries the grain heads in the crude but airy baskets; it dries the sorghum branches, all orange, purple, or white, which the women have saved for next year's seed, stuck up in their thatches. It dries the beans, the piles of split calabashes, pumpkins and cucumbers that the women bring in from the fields in order to extract the seeds, for the massive soft vegetables spoil eventually, but the dried seeds can be pounded to flour and eaten all through the year. The following months will be the dry season, with just a small amount of rain. No crops will be planted, and the cattle, as sometimes happens, may be taken to dry-season pasture. Until the first string beans and tomatoes are ready after spring planting, people will not have fresh vegetables, and until then will depend on their grain.

The wives of a dwelling clear a large area in front of the

storage baskets by the wall of the dwelling and cement the clearing with cow dung smoothed with water, to make a floor. When the floor dries, it is soft and resilient and does not crack under the flails, for the women pile it with grain heads and beat the pile with long sticks—very hard work which makes the arms and shoulders ache, very exacting work, as the women around the pile must time their blows carefully or they will hit each other, and very hot, itchy work, for the dust and chaff fly in the air and stick to perspiring faces. When the breeze blows, the threshers sweep with little grass brooms, gathering the pounded grain heads into a pile. They then stand up to winnow, and the golden kernels pour like water while the chaff blows off on the wind. Threshing can go on until evening, when, from the top of a hill, one can see all of the threshing floors of a neighborhood surrounded by smoldering, glowing rings as the people set the chaff on fire. Even after dark, you can hear the rhythmic thumping of the flails and now and then you can hear laughter and singing too. Sometimes, to speed the work, the men flail also, and sometimes many people thresh together, as the families in a neighborhood take turns helping each other, doing one harvest at a time. These threshing bees are gay occasions: it is cooler at night, and more pleasant because the men are there.

Being the time of plenty, Lara is the season of parties, celebrations, and feasts. Women brew grain into delicious sour beer, thick as cereal, served hot enough to steam. A man may ask his friends to help him with some heavy work —moving a roof, for instance—and then repay his friends in beer, so Lara is the season for accomplishing things. But a man may serve drinks to visitors just for pleasure. Sometimes twenty or thirty men may meet under an etem tree to hear their host's opinions while trying his beer. Or a man might give a small party for a few close friends in the court of one of his wives, where privacy assures that passersby will not join the group to drink up everything, where men and women can sit together informally, passing a warm calabash among them, spending the afternoon. There is an air of relaxation toward the end of harvest. The grain is in the granaries, and the dry, headless stalks rustle in the fields. At this season, for once in all the year, the thornbush fences that surround the fields are opened and the livestock is let into the canes. Thus the fields are cleared for next spring's planting, and the cattle have their harvest festival too.

The year we were there, the rains seemed to let up around the middle of September. Now and then, soft banks of clouds would mass over the Escarpment and drift west to moisten Dodoth. But no big storms came, and presently, the grain in the fields turned brown. Morning and evening, the little gray doves that raid the crops would buzz between the grain stalks, and after dark the crafty monkeys, red and solitary, would approach the fences for the tomatoes and cucumbers that ripened there.

At the end of September, the women of Morukore began the harvesting of their warm fields. On the slope of the hill the two wives of Uri's household carried or rolled their calabash crops to a sunny place within the dwelling wall. In the valley below the hill, Lopore's wives picked their bean crops, the beans multicolored and mottled, the pods ready to split, and every day as people passed their sorghum and millet they examined the heads for ripeness. Toward the end of October, everyone had made a threshing floor. The large rough baskets were built and ready, and people began little by little to cover the bottoms of them with the first ripe heads of grain.

But at the end of October, the weather changed. It was as if the season reversed itself. The little occasional storms increased in frequency and volume until they were no longer brief showers that would make people look up and hold out a palm before stepping under cover, but warm deluges that would leave the fields and the straw roofs steaming and the earth smelling of hot, wet clay. Soon the sky no longer cleared after every rainstorm. In the mornings, fog rolled down the hills and lay in the valleys, and the country became very cold. By the first of November, there was a foggy cover every day and the turning cloud masses changed from dark to pale gray as the wind moved them. The rain came with thunder and lightning and impenetrable black clouds or steady earth-soaking downpours that lasted all night or all day. When the daily temperature dropped, many people who had dormant malaria began to get attacks.

One day, early in the morning after it had poured all night, I went down the hill to visit Lopore's family. The sky was overcast and dark, and all the paths on all the near and far hills showed clearly, silvery and wet with rain. The air was so cold that Lopore's herd had not yet been let out for grazing. The little herdboys were by their mothers' fires, keeping warm. Lopore's old red bull was hungry and had its head out the gate. I went with Nabilo, who, a basin under her arm, was just setting out to harvest the millet in one of her fields. "Only take the ripe heads, not, please, the green ones," she asked me as I followed her down the rockslide into a ravine. Her field began at the water cut in the ravine and ran up the south bank. Rengen, Nabilo's best friend and co-wife, cultivated the field beginning at the cut and running up the north bank. We had only begun cutting millet heads here and there on Nabilo's side when once again rain started, and we climbed the slippery bank to find shelter in Nabilo's field house. By then the rain was pelting and a haze of bouncing raindrops stood above the ground. There was a clap of thunder, then another and another, and the wind blew in gusts. Like a snake, a stream of water crept slowly under the shelter's wall, crossed the floor, and went out the other side. Nabilo made a face at the water and lifted her bundle of millet onto her lap.

We heard someone running and Lopore appeared suddenly, to duck into the shelter. He was streaming wet and his cape was dripping. He wiped his face and snapped the water from his fingers. I asked him if he thought the rain would stop. But in Dodoth people do not predict the weather. "The rain is *ekile apolon*, a man," said Lopore. "Who can talk to the rain?"

It stopped an hour later and left a misty, heavy air. Nabilo began to inspect her dripping field. Her millet, no longer green and resilient, but brittle and ripening, was broken down in patches as if a giant had trampled through. Nabilo, soaking wet, tried to stand some of the broken stalks upright. Lopore watched. Each stalk remained standing for a moment, then slowly lay down. "Couldn't the heads be harvested?" I asked Nabilo. "Yes, if they were ripe," she said.

That morning Nabilo lost about a sixth of her field. Later in the day, a little river, made as the rain ran down the hillsides, rushed through the ravine and carried off more millet in its spate, from both Rengen's side and Nabilo's. In Dodoth, women usually plant more than they need, in case of disaster, but in that one storm Rengen and Nabilo lost most of their margin.

The November weather was like April weather. On all the hills the trees that had shed their leaves put out green buds, then yellow flowers. Blue flowers came up in the grass, and the grass that had dried became lush and green. The vines that grew over the roofs and dwelling walls put out new tendrils, and presently, amid so much moisture, the old gray poles at the back of Lopore's dwelling put out suckers near the ground.

Meanwhile harvesting went on as usual. The storage baskets were gradually being filled. When the sky would clear briefly during a morning or an afternoon, people would hurry to turn the grain heads out of the baskets to dry them in the sun, and every night, or just ahead of every rainstorm, the women would hurry to cover the baskets with capes.

But it was not much use. During the next few days, Nabilo and several other women showed me what was happening to their millet. The kernels on the spongy cobs were putting out threads of roots and little green tendrils to point at the sun. It was no wonder. All over Dodoth, even the legs of the storage baskets were sprouting, and every morning, every woman in Dodoth would remove the top layer of grain heads in her storage basket, or the two top layers or the top quarter of her harvest, and throw it away. As women plant more grain than they need, to guard against fires and washouts, so do they plant their fields in stages, so that the entire crop does not ripen all at once. If some is lost, more is coming. But the year we were there, wave after wave of millet ripened and was harvested and rotted in the unseasonable rain. It was important that the people save some of the harvest. Because of the raiding, every family faced the possibility of losing its cattle. Those who lost cattle would face starvation if they had no crops at all, and fearing this, people worked harder than ever. They tried to thresh the millet while it was still wet, and

dry the kernels away from the cobs. To thresh a dry, resilient millet cob is hard enough, but to thresh the damp cobs
with the kernels all but rooting in them is almost impossible.
Nevertheless, the people tried. Usually after dark in those
days the rain would stop and people would thresh their
millet by moonlight, working in large groups, silent and
exhausted, until one or two in the morning. When late at
night the moon was down and the piles of bulrush were
invisible, the threshed grain would be swept into baskets,
the fires would be built up, and in the flickering light
people would winnow with their breath.

At about that time, we took a trip to Turkanaland. We
drove first to Moroto, then to the Escarpment, and from
there, down the steep road into Kenya. The road crosses
the Turkwell River and proceeds through the desert to
Lodwar, administrative capital of Turkanaland, not far
from the shore of Lake Rudolf, a lake of weeds and lotuses,
crocodiles and pelicans, and deep, warm water. Rain or
not, there is water in Lake Rudolf, source of the Blue Nile.
But between Lake Rudolf and the misty green Escarpment
is the Turkana Desert, where in places there is nothing to
see for miles except slick black rocks under the sun, a landscape that looks barren and greasy, like a hot garage floor.
Though the rainy season was in process, the Turkwell River
was a vast bed of sand. The rib-like markings left by water
were visible and showed that a spate had passed not a day
before, but when we crossed, the sand was desiccated and
a procession of dust devils was moving between the banks.
Around the Turkwell was a hot, gray-green bush where
here and there a few camels and a few goats nibbled the
leaves.

In Turkanaland, a devastating drought of the previous
year, during which many families had lost their herds, had

caused a famine which was still in process. As we drove to
Lodwar, we found the skeleton of a woman, dead of hunger, by the road. Near Lake Rudolf, the administrator had
instituted a famine-relief program and was giving away
food to throngs of emaciated people with disheveled hair,
but at Lodwar, that grim prison town and military post
where Kenyatta was held, the paupers' cemetery was being
expanded, and to give hungry people work, the people on
relief had dug new graves which lay open, waiting for the
bodies of anticipated famine victims to fill.

It was no wonder that the Turkanas intensified their
raiding of Dodoth during the last months of the year.
While in Lodwar, we heard that Dodoth raiding parties
were penetrating far into Turkanaland, and by raiding
small groups of Turkana camps, were succeeding in capturing herds. The Turkanas could not afford to lose their cattle
and, during November, retaliated with a raid against
Dodoth almost every day. More Dodoth were made homeless, to become refugees in Kaabong; more families lost
their cattle and became dependent on their crops; more
harvests failed because of the rain, more millet rotted; and
a tension became manifest in Dodoth.

Of all the people we knew, Lokorimoe was probably the
most serene. He sometimes talked of making preparations
to call a meeting of the householders he knew, a meeting at
which a delegation would be chosen to visit Ibongo, who
would be summoned to Lokorimoe's home. When Ibongo
would come, he was to stay as the guest of Lokorimoe
while meeting with the elders to discuss the rain. Ibongo,
Lokorimoe felt certain, would be prevailed upon to use his
rainstones, or something else, to put a stop to the wet season and bring harvest weather again. I don't know the outcome of this plan. No one like Ibongo came while we were

there, and Lokorimoe wouldn't say if he had sent the delegation.

Uri, too, was serene. He did, it seemed to me, what
common sense would indicate. He roofed his storage baskets tightly, he set a field aside for his cattle for emergen-
cies, and he increased his vigilance for raiders. When the
first gray light began to gather in the morning, it would
reveal him seated on a rock on top of the hill. He would be
motionless, wrapped in his cape against the mist that
swirled among the trees. His spears would be propped
against his shoulder, and his eyes, still very sharp for all his
years, would be fixed on the slopes of the far hills. After the
sun was up and the work of the day had begun, when
people who could see raiders for themselves and give the
alarm were everywhere, Uri would come to our camp from
his lookout, lean his spears in a tree, and drink a cup of tea
with us.

Often during those rests of his, he would discuss America. As if to escape for a few moments, he liked to think of
bounty in the United States, and he would ask rhetorically:
"Is there hunger there? Is there raiding? Not in America.
There, everything is good. People eat, then they sleep.
Food, then sleep. Food, and sleep. But in Dodoth there is
raiding, strife, and hunger. That is what we know."

Because of Uri's willingness to acknowledge the advantages of certain customs found in other countries, at least
some members of his family were the exception to his
statement, and did not know raiding, strife, and hunger.
These were the family of his son Carlo, who kept the store.
One day in Kalapata, when the rain was pelting down, Uri
invited us to take shelter in that store. There was not much
for sale inside the little room, which, with its thick mud
walls, was cold and dim and noisy, for the rain banged on

the tin roof and ten spearmen who had crowded in behind us to keep dry spoke at the top of their lungs. In the front of the store was a counter of poles imbedded in the dirt floor, supporting board shelves backed by cardboard. On the top shelf was an ancient, battered, cobweb-covered scale. On the shelf below were two worn bicycle tires and two exhausted inner tubes. From a nail in the shelf's edge hung five strings of beads, and on the shelf below was a card in which twenty or thirty needles were thrust in a circle. Behind the needles was a razor blade, and from the edges of the card hung ten twists of thread. Beside the card was a bag of cellophane-wrapped candies, ten bars of Lifebuoy soap in frayed red wrappers, and a bottle of a patent medicine called Malaria Mixture. That was all. High on the mud wall behind the counter, someone named SIMEON had written his name repeatedly in different color chalk. A friend of Uri's, one of the spearmen, asked for the little glass shard of mirror that Carlo kept under the counter, and while standing there in the shelter, tried on a necklace. Uri indicated the things on the counter to us, and then with a polite gesture indicated his son, who, fully dressed, lay in the corner asleep. His bed was fifteen or twenty gunnysacks full of finger millet on a rack up off the floor. The millet was grown by his wife, the produce of her field, and it had been kept so dry under the tin roof that it crackled when the young man rolled over.

I asked Uri if the millet would last his son throughout the year. "Yes," said Uri, the provident father who had not been reluctant to exchange old ways for new. "More than a year."

One of Uri's breaks with tradition seemed less advantageous. It involved the field adjacent to his house, the field Uri had set aside for his own use. When Uri and his sons

first cut brush to stand in a huge circle for the fence, people
assumed that he was laying out his gardens for the following year. Ordinarily people never fence off pasture, which
is public, for those who live near it to use. But the section
Uri had fenced was a place he would otherwise have cultivated. It was as if Uri had forgone a field to make the
private pasture, not a bad idea if the Turkana riders, made
desperate by their own famine, were to occupy the forest
where Dodoth cattle usually grazed. Such a plan was sure
to rouse jealousy among the people whose cows were un-
protected. When the neighborhood realized what Uri was
doing, some people became anxious and furious. Among
them was Lopore, who, when he felt threatened by the
troubled times, became very conventional and tried to
make other people keep the rules. His anxious tempers
crept up on him, though, and one night he argued with
Uri.

It was a radiant night. The rain had stopped for a few
hours, and far away in the sky the moon shone in the tumbled clouds. Six women, the wives of Uri and Lopore, were
threshing grain together at Lopore's threshing floor. Uri
and Lopore had retired to Rengen's little kitchen, where,
stripped to the skin, they sat by a fire and took turns swig-
ging beer from a jar so big and heavy it was hard to lift.
And all the time Lopore's heart was rankling; shortly after
midnight his angry voice rang around the hills, and shortly
after that, Uri with dignity went home.

Next day, Lopore's cows broke through the fence into
Uri's field. Uri came down from his etem and angrily drove
the cattle back to Lopore's. This in turn infuriated Lopore.
"Am I the herdboy that you blame me?" he cried.

Uri said coldly: "Keep your cattle out of my field, or I
will beat you."

"Am I your wife?" Lopore cried. Enraged, he was like a madman, like a bull. When Uri went home, Lopore vented his rage on the woman who was his wife and Uri's sister, Nabilo. Twice she talked him out of beating her, and at last she called on Mora, her brother-in-law, to take her side.

"People who fight turn into dogs," said Mora, reminding Lopore of the proverb. "There was a time when you, Uri, and I all lived in the same home. Never did we quarrel. Each went to his own bed at night in peace." These remarks brought an end to the fighting, but though Uri and Lopore never spoke about the pasture, the disagreement was not resolved. Every evening just before dark, the little girls of Lopore's house would appear at the far side of the pasture and break some sticks off the fence for their firewood, while at home Lopore waited for someone to make an issue of what they did. But Uri's family found it easier to repair the fence in the daytime, and no issue was made. "How is this sort of quarreling? Is it good or bad?" Uri once asked. "Rain is causing this. Where is the good sun?" he said.

Perhaps a fear of jealousy caused most other people to cope with the trouble in more conventional ways. Because begging is conventional, before the month was out little processions of begging women were afoot around Dodoth. When a woman's fields are burned or washed away, she begs a bowlful of grain from this neighbor and another bowlful from that neighbor, as she needs it. Charity is an important virtue in Dodoth, though it is not always practiced; charity to one's neighbors is more important still. A woman never knows when she may be begging, so she usually gives, and in years of good harvest, no one is altogether without grain. But the year we were there some women, assessing their harvests, realized that any grain they gathered would not last the year, and foreseeing the paths of

Dodoth lined with other women begging from people who
had nothing to give, took baskets and went begging in advance. A sad procession of two co-wives, the mother of one,
and some of their young daughters came to Morukore with
empty bowls. They came from afar; I had never seen them.
They stopped in the wet grass near Nabilo's stile. Nabilo
and Rengen, who were just sitting down to prepare a stew
in the field house, recognized them and greeted them politely but distantly, knowing why they were there. "Awé,"
said the first of the co-wives when she learned she would
receive nothing from Regen and Nabilo. The little girls
long before had guessed the outcome, and to spare themselves the shame of being refused, had started away along
the path. The two wives followed slowly. The very old lady
was the last to understand.

A second conventional means of coping with anxiety is to
find someone to attack. By the end of the month, there
seemed to be many witches. We heard reports of witches
visiting this or that dwelling, and Lomotin visited many a
court and cattle pen to festoon their poles with charms.
Whether the anxiety prevalent in the country prompted
witches to set out or caused householders to see witches
where there perhaps were none is hard to say. I thought
the latter possible when a man privately suggested that I
avoid a certain neighbor and shoot any hyena that came
toward our camp from the direction of that neighbor's
house. He then described, without naming, several of the
neighbors, until the image of one of them creeping near our
camp at night was overpowering. I remembered a time not
long before when the neighbor in question was testing the
balance of his spear. He had held the blade poised by his
mouth, which smiled the sweetest, deadliest of smiles,
showing his white teeth and pink tongue. As he smiled, his

eyes gleamed. Later the neighbor in question came to ask me if it was true that he had been accused of witchcraft. I tried to say I didn't think so, but he brushed my remarks aside. "What does it matter what you think?" he asked with great bitterness. "I am not going to marry into your family nor will your children marry into mine. If L—— thinks I am a witch, so be it. Let him say so if he likes."

Quarrels developed at that season, quarrels which, if the harvest had been bountiful and the raiding had ceased, might never have begun. A man we knew was stoned until his face was unrecognizable and his scalp split open because of a misunderstanding about his goats. Lopore, too, made trouble in the neighborhood. Once, while traveling with him, I saw him lose his temper when he found an old man washing his hair in the river near the spirit pool. The man was using a cake of soap and white bubbles were spiraling in the current under the trees. Lopore spoke so loudly to the old man that he started and the soap slipped out of his hand. Trembling, he groped for it while Lopore raised his stick, but instead of striking, Lopore turned on his heel and walked away, shouting rebukes. The old man waited until Lopore was far from him before daring to bend and rinse his head. As you must not cut wood in a sacred grove, Lopore explained later, you must not defile a pool. He seemed slightly apologetic, though I am sure he did the right thing. After all, the old man was risking the anger of the spirits that control the rain. But I think Lopore regretted his harshness, for somewhat later he told me: "I am an old man now, the age of your father. I assure you that this has been a very difficult year."

The Protectorate government contributed to the difficulties. By October of the year that followed, Uganda would be independent. The Protectorate government in

Moroto, wanting to leave Karamoja Province in order, with the raiding in control and the famine ended, began to pressure the Jackaits and Mkungus to collect taxes and fines imposed for raids. Meetings were held under the thatched Kaabong courthouse, and the town runner, the man who lived in the rocks in the Kaabong hills, was sent with messages to the Jackaits and Mkungus in the far corners of the country. So in December, groups of Jackaits' police went through the country to collect from the people the overdue taxes and fines. Those taxes and fines which could not be paid in money were collected in cattle. Perhaps the Jackaits and Mkungus, along with the rest of the population, were afraid that the Turkanas would take so many cattle that none would be left to pay fines. Or so it seemed, for everyone said the tax collection was exceptionally severe that year. One day in the early part of December, a group of policemen, one of whom had a rifle, marched up to Uri's house early in the morning and at gunpoint confiscated some of his cows. It was a fine, they said, for a raid the Dodoth had mounted on the Jie ten months before. Uri himself was not suspected of having participated in the raid, but the stolen cattle had been traced to his district. As a householder, he was held partly responsible, whether he had joined the raid or not. But then it developed that the raid had not originated in Lokoki at all, but in Kaabong. Uri was registered as a taxpayer in the Kaabong District and thus incurred the responsibility anyway, though he had not lived there for thirty or forty years.

In order to take the cattle, the police had pointed the gun at Uri and his sons, which had terrified the little children and Uri's two elderly wives. There was nothing Uri could do about it afterwards, except to get very drunk. At the end of the afternoon, still drunk, he came to our camp.

There he accepted a cup of tea and began to throw his sandals. The future reflected his bleakness, for he saw the Turkanas passing to the west, and a person dead. Presently he stopped throwing and told us that in fact the Turkanas had already come to the west but had been met on the ridge by Dodoth scouts and warriors and had been stopped for a time. "Send us guns," he asked, "when you go to America. The government is our enemy, but there is no District Commissioner there." He then showed us with gestures how prisoners are hanged and how people are tied lying face down, their hands bound to one post, their legs to another. He showed us how people cry when they are beaten. He spoke of the enemy and of the people who were killed by raids, and he said once again: "In America everything is good. People eat, then sleep, food then sleep, a blissful life. I have heard that in America there are black people too, who will send us rifles. Can this be so?"

Carlo, the young man who kept the store in Kalapata, was also made bitter by the confiscation of his father's cows, and he too was drunk when we saw him on the following day. It was early in the evening. He was passing our camp on his walk from Kaabong home to Kalapata. When Uri, from our camp, saw his drunken son, he called out to him not to go on to Kalapata but to spend the night with him. Carlo stopped and turned when he heard his father, and when he saw us looking at him, he came directly to our camp. He was dressed in a pair of khaki shorts, a ragged sweater, and a pair of knee socks which were sagging down. His eyes were bloodshot and his face angry. As if we had taken his father's cattle, he came to stand very close to us. His English was hard to understand. He had been to a political rally in Kaabong, he said, where they had discussed the two parties in Uganda. One of them was black-red-black, and one was white and green. "Black-red-black," he said, was "Africans who are black, red which is blood. But Africans have black blood," he said. "The green and white is green for grass and white for the Europeans. By this sign the Europeans can go away or stay if they like. No force, no fighting. And there are two countries," he said, "America and Russia. At the meeting in Kaabong, we were deciding which one was right."

As Carlo talked, his uncle, Mora, and his father, Uri, listened to him anxiously. They heard the anger in his voice but, not knowing English, did not understand what he said. Uri gave me a look as if to say: "He's been drinking," and when Carlo and Uri went up the hill together, Mora looked at me closely to see if I was frightened, for Mora was a very kindly person. When Mora learned what Carlo had been saying, he looked both puzzled and relieved.

One thing which may have been discussed at the meeting but which Carlo had not mentioned was the tax reform proposed by the Protectorate government. It was to go into effect that year and was to affect almost everyone. Since the turn of the century in Dodoth, the tax had been a head tax, the only tax the people had ever known. Now there was to be a graduated property tax. Under the new system, a rich man would pay more than a poor man, each being assessed by their Jackait on the number of their cattle, sheep, and goats. Storekeepers, too, would be assessed according to the bulk of goods for sale in their stores. One day in December, a government representative came in a Land-Rover over the muddy roads through the rain and flooding rivers, from Moroto to Jie, and from Jie to Kaabong, to inform the people of the law. In Kaabong he spoke with the appointed chiefs and subchiefs and then went on to Kalapata, where he hoped to find the Mkungu,

Uri's son-in-law, who would be responsible for collecting the new taxes there. But knowing that the new tax would be unpopular, that for many people in Lokoki and Kalapata districts, the graduated property tax would mean a raise in taxes, and hoping to avoid the issue and the blame, Uri's son-in-law went on a little trip, and when the government representative from Moroto arrived in Kalapata, the Mkungu was not there. The government representative went back to Kaabong—a difficult trip, as the road was almost washed away—and there waited to see the Mkungu, who he was sure would return. But the Mkungu did not return to Kalapata until the government representative, unable to wait any longer, had returned to Moroto. Even so, if the people in Kalapata thought they could escape the new tax by not knowing about it, they too were wrong. A few days later the Jackait of Kaabong surprised Kalapata with a visit, and held a meeting then and there.

It might have been better for the people of Kalapata if they had discussed the new tax with the government representative rather than with the Jackait because the representative was a young, warmhearted man from Karamoja, whereas the Jackait was a harsh old man who knew very well that the taxpayers would try to deceive him. The meeting between the Jackait and the householders was held on the bare earth in front of the Kalapata dhukas under the trees, but after the meeting, householders who had been there met again at Lopore's etem on the rocks to discuss the matter with householders who had not attended. As the men talked, they whittled and chopped, for they all enjoyed woodworking. At Kalapata, it was said, the Jackait of Kaabong addressed all the Mkungus of the northern part of his area. Uri's son-in-law, having come

back to Kalapata, was there; so was the Mkungu of the
Teutho—the hunters and gatherers who lived in the woods.
The Teutho, being of a small (if undetermined) number,
have no chief or Jackait. No one even knows how they are
ruled or knows exactly who their government-appointed
Mkungu is in relation to his people. Usually he was as
evasive as the rest of the Teutho and had made so few
public appearances that many people at the meeting could
not remember ever having seen him before. He had come
with a specific mission, however, which was to plead the
case of his people with the Jackait. The householders at
Lopore's etem said that because the Teutho were mobile,
even slippery, and therefore hard to count, and because not
even the Dodoth knew many of the Teutho personally, the
Teutho had been assessed collectively and were together
responsible for raising money for their tax. Their Mkungu
begged the Jackait to change this: his people had no cattle, no jobs, and no money, and therefore could not pay.
But the Jackait was not moved by the Teutho Mkungu.
"The Teutho have only been assessed at eighty shillings,"
the Jackait had said, "and yet they cannot pay it. In that
case, you must pay for them all."

"You are just against me," said the Teutho Mkungu.

Other amusing injustices, according to the householders,
were done that day. Ten miles south of Kalapata, where
there was a fork in the road, stood a little dhuka all alone.
The dhuka had four mud walls, a door, and a tin roof, but
there was nothing inside it. The owner, finding the prices
for store goods high and the demand for them low, had
abandoned his shop and returned to pastoralism, and now
nothing came in or out of the little building except lizards
through cracks in the wall. But to the intense amusement

of the householders gathered on Lopore's rocks, the Jackait had increased the taxes of the dhuka-keeper "because he had a store."

"Four walls and a roof," said Lopore laughing, "and he must pay more."

The comedy of this had everyone laughing. When the joke got stale, the men began to laugh at Lopore's small and kindly in-law, Bilo, who aghast at the unfairness of the Jackait had begged him to change his mind. But the Jackait's clerks got angry at Bilo and threatened to beat him, and in the etem a large man, acting the clerk's part for the amusement of the gathering, caught Bilo by the arm.

But the funny aspects of the meeting did not long sustain the householders. More and more men ceased laughing and became grave or severe, and by and by, the man who had married Lopore's daughter said to Lopore: "If you are wise, you will give your cattle one by one to your friends to keep for you. Then you pay nothing."

A middle-aged neighbor who was preparing to marry his third wife, a daughter of Nakade, asked the gathering: "What about a man preparing for marriage? You have to pay as though you owned all those cows, yet when your father-in-law gets them, you have nothing. If the Mkungu comes to count my cattle, I'll say that they're not mine— they belong to Nakade."

Lopore said: "I may be marrying again, too."

But the neighbor was too absorbed to hear this announcement. "How can I pay forty shillings," he asked the gathering, "when some of my cattle are to be given away?"

Uri, wearing a cape and a chain belt, was walking slowly up the hill to join the men on the rock. "Hide your cows," said the neighbor to Uri.

"How can you hide what is seen by many people?" asked

Uri. "And if you give your cows away, where will you get milk?"

"The government is trying to finish cattle here," said Lopore gravely. "If you have to pay tax, you have to sell an ox to get the money. And the more cows you have, the more the government wants to take them away."

At the beginning of December, for about ten days, the rain seemed to be stopping. The clouds which would build on the horizon would dissolve into a high fog by the end of the day. The weather was hot and the earth steaming. As far as I know, the only wedding held in the entire district of Lokoki during that year of deprivation was held during those few days. The rich man Lokorimoe had a party attended by most of the neighboring householders, and also by a flautist from Acholi, a nice young man named Marco Pole. The rich man Akou, whose camp was near Mora's house, also had a party. Though he himself was not able to attend, he gave a barren cow for the neighbors to slaughter, roast, and eat. The neighbors slaughtered the cow in a clump of bushes, roasted it in a clearing nearby, and gave the cow's cooked, blackened head and some of its ribs to some of the rich man's wives. We attended both these parties and many private parties in people's homes as well. We drank beer from huge calabashes, from cups, from pots, from small enamel basins, beer hot enough to burn our throats, intoxicating in the hot sun. The Acholi flautist Marco Pole, who attended most of these parties in Dodoth attire (though he put on European clothes when he went home), was a Catholic and would cross himself before taking a swallow of beer.

And then one day, because we would soon be starting home and wanted to repay the people of the neighborhood in some part for their extreme kindness and hospitality, we too gave a party. We invited forty people, but more than one hundred came. Like the rich camp owner who lived near Mora, we did not try to serve beer to the large gathering; our feast was a bull and a barren cow. That we bought both from the neighborhood was welcome because people needed money for the new tax. Mora sold us the bull and thus got money which he would otherwise not have been able to raise. A young man named Rogo who was in trouble because of delinquency with taxes sold us the cow. Before sunrise on the morning of the party, he made a point of driving his herd by our camp. As the herd appeared out of the mist, he chased the cow toward us. She was already paid for, but lanky and tall, she was trying hard to rejoin the rest of the herd. "How can we keep her?" we asked Rogo. "Kill her," he said. "Bring me a spear." We did. The cow's eyes rolled with terror as Rogo's little brothers chased her around and as the herd boys from various passing herds helped make a barrier of arms. Even though Rogo needed money badly, he did not want to kill her. He feinted a long time before stabbing her with his spear. Then all at once he stuck her in the side. Moaning and struggling she fell, but she was not a very strong cow and did not rise again. Even so, it took her a long time to die, and Rogo did not like watching. To hasten the process, he plunged the spear up and down in her wound, which caused her to cry. Our son, two years old, also cried. "Don't let them kill her," he wept, but no one listened, for children in Dodoth do not act this way. A few Dodoth boys his age were looking on in silence with blank, emotionless eyes.

While the cow was being skinned, Mora sent his two sons after the bull, which they chased up to the camp and speared. It stood trembling, blood coming from its nostrils, for twenty minutes, watched by very few, for most people were busy with the cow, whose muscles were still twitching. The bull moaned and lay down. Mora's son pulled its hind quarters around to get it in a better position for skinning, but it got up again and stood, head drooping, for ten minutes more. When it lay down again, someone pushed it over. Then no one paid it much attention, and the next thing we knew, it too was being skinned.

Large numbers of people began to arrive. Men came in groups, men came with their wives, and older women came with their younger co-wives and daughters. Householders of Kalapata and Lokoki came, many dressed in their finest clothes. Some wore plumed, feathered wigs, some wore immense, heavily plumed ceremonial headdresses and ceremonial leopard-skin capes. A few schoolboys came from far up north at Kamion; Uri's son Carlo came with townsmen friends from Kaabong. In the crowd I saw the Jackait of Loyoro, a few policemen, a few askaris, a few teachers from one of the mission schools, and I thought I even saw the Teutho Mkungu. Lomotin, the emuron, came by himself and sat under a tree at a distance. Presently almost every important person in the neighborhood had joined him there. Perhaps in the crowd there were even witches— there usually are in troubled times, the Dodoth say; their malevolent influence accounts for the absence of little children. That day the babies were the only ones not present; they were kept safe at home.

Before the sun was high, the bull and half the cow were already cooked and eaten. Dark clouds were looming nearer and nearer, and the party, which had begun pleasantly enough, suddenly took on a note of emergency as people hurried to finish eating before it rained.

By ten o'clock the clouds were over us and people were

bolting down the last bites and running for shelter, and by the time the heavy rapid storm was over, the guests had disappeared. At that point Lokorimoe, the rich man who lived on Kailele, arrived. It had taken him two hours with his swollen ankles and his rheumatism to walk from his house to our camp. He sat on his stool to rest himself and to wipe the perspiration from his eyes. We thought he would be there alone, but before long the other guests began to return, from Uri's house, from Lopore's house, from under the tent flaps in our camp, where they had taken shelter, and the dancing began. In no time, the clearing around our camp was crowded with dancers who formed in two close-packed circles, one for men of twenty to thirty, for boys and children, for little girls, and for the young men's fian-cées, lovers, and brides, all of whom danced vigorously and beautifully, groups of the girls leaping with each of the men. The other circle was formed by the older men, the householders, and their elderly wives, who held hands and swayed from side to side very decorously as the old men leaped on their spindly legs. When one of the circles would become too large, another circle would form, and by the end of the day there were many circles. Everyone was dancing—Lopore and his neighbors and their wives were dancing; Nakade was dancing; Lomotin was dancing with his knobby knees. I danced, my children danced, Tom and Kirsti danced, Tim Asch danced; David our interpreter, and our cook were dancing; the schoolboys were dancing; the police—using their rifles to gesture as men use clubs—were dancing; the Jackait of Loyoro and his askaris and the man who was possibly the Teutho Mkungu were dancing too. When the sun went down and the vultures who had settled in the trees began to drop heavily to the ground, the singing was at its loudest and most vigorous, and the sunset made the dust a pink cloud. After dark, people began to go home. The teachers rode away on their bicycles, the little schoolboys, having formed one of their processions, started off along the road, and lines of householders and their great families took the various paths. The man who may have been the Teutho Mkungu vanished as though into thin air, and the Jackait of Loyoro, with his retinue, took up their bedrolls and went home with Uri.

In the morning, the Jackait and his police came back from Morukore and threw their bedrolls down beside the road. The Jackait then sat on a bedroll while the two policemen went off past Lopore's house and fields and crossed the plain to the home of Rogo's family at the foot of Kailele hill. Rogo's family had not paid its taxes, and the policemen were going to confiscate the family cows.

Rogo was young to be a householder. He and his brothers had formed a compound dwelling which included Rogo's wife and baby and his younger brother, Kalingemala who was gathering cattle to give for a bride. Neither Rogo nor Kalingemala had felt he could afford to sell cattle during hard times in order to pay taxes, but this had been a poor decision. The two young men now owed not only taxes, but a fine.

When the policemen came, Rogo had the money we had paid him the day before, and gave that to save his cattle, but when the policemen asked for Kalingemala's money, he had to say he had none.

It was very early. Mist still hung in a cloud over the fields, and through the damp grass, the cattle were just starting to pasture. Within minutes, the police had surrounded Kalingemala's cattle—he had eight head—and were driving them toward the Jackait near our camp. Just after sunrise they arrived at the road. Behind them walked

Kalingemala, who forked off the path into our camp and, very discouraged, threw himself down. Kalingemala had helped us build our fence and put our tents up, and had asked us to save his salary for him. He wanted it now. When we gave it, he took it to the policemen at the roadside, who were already employing a passerby as herdsman to take the confiscated cattle to Kaabong. The little cattle did not know what was happening and were gazing around through the misty air among the trees. The policeman, who wore a red fez, an army coat, puttees, and rubber-tire sandals and who carried a spatter gun which had a huge, open magazine that could hold several shells and fire in a burst, pocketed the money Kalingemala gave him and instructed the herdsman to proceed toward Kaabong.

At this point, the Jackait arrived, turning up his collar against the chilly air. Several early risers arrived with him to see what he was doing, roaming the country just after dawn. Usually in the cold morning people crouch and hug themselves, but Kalingemala, who wore only a cloth cape and had gooseflesh, stood up straight. The policeman gave the money to the Jackait, who counted it, then said to Kalingemala: "This is not enough." To the assembled people he said: "He owes another thirty-one shillings for 1959."

"Is this true?" we asked Kalingemala, and Rogo, who had followed him, answered: "It is. Kalingemala gave thirty-one shillings to our brother in 1959 to pay the tax then, but our brother used it for something else."

Kalingemala stood apart from the gathering, beside his little cows. He was twenty or so, with a young, rugged face, a man so tall that the backs of the little cows hardly came to his waist. His bones were large, his hands were broad and muscular, and his fist could almost hide a cow's ear. He stood very still, thinking as he stroked the little cattle. Presently he brightened and asked if we would buy his spears. We would, we said, and he ran home to get them. He was gone a long time. "Be sure they don't take my cattle," he said to me as he was leaving. "I will," I said and went to stand with the herd. The Jackait and the policemen had joined Rogo at a tiny roadside fire of dry twigs. Meanwhile, the confiscated cattle were slowly drifting into Uri's fenced-off field. "What cattle are these?" we heard Uri shout from behind the trees.

"Government cattle," said the Jackait.

"The government can't keep cattle in my field," said Uri. "Get them out." The neighbors who had gathered exchanged glances, but no one said anything until Uri cried: "I will beat this man!"

"Beat him," called one of the neighbors enthusiastically. The Jackait, the policeman, and their herder, sensing trouble, had got to their feet, and the little herd, chased by Uri, came drifting back toward us. The Jackait, the policeman, and the two herders then started toward the road, driving the cattle before them. "Wait," we called, "where are you going?"

"It is getting late," said the Jackait. "Rain is coming and we have to go all the way to Kaabong." We urged them to wait, saying that Kalingemala would probably not be long. The Jackait and the policeman sat down uneasily in the middle of the road. Rogo had said nothing, but he ducked his head and looked at the policeman in a most sinister manner, smiling a little, bitter smile. The policeman looked around uncomfortably. The Jackait, jingling the money in his pocket, looked up at the sky. He seemed afraid of nothing, least of all Rogo, whom he presently sent to look for Kalingemala. Just then we saw Kalingemala running back, two spears in his hands, and when he arrived, all out of breath, we went straight into camp, where we paid him for the two spears. Kalingemala was extremely happy. He shook everyone's hand and smiled and, taking the money, ran out and thrust it at the Jackait. The Jackait took it, examined it carefully, put it in his pocket, then said to Kalingemala: "But this is not enough. You owe thirty-one shillings more as fine for two years at fifteen fifty a year." Kalingemala's smile faded; there was a momentary flash of disbelief; and then, as it came to him that his money was gone, that he had nothing else to sell, and that he was still going to lose his cattle, he suddenly turned, marched into our camp, and came back in a moment, rage and despair in his face, and the two spears in his hands. Running into the little herd, he confronted his cattle with upheld arms to make them wheel and trot home.

"The guards are off his spears," someone shouted, and so they were. We could see the razor edges of the blades. Kalingemala and his cattle came toward us, and the policeman efficiently and calmly stepped to one side of the little crowd, fished in his pocket, and filled the magazine with shells. He worked the bolt, filled the chamber, and calmly raised the gun. Kalingemala saw this. His eyes filled with tears and a look of deep, black despair came upon his face. Then, bare spears raised, he ran straight for the policeman. Everyone shouted at once.

"We'll pay his fine," we shouted to the Jackait.

"Take the shells out of the rifle," said Tom Johnson to the policeman in English. But the policeman paid no attention; he did not speak English. Tom walked up beside him. "Take the shells out of that rifle," he said again. The policeman could not help but guess his meaning, and miraculously he obeyed. In the pause, Carlo took the two spears from Kalingemala and gave them to me and I stuck them in the fence. But feelings still ran high. We found thirty-one shillings and gave them to the Jackait, who paid no attention to the money, but insisted: "What about a man who shows me his unsheathed spears?" His voice, as he spoke, shook with emotion. And he was right. Dodoth do not raise their spears against each other, ever. It is reserved strictly for foreigners, aliens, *ngimoe*. Kalingemala sat down trembling amid his cows, who began to graze.

"Take the money and go," came Uri's voice from the little forest. All this time, he had remained directly behind Kalingemala, in the line of fire. I persuaded the Jackait to sign a receipt for the money. Coming to himself again, he said he preferred to sign with his thumbprint. He washed his thumb with his tongue, dried his thumb on his pants, and let me ink it for him with a ball-point pen. His print made, he stood erect and called his men together. They took their bright bedrolls and rifles, stood, and were ready. Now Kalingemala recovered: "Look for me in Kaabong," he said, "where I will come to kill you."

"Never mind that," we all said, "go and get your cows." The herdsmen, who seemed to have misunderstood everything, had collected the cattle again, and were trotting them toward the road, but Rogo was after them, and in a moment we saw him far away among the trees, cutting Kalingemala's free cattle from the herd. Kalingemala followed slowly, watching from a distance as his brother settled things with the herdsmen. Rogo and the herdsmen discussed the cattle calmly while the Jackait and the policeman went to the road by another path and Kalingemala stood among the wet trees of the landscape, absently gaz-

ing at the figures of cattle and people moving by. It made
me sad to see him standing alone among the trees, with his
strong shoulders, his large heavy head and hands; he
seemed young, a little clumsy, and exceedingly brave. But
his strength and bravery might have been for nothing, and
if another year comes and he, for all his honor, does not
have the money for his tax, he may risk his life once more
for his cattle and be killed.

That marked the end of talk about taxes in Kalapata and
Lokoki districts, and also the end of the short dry spell.
After that, the rain began again in torrents and came down
both night and day. Also the Turkanas, who seemed to have
taken a vacation, began to raid once more. Two nights
after the episode with Kalingemala, the women went back
to pounding their bulrush and the men to looking after
their herds, and three nights after, we went to visit Lopore
and found him in his etem with his spear. It was evening.
The sun in the far distance shone red behind the thousand
little wraiths of vapor that were rising from the land like
smoke. Lopore, facing the valley with his spear on his
shoulder, seemed preoccupied.

"Will there be more rain?" I asked him.

"It's bad to predict the weather," he answered absently.
"Who can talk to the rain?"

Nabilo came out of the dwelling to greet me, but stopped
when she saw Lopore.

"What are you doing there?" she asked suspiciously,
squinting her eyes to see.

"Nothing," said Lopore.

"Turkanas? It's evening now. They'll find the cows at
home," she said. He didn't answer for a moment.

"They won't come," he said finally. "They'll be tired and
stiff. They've been in the forest two days and two nights in

the rain. We've been at home beside fires, under cover. If they come now, they'll be killed."

"Then why are you waiting?" asked Nabilo.

Lopore sighed. He turned, and once again began to look out over the valley. Nabilo waited behind him for a moment, then walked past him to the door of the dwelling, ducked, and went in.

CHAPTER EIGHT

Turkanas

It usually happened that a Turkana raiding party entering Dodoth came by way of a topographical feature which, as far as I know, has no name in English. In Dodoth the word is *ngapulei*. These are the involutions of the flat Rift Valley between the precipitous slopes of the Escarpment hills. Some involutions penetrate Dodoth, and by keeping to those ngapulei that end near settlements, the raiders can get near their quarry while remaining on their own ground, as it were, unseen.

There was an involution near Kamion in the northern part of Dodoth, long since evacuated by all but three Dodoth families and now part of the vast expanse of wilderness reaching over the Uganda border into the Sudan. Except for the three families, the only other human inhabitants of those lonely forests were the Catholic schoolmaster of a tiny mud schoolhouse, his twenty little pupils, and a band of Teuthos, who had a little village near the school.

The village was unoccupied most of the time. Once, while driving up to Kamion we stopped to see the village, which was very near the road. It was a puzzling mixture: there were several square courtyards containing what must have been Teutho houses, rectangular and pitched-roofed, with built-in seats and sleeping platforms; then also round courts like Dodoth women's kitchens, and half-spheroid thatches like Turkana women's domes. I wondered if Turkanas might be staying there. The Teutho all were gone.

From time to time, various other groups of people stayed near Kamion in the wild hills. One such group was a company of British Army Engineers. They camped in an immense brushwork while building a road leading over the Escarpment cliffs into the Rift Valley so that escaping raiders could no longer simply vanish with impunity over the Escarpment's rim. Though the engineers did no fighting, the raiders learned of their presence and avoided them, so they were there alone. The crowd of pink, pale men, the rumbling of their trucks, and the blasts of dynamite that the construction workers would set off caused the Teutho once again to leave their homes. I think, however, that some Teuthos would come back from time to time, perhaps at night, to harvest their tomatoes. But before the road was finished, while it was still a rocky slope so high and steep that only the most courageous of the engineers would dare to drive it, there was trouble in Kenya, in Aden, and in Berlin; the British engineers were recalled, the Teutho became aware of the silence and returned to their homes, and once more the Turkana raiders climbed the old paths up the Escarpment. Once at this time we visited Kamion and on one of the most northern promontories, from which one could see the huge stretch of the wild valley below, we found a fire, the coals still hot. It was a little camp fire

abandoned moments before. Whoever had left it had probably assumed that we were police. We assumed that the
Turkanas had left it and, lest they shoot us, ran away as
fast as we could go.

In early December the Turkanas mounted a raid so large
that if one could have stood on the promontory to see the
files of men climbing the hill, one would have thought
them an army. They must have climbed at night and during the next day sent a group, perhaps an arm of the formation, all the way across northern Dodoth to the western
border at Napore. The other arm of the formation went
south to attack predetermined places in the north-south
settlement line, the southernmost point of attack being a
place called Koputh, south of Kaabong. During the raid,
many Dodoth were killed at Koputh, among them a baby
who was pinned to the ground by a spear. Many dwellings
were burned when the western branch of the formation
attacked at Napore. Out there, though, a Dodoth woman
killed a Turkana, spearing the nape of his neck as it appeared in her tiny door. During this phase of the raid, more
than a dozen people were killed and more than a hundred
cattle stolen. By studying the footprints of the raiding force
after it departed, it was estimated that the Turkanas were
almost one hundred strong.

After that, a second group, a detachment of the King's
African Rifles, came to occupy the woods. Their presence
not only would protect the empty country against occupation by Turkana raiders and herdsmen, but would provide
a readily available defending force which, upon learning of
a raid, could give chase right away. The K.A.R. built a
large and sprawling camp near Kalapata, with truck tracks
everywhere and little khaki tents pitched on the flat spots,

the guy wires festooned with drying socks. The soldiers themselves seemed extraordinary. They came from all over East and Central Africa and seemed to have been chosen partly for size, for they were all huge. In a group they looked bigger than they were, for their voices and their jokes were loud, and their gestures expansive. They wore heavy boots into which they bloused their khaki trousers, and they covered their heads and faces with floppy, wide-brimmed hats.

Periodically, the K.A.R. would travel in convoy between Kaabong and Kalapata. The men carried Browning automatic rifles and sat in rows, army style, in the backs of the transport trucks, singing in Swahili. "Nobody can climb Mt. Kenya except for the K.A.R. Jinja," was one of the rollicking, aggressive songs that would float out over the hillsides as the convoy roared along the road, scattering everything in its way. If a river was full, the driver would splash the truck right in, maybe to emerge, dripping, on the far side, maybe to stick fast on the bottom. If they were stuck, a group of the enormous soldiers would leap out, heave the truck up onto the bank again, and climb back in, kicking the tires, banging the metal body with their rifle stocks, and shouting pleasantries to their driver, who would answer with a blast of the horn. These noisy companies gave the impression of being just barely in control. They were never quite in step while marching; some of the men would carry their rifles by the muzzle over their shoulders; and I sometimes had the feeling that it was quite within their power to overcome their sergeant, a short, frail man.

We saw the K.A.R. performing on the day of the Jie Agricultural Fair. Under the aerial cover of a little police plane, which was dropping thunder flashes and parachutes floating down with flares, a group of camouflaged soldiers, crouching over their rifles, gave a demonstration of the K.A.R. in an advance. Firing blanks, the soldiers crossed the mission's playing field, the center of the fair. Kneeling, standing, crouching, crawling, the soldiers advanced under the cover of other soldiers firing over their heads. The Jie spectators, for the excitement of it, were massed at the end of the field, to see what it was like, being charged by the K.A.R. But as the thunder flashes and the little drifting flares, blown by the wind where they were not expected, began to explode over the crowd, panic began. People were jostling and trampling, giving way to the terrifying on-slaught, and in their midst, the soldiers broke through the barrier which the clawing people had formed. Then, in-stead of stopping where the demonstration was to end, the soldiers got carried away by their performance. As if it was the real thing, not a demonstration, the large group of rifle-men swarmed out beyond the fair, and as if they had for-gotten that they were just performing, did not fetch up until they were a quarter of a mile away, out of sight among the trees. I could imagine them attacking and com-pletely overcoming a force of Turkana raiders, then charging beyond them to conquer Kenya as well. With Independence, the K.A.R. became the Uganda Rifles, some sections of which mutinied in 1963.

The K.A.R. established a patrol between the north-south line of habitation and the Escarpment hills. The convoy of trucks would pass us going north in the morning and south at night. If word came that a raid had taken place, the convoys of trucks would go by road as near to the scene as possible, and then the soldiers on foot would fan out in the bush to hunt the raiders. The soldiers, armed with automatic weapons, were fearless, and if the Turkana raiders were afraid of anybody, it was of them. Some Dodoth were afraid of them too, sometimes with good reason. "Don't wear brown," a soldier once said to Lopore. "You could be shot for a Turkana."

Perhaps it was not surprising that there was no real rapport between the Dodoth and the soldiers. Though the country seemed full of soldiers, the householders continued to stay in their lookouts and the young men continued scouting. If the rumors of a raid came, or if the scouts found the footprints of a raiding party, they would tell other Dodoth, but not the soldiers.

One afternoon, far out on the orchard plain, I met a scout who had seen the Turkana. A small raiding party was massing in the north, he said, and he was on his way to warn the district. He was a young man, very slender. His weapons were a leather shield and two spears, one for throwing, one for sticking at close range if he should need it. I asked him why he did not report the raiders to the K.A.R. He looked surprised, as if he had never thought of it. "I don't know why," he said.

One day, so said the Dodoth, a very large raid was mounting. The raiders were already at the top of the Escarpment and were expected to come somewhere between Kamion and Kalapata. To do what they could, the people of Morukore and the surrounding neighborhoods held a sacrifice beneath the sacred trees on the river. After the elders had drunk the blood of a black ox, reddening their chins and lip plugs, they took the integument and the intestines to the table of the swollen rumen, spread it out, and found little groupings of polyps or tumors or cocci ulcers, each of which meant a death. They must have been

Turkana deaths, for the natural strings in bunches between the integument and the intestine itself were the living Dodoth. Judging from the divination, no great harm was expected to come to Dodoth, and the men crouching around the integument looked on calmly. One man felted another man's hair, and two little boys from the school at Kamion, who had come to our camp in the morning with a note requesting that we take them to Kaabong, were practicing their English. "Wha is dis? Dat is ah chaiah. Wha is dis? Dis is a book. Wha are you doing? I am sitting on da chaiah. Da chaiah. Da chaiah." We asked in a whisper why they were going to Kaabong, and they replied that they were going for cornmeal because a raid was coming and there was no food in the school.

After the divination, prayers were offered for the well-being of Dodoth, and it was decided that two more sacrifices would be held, one in the eastern and one in the western neighborhood. A prayer was offered for the owner of the sacrificed ox and the ceremony came to an end.

The raid, which was expected within a day or two, was delayed. Suspense mounted, then subsided, though no one doubted that in time the raid would come. Then one day a scout reported that the original raiding party in the forest had been joined by fifty new men, and for the first time the Dodoth seemed uneasy. The following evening, a scout reported that the entire party had disappeared—which meant that they had fanned out into the bush. People knew that a raid was imminent, and in every household in the area that night, a few people stayed up to listen.

Early the next morning the schoolteacher from Kamion came bicycling into our camp to tell me that a man who had been speared was waiting for me by the road. We got in the car and, at a bend in the road a mile south of our camp, we found Toperi-peri, the Teutho youngster, all alone beside a fire. He had been speared in the shoulder, and a gaping three- or four-inch wound showed the muscles, red and bulging, under his skin. We helped him into the car. Several Dodoth had also jumped in at the last minute, to profit from Toperi-peri's misadventure and ride to Kaabong, but when they found the car filled with the smell of human meat, a bad, sweet, heavy odor, they asked that the windows be opened and held their hands over their noses. This might have embarrassed Toperi-peri had he not been in so much pain. He was brown with the blood that had dried all over him, and he cradled the elbow of his wounded arm. As we drove, he told us that his attackers were Turkanas, that during the night he had surprised them in their camp, which had not been near the Escarpment, as one might have expected, but in the forest not two miles east of the road. Being a Teutho, Toperi-peri did not have a shield, but only courage and his spear, which, as he said in order to impress the Dodoth passengers, he had flung at the Turkanas. When he was struck in turn, he had picked the spear from his shoulder, thrown it back, and run to a place where he knew he would be safe. There, he began to bleed, and in the dawn he made his way to the roadside, where the teacher found him. Taking a chance that we would help him, he had asked the teacher to tell us.

The jiggling of the car had made his wound bleed again. Though he held the gap shut, blood oozed between his fingers, and at least one woman in the car snickered as she held her nose. After all, the Teutho are inferior to the Dodoth. I was worried about his shoulder and did not try to drive more slowly over bumps and rivers, but rushed toward Kaabong. But the lurching car so pained Toperi-peri that his confident smile became a grimace, and I had to slow down. When we finally reached the dispensary, he seemed faint. We helped him from the car into the dispensary, where he slumped against the wall. There he learned that the dispenser, by law, could not fix him up until the police had first seen him. Leaving Toperi-peri, we rushed in the Land-Rover to the police station and urged a sergeant and the interpreter to come back with us. Toperi-peri spoke both Teutho and Ngadodotho; the interpreter spoke Akarimojong and Swahili; the sergeant spoke Swahili, but wrote his report in English, a statement in the first person singular, signed by Toperi-peri's thumb.

The report itself was moving. It stated that "I, a Teutho, was walking in the bush to the east beyond the mountains looking for honey at night. I came upon a band of armed men. I didn't know if they were Dodoth or Turkanas. It was impossible to tell at night. One threw a spear. It hit me in the shoulder." That was the end of the report. The policeman inked Toperi-peri's thumb and pressed it on the paper, and Toperi-peri, on the cot, lay still.

Meanwhile, the dispenser was trying to clear the dispensary of spectators so he could stitch the wound. His surgery was filled with people who had to be half-pushed out the door, his implements had to be sterilized, and a clean bed had to be made. Meanwhile, Toperi-peri was left alone in the back room, behind a closed door, but when the dispenser was ready and opened the door to call Toperi-peri, he found no one. Toperi-peri had taken the pillowcase to bind his arm, rolled off the cot, slipped through the window, and was gone.

Perhaps he was afraid of the police. Perhaps he was

afraid of the dispenser. Perhaps he was afraid he would be
made to report to the police whether Turkanas or Dodoth
had wounded him. I know that he would rather we had
helped him privately than have taken him to the dispenser
and involved him with the Dodoth, the government, and
the police. He was an independent and a brave young person. I hope that he survived the bleeding, but I can't say
what happened because no one we knew ever saw him
again.

During the next few days rumors of a raid came from
all directions and it became apparent that a raid was massing not in one place, but everywhere. One night in my tent
when I couldn't sleep, panic overcame me and I thought of
moving to Kaabong. Early the next morning I went to
Lopore's house to see what he thought about it, and found
the corridor between the courts and the cattle pen so beautiful with its splendid pink view of the valley in the early
light before the ancient sweeping mountains, with hawks
above in the clear air, that I sat down with his children and
grandchildren as if nothing was wrong. The little baby
Iloshabiet sat in her mother's lap while her mother,
Chuchu, sang this song: "Emoit, ngimoe; emoit, ngimoe."
Enemy, enemies; foreigner, foreigners. In the cattle pen,
Lopore's ten-year-old children were milking the cows,
which Lopore was keeping at home because of the raid.
Torori found a calabash the size of a teacup, which he filled
with milk to share with his sister Chuchu, and when she
raised it to her mouth, a white cabbage moth flew from the
little gourd and landed on her hair. Everything was so
pleasant in Lopore's corridor that I forgot anything was
wrong. But by nine in the morning the alarm was sounding,
and the raid had begun. Torori ran by with two spears and
a shield, his face filled with anger and despair. Everyone

was arming, then leaving; some men were going to protect their herds and herdboy sons, and other men, in small armed groups, were taking the direction in which the enemy were thought to be. Then came word that it was nothing. The Teutho in the woods had started an alarm because they had seen the Turkanas coming, but the alarm supposedly was premature; the Turkanas were still on their way.

In the middle of the morning that terrifying day, a sick woman with three children came by our camp. In the pouch of her cape rode two pumpkins and her baby; by her side ran her daughter, a six-year-old; and in front of her, a skin-covered skeleton, walked her four-year-old son. Dysentery had emaciated him. His flesh was almost gone, and he was so weak he could barely stagger. The sick mother, who had to carry food and a baby, was using a switch to drive the dying boy on. She looked neither right nor left but made the children hurry.

As the little procession passed, Rengen saw them. She was wrapped in her cape, standing almost hidden by the trees, the smoke from her clay pipe rising. Seeing the distress of the children, she strode down the path after the mother to ask her to stop. We, too, ran after Rengen. I asked the woman her name.

"You know me," she said. And so I did, though I had not recognized her, the daughter of Lomotin. When I had first met her, she was well enough, but now, as if a witch were trying his power against her father, her eyes were bright with disease. I offered her food and cocoa.

"I have food," she said. She opened her cape to show me ground millet in a calabash and the two pumpkins in the cloth. I asked where she was going and she answered: "To Kaabong." I offered to drive her, and she accepted, but when she found that we would not be leaving for another hour, she decided not to wait. As we talked, the little skeleton sank to the ground. Harshly she ordered him to his feet again. He cried weakly, but obeyed.

Her little girl spoke up loudly and begged her mother to wait. The mother refused. The little girl then begged her mother to accept the rest and the cocoa, "not for me, for him," she said. Again the mother refused, saying there was no place to stop. I offered her our camp. She didn't answer, but turning the children so that they faced down the path, she made them hurry on. I trotted beside her. "What is your hurry?" I asked.

She looked at me with fatigue and terror. "Isn't there going to be a raid?"

"Stay and have tea with us," I urged her. "I'm driving to Kaabong."

The little girl was getting stubborn. She turned when I said this, and came straight back toward our camp. When her mother called her, she indicated her brother, who had collapsed under a bush, as he did every time the procession halted, and she begged: "Let him have cocoa! Let him have food!" The mother hesitated. She wanted to; she even asked if we had water. I said we did and offered to make tea. The interpreter did not translate the part about the tea. I urged that he do so, which was wrong; her judgment got the better of her and she started away firmly.

She was, the interpreter told me later, under an injunction against witches, strangers, foreigners, and had to escape malevolent influences as well as escape the raid. When I saw that she was determined, I ran back to camp to get the Land-Rover, but by the time I brought the car around, she was already far down the road. I pulled the car up beside her and stopped and opened the door—but only because her little girl begged her so, and finally began to push the little boy toward the door, did the mother consent to get in. They asked to get out by the Kaabong court-house, and as the children climbed down, they looked through the car window at me, wide-eyed but very briefly, as drowning children might look up at a person in a boat.

A meeting was being held in the courthouse. The representative of Dodoth was there, and someone was saying not to raid the Jie. "How can we not?" the Jackait of Kaabong asked, "when the Jie raid in motorcars and use their police and all?"

"Let us move to class the Jie with the Turkana," someone else proposed, "because they raid together." That was all we heard of the meeting. The woman and her children had vanished around a bend in the path, and being afraid the raid would come to our camp in our absence, we had to go home.

We found a group of men assembled at Lopore's lookout in the rocks. Uri was saying: "Remember that the enemies are still coming, even if they don't come today. Some Teutho say that men are not to sleep at home because the enemies are so many. All the enemies are the same as you. So why are you afraid of them? Where are we going to put our cows if we are all afraid?"

A man I didn't know said: "Why can't we go in a group to find them, instead of waiting here? If we find them, we'll fight them instead of letting them come to kill our people."

"Let the women and children go elsewhere while we wait at home to fight them," said Lopore.

"Let us go to the river," someone else said. A sacrifice, I learned, was already in process.

When we went, we found the riverbank like the encampment of a battlefield. Men with spears stood or sat and talked by little campfires. When the group from Morukore arrived, a man came up to tell them that in the intestines of the sacrifice it had been seen that the enemy would come to Morungole and Lotim. The news relieved the minds of the Morukore group, for Morungole and Lotim were rather far away, but just as a precaution, the members of each house divided up when night came, some to stay in the camp by the river, some to guard the home. The people at the river were to stay awake all night, keeping warm beside the fires and consuming the sacrifice.

Early the next morning, we drove to Kalapata to ask the soldiers what was going on. The sergeant said that he doubted a raid was coming; he had heard nothing whatever about it. Then, all of a sudden, before we knew what was happening, the soldiers seized a thin young man who was standing by a dhuka, and flung him in chains. He was a spy, said the sergeant—a spy working as a houseboy for the dhuka-keeper. Perhaps they wanted to question him. I asked the sergeant how he knew the young man was a spy.

"He is a Turkana," said the sergeant.

I asked how the sergeant knew that; the boy wore no ornaments, only a plain black cape and a simple haircut. The sergeant said he knew because of the haircut and the missing teeth in front. "But the Dodoth do that, too," I said. "Well," said the sergeant, exasperated, "he is known personally to everyone here."

When we returned to Morukore, we found that the people were going to sacrifice again. In times of extreme suspense, people sacrifice day after day until the raid is over. Now it seemed that it wouldn't be long; at the river we learned that three young scouts had seen the Turkanas. Some Teutho had pointed them out to the three Dodoth boys at the Escarpment. The Turkanas, who had been reported already in Dodoth, were actually seen in their own country, and were seen from the top of the ridge. Far below, in the bushes of the valley floor, the Turkanas were sitting down and resting, the scouts said. It had been thought that there were a great many Turkanas, but the young scouts said there were only a few. Perhaps the Turkanas also had felt apprehensive or had had a sign that bade them go home.

Before noon, enough people had assembled by the riverbank to hold that day's sacrifice, and by one in the afternoon an ox had been selected. By two o'clock the owner of the ox had been found and persuaded to let his ox be speared, and by three o'clock the sacrifice was being eaten. By four it was gone; by five the speeches had been made, the people of the western neighborhoods had been berated, the prayers had been offered; and by evening it was learned that the raid had already taken place, almost exactly where the first sacrifice had predicted, not quite at Lotim, but west of Kamion.

While the householders of Lokoki were eating their ox, the twenty or thirty Turkanas the scouts had seen had climbed between the cliffs of the Escarpment and up a gradual slope that came to an end in the middle of three dwellings. The dwellings were isolated—it did the householders no good to shout the alarm. The three men and their sons took up their spears, to fight as well as they were able, but the Turkana warriors swarmed over them, stealing all their cattle and spearing one of the householders in the leg and upper arm. The femoral and brachial arteries

were severed—the householder, a man of forty named
Lopole, dragged himself home. His little boy, however, had
been in a sorghum field, and when the raiders sprang out of
the bushes and the fighting began, he ran as fast as his legs
would carry him to the school hut at Kamion. There he
found the teacher (the teacher showed us later) sitting in
front of his door on a bed of portulaca, which was used as a
seat in the midst of whitewashed stones. When the teacher
heard the breathless story, he reached for his bicycle and
pedaled hard to Kalapata, where he told the K.A.R. A pla-
toon of the soldiers got into a truck and set out at once. As
the heavy truck groaned over the ruts in the edge of Kalapata's clearing, several of Kalapata's householders, armed
with spears, caught up with the truck and flung themselves
in with the soldiers, and they all rode slowly to Kamion.
The Turkanas had bundled about a hundred cattle back
down the hill again, and were by now lost from sight in the
valley. The soldiers did not follow on foot, but wheeled
about, drove to the new road over the Escarpment, drove
the dangerous, slippery, steep way, with the truck's body
sometimes almost perpendicular. They had hoped to intercept the herd, but the Turkanas had gone. The tracks of the
cattle at the foot of the slope showed that the herd was
already on its way to the border. The K.A.R., the dhuka-
keepers, and the householders all climbed out of the truck
and ran after them, and came back twenty-four hours later,
dragging the body of a man.

The soldiers had been victorious, they reported to their
officer, who by this time had arrived in another truck. They
had engaged the enemy after dark, had met with no resistance, had recovered all the cattle, and had suffered no
casualties. On the other hand, three Turkanas had been

killed. Two, they said, were eaten by wild animals during
the night, but the third, a man of twenty-five, they had
brought with them for conveyance to Loyoro, where he
could be examined for "tribal markings," to determine from
what part of Turkanaland the raid had sprung. This
seemed futile. The photographer of our group, Tim Asch,
was in the valley when the K.A.R emerged from the bush,
and he photographed the body, which was absolutely
naked, without ornaments or headdress, and had no dis-
tinguishing marks whatever, only some white patches
where his skin had peeled off, and the hole where the bullet
had gone in.

The encounter, said the soldiers, had taken place just
inside the Uganda border. This was lucky for the householders who had lost their cows, because if the encounter
had taken place in Kenya the cows, as a precaution against
hoof and mouth disease, would have to be killed. As it was,
the cows were on their way back through the forest, driven
by a few of the Dodoth. The column of soldiers had hurried
on ahead of the cattle to make the report. That was the end
of the matter. The stiff corpse was flung into the back of
one truck, the soldiers climbed into the back of the other;
both trucks were started and driven up the Escarpment;
and officially the raid was at an end.

Meanwhile, however, the householder Lopole bled to
death in his wife's house. When he was dead his eldest son
lifted him in his arms as one lifts a child, and carried him to
a clump of bushes near the home. There we saw him. We
had gone with the teacher to the scene of the raid to see the
cattle returning, and saw Lopole's round hip and shoulder
among the leaves. He lay on his side, still in the position of
being carried. Everything movable had been taken from his

body, as is the custom, and except for his headdress, he was as he was born.

It was evening. A great pile of sunlit clouds showed over the hills. In an hour night would come, and in another hour, the hyenas, and in the morning, the little brown hawks and vultures. The teacher, a friend of Lopole's, looked up at the sky and sighed, and turned to go home. On the way we saw a herd coming through the bushes. A herdsman with a stricken face followed it blindly. Lopole's cattle were being returned.

Not long after the soldiers came back, and the Dodoth who had accompanied them had a chance to tell their story, I became aware that the episode in the valley was being called "the K.A.R. raid on the Turkanas." I asked around and discovered that a story was slowly spreading, perhaps changing as it went. I was able to find five eyewitnesses, whom I interviewed separately, but on the same day. Four were Dodoth men who had gone from Kalapata, one as a guide to the K.A.R., three who wanted revenge on the Turkanas and took the opportunity when protected by soldiers. The fifth eyewitness was a householder from Kamion who, with a group of neighborhood boys, had given chase on his own.

After the K.A.R. had driven to the foot of the Escarpment, said one of the eyewitnesses, they found the track of the stolen cattle easily because the cattle were being forced to trot and were trampling bushes and grass. The valley there is one of the wildest in East Africa; neither Turkanas nor Teutho nor Dodoth live in it, and from the top of the Escarpment one can look at its limitless gray bush, lying empty to the north and east as far as the eye can see. The soldiers and Dodoth saw many wild animals, especially

lions and buffalo. The lions were all tame, said one informant, and watched the procession unafraid.

After walking for several miles, the soldiers met the
group of Dodoth from Kamion, and the two groups joined.
In the lead went the soldiers, their rifles ready. In the middle went the Dodoth spearmen in Western clothes, and at
the end went the Dodoth in capes, for night was falling and
the soldiers did not want to confuse the Dodoth with the
Turkanas after dark. Unaware that they were being followed, the Turkanas had slackened their pace. Just after
sunset they crossed the international border and an hour
after that they reached their camp, and the soldiers saw the
lights of their fires.

The soldiers sent a scout to see what was happening, and
the scout came back to say that the camp was in an inlet,
one of the ngapulei, the steep sides of which formed a
large, natural pen that kept the cattle from straying. Even
though the spot was in Kenya, the soldiers fell back half a
mile, decided on a formation, and prepared to attack. As a
precaution, they waited for the Turkanas to be disarmed,
and perhaps resting. At nine o'clock—by the watch worn
by one of the soldiers—the soldiers and the Dodoth approached within sight of the Turkana campfires. Some of
my informants, a few paces behind the soldiers, saw people
sitting and eating, with their spears stacked in the trees.
Being over the border, the Turkanas felt safe; their capture
was now a problem for the Kenya police, not the Uganda
soldiers. The soldiers were counting on this. One of my
informants then noticed the gleam of neckrings in the firelight, and tiny shapes among the grown figures, and he
realized that there were women and children with the men.
This, he said, was because of the famine. Hungry Turkana
families would climb the Escarpment to harvest the

Dodoth's lush, abandoned fields. The presence of the women and children explained the Turkana footprints recently found north of Kamion but not followed by a raid.

My informants took seriously the advice of the soldiers. When the soldiers went forward, scatter guns ready, the Dodoth took the guards off their spears, just in case, but they stayed very far behind. When the Dodoth heard the rapid, hammering fire of the scatter guns and the screams of the Turkanas, they crept forward. They saw the Turkanas leaping and falling against the firelight, some trying to escape, some trying to reach their spears. Only one Turkana, according to one informant, was able to reach his spear and throw it out into the dark.

In moments the attack was over. The soldiers, their rifles ready, walked into the camp to inspect the dead, and some of the Dodoth ran through the trees to kill any escaping Turkanas, some of whom were wounded, all of whom had run without their spears. The Dodoth from Kamion followed the soldiers in at once and went to the back of the U-shaped valley to see their cattle again. Most of the Dodoth from Kalapata waited in the dark bush for perhaps three quarters of an hour until there was no longer any danger of their being confused with the Turkana. After the last burst of rifle fire, and after the last screaming person was dead, three of my informants and several of their friends went to the camp to see what had happened.

There, the soldiers were collecting spears. My informants and their friends found their way among sixteen sprawled corpses, three of them women, two of them children, and as they did, they counted fourteen more trails of blood, drops and splashes on the bushes, showing the paths of people who were shot and had run. The soldiers eventually recalled the Dodoth who were chasing the wounded, saying that these people were not dangerous and that the wounded would not live to get home.

One of my informants noticed at the edge of the firelight a Turkana woman with a little girl. The woman, who had been shot, was dying, and the little girl, a two-year-old, clung to her. One of the soldiers also saw them, and approaching the pair, inspected the woman and caught the little girl by the arm. The soldier then summoned my informant and told him to kill the child. My informant refused. The soldier then sat down on a rock, and pinning the little girl with his feet, her legs under one boot and her neck under the other, he broke her back with a stone. She cried, said my informant, when the soldier began to beat her.

That night the soldiers camped at the scene of horror. In the morning they collected and burned most of the spears, the shields, the bags of millet which the Turkana women had harvested and would have taken home, and even the remaining meat, so that any wounded person who might drag himself or herself into the camp would find no food. Taking the few Turkana rifles and one of the corpses, the soldiers then started back. They walked all morning and arrived at their truck again at noon.

I asked each informant what he thought of the massacre, and most agreed that it was good to eliminate Turkanas. But one said: "The Kenya government won't like this. They will ask: 'Why did you kill my people?'"

When I asked the man who had refused to kill the girl if the soldiers had told the truth to the officers, he said very bitterly: "Ah no! They said nice words! On the way home they decided to report killing only three or four."

The soldiers emerged from the bush at noon, and by night were arranging to leave Kalapata for the south. The transfer, I think, was decided on previously and was not related to the massacre. We went to see the preparations on our way back from Kamion, where we had gone to see the returning cows. The camp at Kalapata was lit by fires. Some soldiers were packing, others were cleaning up, for their hands and arms and boots and one of the trucks' rear fenders were red with blood. In return for their recapture of the cattle, the K.A.R. had rewarded themselves with two of the Kamion cows. They had singled them out of the returning herds, brained them, then heaved them on a tailgate to slit their throats, while their owner, a Kamion householder, stood by, wringing his hands. He knew better than to complain, though, and presently he gave up his vigil and went home.

The first truck of the convoy had already started, and stood in the road, the headlights on and motor running, as the second truck pulled up behind. Bundles and tents were loaded, the campsite, bit by bit, was cleared, and the soldiers, their rifles on their shoulders, climbed in. When everything was ready, a driver gave a signal and the first truck pulled away, followed by the second, the third; the soldiers in the back were singing; somewhere, wrapped in something, lay the dead Turkana, and alone in the last truck, in their own thick, slippery blood, rolled the two cows.

The departure of the soldiers and the murder of the people in the Turkana camp left the northern part of the country empty and silent again. In the stillness, the Teutho crept back to their village and some young Dodoth, who thought it might be politic to follow the K.A.R. raid on the Turkana with a raid of their own, were captured by the very angry Kenya police and flung into jail. Raiding was ended, for a time at least. People in Dodoth went back to harvesting their wet gardens, and things seemed more or less normal, but for more than a week after the massacre, if you stood on the promontory of the Escarpment and looked at the distant involutions, you would see birds over the one in which the raiding camp had been.

CHAPTER NINE

Lopore

MEANWHILE, in a remote dwelling on a mountain, the famous emuron who may have been Ibongo had a prophetic dream. He did not dream of raids or soldiers or of famine or rotting grain, and he did not, as Lokorimoe's delegation may have asked him to, dream of a way to stop the unseasonable raining, which went on to wash out roads and bridges, marooning whole towns all over East Africa, and continued into what should have been the depth of the dry season, after the turn of the year. Instead, the emuron dreamed of a disease which he saw would overcome Dodoth unless measures were taken against it. He saw sacrifices in his dream, and smoke, and women and children moving in the smoke, and when he awoke he told his dream to his neighbors and associates very much as Lomotin told dreams to Lopore. Soon each householder and elder in the country knew about it. The dream achieved a national reputation and for a time was the subject most generally discussed.

Though it often stormed at night, a part of every day was sunny, with fresh air, blue sky, and little white clouds. During these clear hours, while the women turned the wet grain out of their storage baskets to dry it in the sun, the men would sit among the boulders of their etems, speculating on the implications of the prophecy. The disease which the prophecy would avert was a disease of coughing and pains in the chest that afflicts first cattle, then people, a disease which weakens the bones, attacks the head, and causes many to die. I wondered if it were anthrax. Pulmonary anthrax still exists in East Africa, and I once asked the men at Lopore's etem if somewhere the disease had already begun. "Isn't it enough to dream about it?" Lopore cried.

The form of the protective sacrifice was quite specific. Elders were to preside; women and children were to attend; the ox was to be black; and clansmen were to sacrifice together. Every district in the country was to hold such a sacrifice; not all districts at once, but one after the other. The sacrificing was to move northwest clockwise, and a ring of protection would thus be cast over all Dodoth, as a ring of protection is cast at a sacred place by a dying ox.

The sacrificing seemed to begin near Loyoro, in the south of Dodoth. Though Kaabong is the capital of Dodoth, Loyoro is, I think, Dodoth's true center, for it may be that when the Dodoth first occupied their country, they settled around Loyoro, and even today, the primary sacred groves of many different clans are found there. The charmed ring of sacrificing then came up toward Lokoki. There came a pause in its progress, however: it had not been decided whether the sacrifice would be in the east of Lokoki or in the west. I didn't understand the hesitation, or

the reasons for it, and I became worried that we would
miss the service, as we were about to leave. Shortly, however, it was decided that the service would be held in the
west because Lokoki's two most senior elders, two brothers-
in-law, lived in the western section, on a hill called
Morunyang, and wanted the sacrifice in their sacred grove.
In the face of raids, alarms, tax collectors, and soldiers,
these two old men had seemed aloof and remote. But when
at last a matter came that called for them to preside, they
had only to say when and where the sacrifice would be and
everyone did just as they said.

The names of the elders were Angerengmoe, which
comes from *angerer*, to eviscerate, and Bakimoe, which
comes from *akibak*, to stand in line. Their hill was high and
steep and very stony, covered with thornbush and little
trees. Though its name meant Yellow Mountain—perhaps
it was first discovered in the dry season—it was lime green
when we approached it early in the morning of the day of
the sacrifice. The hill seemed pale and ethereal against the
mass of the dark mountain range beyond. At the foot of the
hill on the eastern side were a few new dwellings. At its foot
in the west was the sacred place, a grove filled with long
shadows in the rosy, morning light.

A winding path led up the hill among the trees. It led by
Bakimoe's dwelling and his threshing floor, where in the
fresh breeze two of his wives were winnowing, and beyond
his granaries to Angerengmoe's wall. Beyond the wall, the
tree line ended and the path emerged on the bald summit
of the hill, the etem of Angerengmoe, where even at that
early hour fifteen householders and elders sat among the
stones.

The men sat with their backs to the pathway, their faces
turned to the view, the widest in Lokoki. The range of hills

curves out at Morunyang, and the men on the summit could see south to the very distant blue of the Kaabong hills, north to the tiny, shining roofs at Kalapata, to our half-razed camp on Morukore, to Lopore's dwelling sprawled on the slope beyond, to Kailele and the vast fields of Lokorimoe, and to all the dwellings far across the plain.

Somewhere in the landscape a black ox grazed. The men were waiting for it. A boy had been sent to find the herd; he would then have to find the owner to announce that the black ox was wanted, and the owner's permission would have to be obtained. All of this would take time, and the men knew it. They were as patient as a pride of lions on the hilltop. They spoke softly and passed snuff while the plumes of their headdresses stirred in the wind like manes.

Bakimoe and Angerengmoe turned to see who had arrived, then stood up and came toward us. The two old men were very frail and therefore moved quite slowly. Both were naked except for the gray capes over their backs, and both were without plumes or headdresses, but only their own gray hair. Their wrinkled skins, as thin and loose and delicate as the skin beneath an eye, were covered from the waist in back up over the shoulder and down to the waist in front with the intricate linear scar patterns for enemy victims, but the scars were so old and small they were barely visible, and lay over the elders like hair veils.

Angerengmoe took my hands and over my face he spat a misty blessing. "I pray God that all people may live together peacefully," he said, a grave and formal greeting for a foreigner. He then said: "The ox is soon coming," and invited us to sit down.

"The ox is sent for," said Bakimoe with formality as we sat next to him. Then silence fell, and we began waiting too. The sun climbed higher. The ethereal light and hazy air that hung on Morunyang gave way to glare and shadows, and the day became hot. Some of the waiting men wrapped themselves in their capes and lay down to sleep, some moved their stools back into the shade of the trees. Some, like Angerengmoe and Bakimoe, remained impassive among the rocks, their eyes scanning the green landscape or following the flights of birds which flashed up from the nearby trees and slipped through the air down the steep hill.

The men belonged mostly to two clans: Ngidiko—They of the Warthogs—which was the clan of Bakimoe; and Nginyangatom—They of the Yellow Trumpet—the clan of Angerengmoe. That, according to Neville Dyson-Hudson, might be a very ancient clan, perhaps deriving from the time the Dodoth left Karamoja, where the yellow trumpet is used symbolically to lead the herds departing for dry-season pasture. As it leads herds and their herdsmen today, it could have led the departing herds and people who came to colonize Dodoth. Lopore was a member of clan Nginyangatom although he wasn't present. Uri, who was, belonged to Ngidiko.

I wondered if Lopore was planning to attend. When we had passed his dwelling early in the morning, we had found him in his old cape with a calabash of medicine with which he was planning to dose his bull. I had thought he might be planning not to come at all, so much did he resent the western neighborhoods for their self-seeking ways. But suddenly there he was, standing in the midst of the patient, waiting people. He had bathed and changed his clothes and now wore a new white cape and the cap of red feathers which he had taken from the Turkana on the day of the June raid. But no one greeted him. He glared at the gathering, his heavy brows drawn, and presently he sat down, not with his age group but near to Bakimoe in the circle of elders. No one paid any attention. After waiting many minutes while still no one greeted him, Lopore said loudly: "Bakimoe! I have come!"

"Eh," said Bakimoe, gazing into the distance and picking his teeth with a straw.

Lopore looked as if he had expected another answer, though I don't know what else it could have been, after he had so frequently and publicly called the people of the western neighborhoods cowards and women. There was a short pause and he tried to engage Bakimoe again. "There are many people now waiting here," he said rudely, "but no ox has come."

Bakimoe spoke blandly with Angerengmoe about another matter, keeping his voice so low that Lopore could not hear him. As he did, three newcomers appeared on a footpath approaching the top of the hill. "Who are those men?" Lopore demanded.

"Visitors," said Bakimoe in a distant, superior manner. This gave Lopore the opening he had been waiting for.

"Are they visitors or are they Turkanas?" he yelled.

Having said it, Lopore got up, took his stool, and moved to join his age group, where he began the long, formal greeting with one of the men. Lopore was not very warm toward anyone present and gave the greeting in a perfunctory manner, without letting the man respond. He then left the man abruptly, went off a certain distance, and lay down.

It was now early afternoon, and the sun blazed in the sky. The fifty or sixty men who were in Angerengmoe's etem sought the shade. No gathering is as sedate as a group of Dodoth men waiting for an ox, and no conversations—

about events of the day, news, cattle—are as conventional. People were all the more surprised, therefore, when Lopore suddenly jumped to his feet and, pointing to the naked back of a householder who was sitting soberly on a rock, cried: "Who is this man?" People turned to stare. Lopore continued: "Some say he's of clan Ngidiko, but clan Ngidiko counts him as one of clan Nginyangatom." Lopore thrust his pointing finger into the householder's face and shouted rudely: "Which?" The householder rose abruptly, hooking his fist to catch Lopore with an uppercut under the chin. Lopore's head snapped back as he and the householder grappled, fell, and began to roll slowly and clumsily down the hill, bits of grass and red feathers from Lopore's headdress rising into the air.

The gathering had not expected anything like this. Though Bakimoe and Angerengmoe merely glanced around to confirm their suspicions that the disturbance was caused by Lopore, some other elders and householders openly stared, and some even stood up to see. In the high grass at the foot of the hill the men's locked bodies came to a stop. They separated, sat up, and looked at each other. "A few years ago I could have thrown you," said Lopore.

"We are both getting old," said the other man, standing up. Slowly, side by side, Lopore and his clansman climbed the hill. "I was waiting for you here since early morning," said the clansman. "Why didn't you come?"

"Because you people on this side are jackals," said Lopore.

"Then why are you following me?" asked his clansman.

"Because you have snuff."

Realizing that a fight had not really been in process, the observers took their seats again. Once more, people pretended to ignore Lopore, but this was now more difficult and when Lopore sat down at the rim of the hill with his back to everybody but his clansman, it was almost as if he was ignoring them. Perhaps the slight victory softened Lopore. Perhaps meeting with his clansman reminded him of the past. But not long after the mock fight, Lopore came to sit near me to tell me that it was Angerengmoe who under another name, fifty years ago at Okware's dwelling, had been with Lopore's first raiding party; he was one of the askaris who had served as Lopore's witness when Okware would have confiscated the captive goats. Angerengmoe overheard the story and looked at Lopore, and the two men, smiling slightly, exchanged a glance.

At half past four that afternoon, a herd appeared in the trees below the hill. The herdboy tried to drive the cattle out of the woods. Among the mass of trotting beasts that like a wave flowed up over the slope of the hill, and down into the woods again, ran a little black ox. "There," said some of the men as calmly as if they had not been waiting nine hours to see it, and taking up their stools, began to saunter down the hill. Soon only Angerengmoe and Bakimoe remained on the hilltop; they finished their conversation, stood up, and in the most leisurely manner, their capes billowing above their ankles, they walked slowly after the others and vanished among the trees.

The sacred place, which stood in the valley by the water-cut gully of a stream, was a parklike grove of small acacia trees. Young men, householders, and elders sat or stood among the acacias, forming a circle in the center of which was the black ox, its head lowered and its tail arched.

It was one of those beasts which is called *emong*, translated as "ox," but which biologically is a bull, and it seemed angry. It flung the dirt up over its shoulders and shook its horns.

Its owner seemed angry too. He sat firmly in the very center of the glade and absolutely refused to let anyone spear his ox unless the spearer paid him a heifer within two days. "Two days!" he said hotly. "I want the heifer in two days."

Near me, Angerengmoe remarked to Bakimoe in a tired voice: "All oxen are paid for eventually."

But across the glade Lopore was shouting: "Kill it! Why is it here?"

"Or drive it away," cried someone else.

"You can't drive an ox from a sacred place," said Lopore.

"Kill it, drive it," said Bakimoe to Angerengmoe. The two old men gathered their capes about their legs and settled down for another long conversation. They were so composed and dignified that it bothered them not a bit when the bull suddenly charged them, causing them to snatch up their stools and run on spindly legs, their capes streaming, into the trees. They merely raised their voices, continuing their conversation as they ran. Inasmuch as they could, they ignored the bull and when a householder suddenly decided to pay the heifer and called the news out to his son, who then speared the bull, dropping it instantly, Bakimoe simply stopped running and walked back a few yards to kneel behind the dead bull. He raised his arms, hummed a few bars of a very sober hymn, and began to pray.

"All bad things will end today."

"They will," answered the group of men who were slowly kneeling around him.

"All bad things will disappear."

"They will."

"Let all bad things go with the sun."

"They will."

"The father of this ox is here."

"He is."

"His people, they are here."

"They are."

"Let them always be here, and in their camps."

"Let them be here."

"Is this not good?"

"It is."

"It is," said Bakimoe, letting his arms fall.

"It is."

Angerengmoe stood at the tail of the bull while younger men bent to start the butchering. As their spear tail swung, Angerengmoe said to them: "This ox is for Ngikido and Nginyangatom. You are butchering too slowly. You are letting the sun go down." As he spoke, the bull's ribs and front leg were lifted off. Angerengmoe knelt and put his lips to the hot blood in the bowl-like cavity, wiping his mouth on the stiff hairs of the thigh. Bakimoe drank next; then, one by one, the other members of the senior generation, some of whom ladled blood into the neck cavity for the junior men. The divination was held, and the legs divided. The fire was built and the men began to eat, and suddenly, in the golden haze that had settled in the grove in the evening, three groups of women and children appeared, walking quickly and quietly, all in a line. They were the mothers, wives, and children of the clansmen of the western neighborhoods, and because it is against tradition for women to come to a sacred place, they were uneasy. They tried to look straight ahead or at the ground, as some of the young men shouted: "Beat the first one!" or "Run along!"

But Bakimoe raised his arms so that his cape fell like sleeves, and with the evening sun in his face, giving his skin a violet cast, he showed the path the women were to follow. Quickly and quietly, their leather skirts asway, the women walked in a circle around the raw meat, the wood that was to burn, and the fire where the meat was roasting, and the cloud of smoke from the meat and fire encompassed them all. The women hurried through the yellow haze until they had completed their circle, whereupon they broke and ran.

"Disappear," called a youngster as the group was passing.

"Hello there, Importance," murmured one of the older women as she hurried by the rude young man.

But Bakimoe was praying, and with his arms raised he said: "Bad things will go forever from our trees!"

"They will."

"Bad things to Dodoth will disappear."

"They will."

"Those who speak ill of Dodoth will disappear."

"They will."

"The ngipian will send thunder against them."

"They will."

"Our cattle will live here in peace."

"They will."

"With grass and water."

"They will."

"They will."

"They will."

The sun lit all the little ridges with their tumbled trees and gleamed on the spear blades held straight up by the prayerful people, and as the last of the women and children vanished over the hill and the column of smoke billowed

empty and slowly on the ground, it came to me that what
we saw had been seen before, almost exactly, by the
emuron in his sleep. It was strange, to be watching someone else's dream, just as night was coming.

After dark the sacrifice disbanded and the people began
to go home. "I thought you had a flashlight," said Lopore to
me as the group from Morukore organized for the five-mile
walk.

"I didn't know you were expecting it," I said.

"Oh yes, I was," said Lopore. "If I had known you didn't
have it, we would have left earlier."

"We'll have to use the starlight," said Lomotin, ending
the pointless conversation. "And hope we meet nothing on
the way." He led off into the darkness, followed closely
by the others. "Look out for the spear points," said he.

Judging from the group of men who visited Lopore's
etem in the morning, he was not the only person who resented the fact that the western neighborhoods alone were
benefiting from the sacrifice. There were always four or
five people visiting his etem, but before the sun was well
up that particular day, there were at least twelve men waiting. More came as the day began to warm. Lomotin, his
special, broken spear and dreaming stool in one hand,
crawled out Lopore's door; he had spent the night with
Lopore, wanting to be present when the neighbors gathered there. Lopore and his son-in-law were busy serving
the visitors with an enormous roast, part of the sacrifice,
which Lopore had carried home the night before. It is un-
common, sometimes forbidden, for a man to carry away
part of a sacrifice; all of it must be eaten in the grove. But
though Lopore may have broken a rule, he kept the prin-
ciple of it: he had hidden the meat overnight in a deep

cleft in some boulders and did not bring it into his home. If the people of the eastern neighboorhoods ate this meat, it would be a bit like having attended the service itself. As they ate, Lopore stood up to address them, and having repeated once again all the complaints he had against the western neighborhoods—"those people are nothing," he said, "they won't even spear the ox when they get it"—he proposed that within the next few days the people of the eastern neighborhoods hold a sacrifice of their own. I doubt that it was this the dreaming prophet had intended. Nevertheless, as Lopore spoke and paced against the rainy sky, flinging out an arm and crying: "We will do the same as they did to the women. We on this side are one people, all these dwellings here," a murmur of assent rose from the men.

The remark was his climax. Saying: "I have put the matter before you—if you don't understand, that's up to you," Lopore wrapped his cape around himself and sat down near us while the men put their heads together and in whispers talked over what he had said. "Do you think I'm an elder because I am speaking of these matters?" he asked us. "I'm not, but I'm not bad, and I can say what I like."

Presently Lomotin arose and said in his soft manner: "We will do it within the next few days. We will not look far for the ox but will take it from among our own neighborhoods. Let it be as Lopore says." He sat down as the crowd murmured their agreement and approval, which Lopore acknowledged with a nod.

A young man leaned forward and spoke to us earnestly. "Lopore says he's not an elder, but around here he's very important, a very important man."

Wondering if he had heard this, I looked around. But he was not listening. Having gotten to his feet, he was button-

ing on the overcoat, gift of Nabilo, and taking up his club
and spear. The men were so occupied with their talking
and eating that they hardly noticed him slip between the
boulders and start down the rockslide, which at that spot
was as steep as a stair. The blue summer flowers which
grew in the rocks, and which had bloomed again because of
the rain, were knee-high to Lopore and swayed as he disturbed them. When he reached the foot of the hill where
gray mist was swirling, he looked back, and seeing me
watching, waved for me to come. I followed through the
decapitated grain stalks in the field below, along a footpath
to the cattle road, and along the cattle road to a dwelling
partway across the plain. There were too many people at
his home, he explained when I caught up with him. They
wouldn't leave until evening. He was tired of talking and
was going to visit a friend.

The friend and Lopore knew each other so well that
Lopore didn't announce himself at the outer wall but went
straight to the doorway, dropped to one knee, and ducked
in. He made his way through the maze of passages until he
dropped again in front of an inner door. When he rose this
time he was in a little courtyard where a woman knelt,
grinding flour with a stone. She was a slender woman of
forty-five or fifty, with a sensitive face and delicately wrinkled skin. She looked up when Lopore entered, and putting
her grindstone by, she folded her hands. Lopore casually
stood his club and spear in a corner and flung down his
stool as he introduced her. "My wife," he said, "Kiten."

I was so astonished that I couldn't help but ask about
her, which she didn't seem to mind. While Lopore answered, she looked down modestly and smiled. She was, he
said, his brother's widow, and had been living elsewhere

for a very long time. But lately she had begun to think of living with Lopore, and until a court could be built for her, she was staying as the guest of his friend. She was going to start a garden near Lopore's house, however, and it would not be long before she would move in.

"She has four children, a girl, a boy, a boy, a girl," said Lopore. "Ask her their names. She'll tell you anything." So I did. Then she and Lopore began to speak of other things. They sat very close together, he on his stool, she on the ground, with her outstretched feet under his knees. She would touch his sandals now and then and would look down, smiling, when he teased her. Presently she indicated me and said: "Since she can read, ask her to tell me when I will die."

Lopore reached down and took one of her legs, which he crossed over the other, and holding her ankles tightly between his large fingers, he gave her feet a shake. "You are a great liar," he said. "She can't tell you that. If Europeans knew things like that, they wouldn't die themselves."

"But," she said, looking at him evenly, "there was a clerk in Kaabong when I was young, working for the government. One day he said he was going to die at noon. No one believed him. He took a chair, sat in it beside the door, and waited. At noon, he fell over dead. People then believed him."

"How did he know?" asked Lopore.

"Because he could read."

"She thinks," he said to me, "that you are refusing to tell her. It isn't good to speak of dying."

"But what else can we speak of?" Kiten asked. "There is no sun to dry the bulrush. What will we do if there is no bulrush and if the cattle are taken to dry-season pasture?"

Lopore smiled down at her with protective affection. "My herd will stay," he said.

We packed the next morning, and by afternoon we left, so we don't know what happened to Kiten and Lopore. We left self-addressed, stamped air letters in several homes, but to date we have received only one. "Lopore greets Thomas," it says, but it contains no news. We had hoped to get news from David and the Verona Fathers in Kaabong, but David got a good job in Moroto which seldom takes him north of Kaabong, and the fathers and we didn't know the same people. The only news we received of a personal nature came by mail from an American studying in Uganda, who quite fortuitously stayed one night at Uri's house. At the time, we didn't know the young man; it was Uri who suggested that he write to us. In this way, Uri sent greetings too.

For general news, we rely on David's letters and on *The New York Times*, which now and then gets news of Kara-moja from the United Press and Associated Press people stationed in Nairobi. From these sources, we heard about the Independence Day celebration in Moroto, about the good harvest the following year, which helped make up for the bad harvest, and about the fact that raiding had, for a time, been stopped.

One day in New York, our phone rang. It was a friend from Moroto who was calling from Washington, where he, with a group of young Ugandans, was on a study grant. A holiday was coming. They wanted to spend it in New York. We invited our friend to stay with us, and when he came, I'm afraid I plagued him for answers to questions I hadn't hoped to have answered before. I wanted to know what had happened to the people I knew, of course, but he only knew one of them, a graduate from the Kaabong mission school. This man could have had an excellent job with the new government if he had chosen to remain in Dodoth. But the glamour of the city drew him—the top life, which is night life—and though the title of his city job was quite impressive (he was "with the meteorological department"), his pay was low, for his work was to measure the level of rain in a rain barrel.

I asked about the jobs held by the more dedicated people with educations, and instead of wasting very much time explaining, our guests introduced us to his friends. They were, without exception, extraordinary people. Amusing and intelligent, any one of them could probably have found a good job in a city. But each of them had chosen to serve his own people and work at home. Intertribal hostility such as the raiding in Karamoja does not effect young men like these, who are able to remain on good terms with each other. This in itself will serve the nation well.

The rest I asked our friend was odds and ends—about the old-fashioned ways of building houses and the derivation of certain words. But one night at a party it occurred to me that I knew very little about the stars. There are not many stories in Dodoth about them, and people went to sleep early at night, so I never even learned the names. Our friend said that he was not really familiar with the subject, but he agreed to tell me what he could, and later, coming home in a taxi, he tried to point out several stars as they flashed between the West Side blocks. But this was not successful. He tried again in front of the building, and again from our apartment window, but always too small a patch of sky was showing. In the end, we went out on the roof. From there, the view was perfect, and as it happened, we looked up to see a brilliant Echo drifting over Ninety-sixth Street, far and high. These satellites, our friend said, were thought to be planes by most people in Dodoth and Karamoja. He then showed us, in the haze over the city, the difference between the tiny, bright type of star called *akachierit* and the large, soft kind of star, which is called *etop*. Planets are among the bodies called etop. A shooting star is *aremong etop*, which seems to have the word for "ox" in it, and which shoots toward a place where a raid or a disease may come from, as the star is a message from God. An eclipse is "when the sun died; when the moon died," and is caused by God before he sends disaster. The only other thing about the stars that our friend could think to show us was the seasonal position of the Pleiades, the constellation Ngakuliak, by which the Dodoth mark seasons, and after looking for a time we found them high in the air above the Spry sign, marking the start of the year.

A NOTE ABOUT THE AUTHOR

ELIZABETH MARSHALL THOMAS was born in Boston, Massachusetts. She was graduated from Radcliffe in 1954. She accompanied three expeditions to make anthropological studies and films in Namibia and Botswana in 1951, 1952–53 and 1955. Her first book, *The Harmless People*, published by Knopf in 1959, was a highly acclaimed account of life among the San or Bushmen, the hunter-gatherers of the Kalahari Desert. Her articles about southern Africa and Uganda have appeared in *The Reporter*, the *National Geographic*, *Mademoiselle*, *The New Yorker*, the *Atlantic Monthly*, and the *Smithsonian Magazine*. Mrs. Thomas makes her home with her husband, Stephen, in Virginia.